1954

ALSO BY BILL MADDEN

Steinbrenner: The Last Lion of Baseball

Pride of October: What It Was to Be Young and a Yankee

Zim: A Baseball Life (with Don Zimmer)

*Damned Yankees: Chaos, Confusion, and Craziness
in the Steinbrenner Era (with Moss Klein)*

1954

**The Year Willie Mays and the
First Generation of Black Superstars
Changed Major League Baseball Forever**

BY
BILL MADDEN

DA CAPO PRESS
A Member of the Perseus Books Group

Designed by Linda Mark
Set in 12.5 point Bell MT Std by the Perseus Books Group

Library of Congress Cataloging-in-Publication Data

Madden, Bill.
   1954 : the year Willie Mays and the first generation of black superstars
changed major league baseball forever / by Bill Madden.—First Da Capo
Press edition.
      pages cm
   Includes bibliographical references and index.
   ISBN 978-0-306-82332-9 (hardback) — ISBN 978-0-306-82333-6 (e-book)
   1. Baseball—United States—History—20th century. 2. African American
   baseball players—United States—History—20th century. 3. Discrimination
   in sports—United States—History—20th century. 4. Mays, Willie, 1931–
   I. Title.
GV863.A1M28 2014
796.357'64097309045—dc23

                                                             2014000774

First Da Capo Press edition 2014
Published by Da Capo Press
A Member of the Perseus Books Group
www.dacapopress.com

Da Capo Press books are available at special discounts for bulk purchases
in the U.S. by corporations, institutions, and other organizations. For more
information, please contact the Special Markets Department at the Perseus
Books Group, 2300 Chestnut Street, Suite 200, Philadelphia, PA, 19103, or
call (800) 810-4145, ext. 5000, or e-mail special.markets@perseusbooks.com.

10 9 8 7 6 5 4 3 2 1

For Jackie, Larry, Willie, Campy, Monte, Hank, Ernie, and Minnie: They turned seventy-eight years of baseball's injustice into a collective triumph of the human spirit.

TABLE OF CONTENTS

INTRODUCTION

A FEW DAYS AFTER THE 2000 "SUBWAY" WORLD SERIES BETWEEN the Yankees and the Mets I got a call from my agent with an intriguing book proposal. "Larry Doby wants to write his autobiography," he said. "He's never told his story, and he specifically wants to know if you would be interested in doing it with him."

I was both interested and flattered. As a player—a renowned slugger for the Cleveland Indians and Chicago White Sox from 1947 to '58—Doby was one of the heroes of my fifties youth. It was only long after he'd retired and gone to work as a special assistant for American League President Gene Budig, however, that I got to know him as a friend. I interviewed him a few times at his office on the twenty-ninth floor of the Major League Baseball headquarters at 350 Park Avenue in Manhattan, where the subject invariably always got back to his trials in 1947, when he became the second black player in baseball and first in the American League, and then the joy of 1954, when his Indians won an AL record 111 games, dethroned the five-straight world champion Yankees, and went on to play Willie Mays's Giants in the first World Series that featured players of color on both teams.

"You know all those stories about '47 and '54," Doby was saying when my agent, Rob Wilson, and I visited him at his house in Montclair, New Jersey. "Well, now I want to put them in a book so they're there—for the record."

"They need to be, Larry," I said. "Everybody knows Jackie's story. But not enough people know yours."

Doby smiled in appreciation. We shook hands and agreed to talk further to put a proposal together. What I didn't tell him was that for years I had wanted to write a book about the 1954 season, about how it was a watershed season for baseball in so many ways. For Doby, it was his peak season as he led the American League in home runs and RBI and, on the last day of July, made what witnesses said was one of the greatest catches ever by a center fielder. But seven years after Jackie Robinson had broken the baseball color line, 1954 was also a triumphant season for black players—and, in a larger sense, for baseball and the country as a whole.

For if Doby was the dominant player in the American League, Mays certainly emerged as the preeminent player in the National League, only with a flair and boyish innocence that all fans, black and white, quickly came to embrace. In blazing their own parallel trails, however, Robinson's and Doby's personalities did not lend themselves to affection from the fans. Jackie was outspoken and confrontational, whereas Larry was introverted and seemingly always angry. But affection was not what they were seeking; rather, they wanted acceptance and respect and in that regard, they accomplished their mission for all their black brethren.

Mays, however, was almost instantly beloved in 1954, much of that due to how seemingly easy it was for him to live up to the effusive buildup from his Giants manager, Leo Durocher. He just didn't realize it. He didn't want to know about race issues or social injustice, and he seemed immune to the indignities and epithets the other players of his race had to endure. All he wanted was to play.

Nearly sixty years later, when I interviewed Mays for this book, he had not changed. We were sitting in a room off the lobby of the Otesaga Hotel in Cooperstown, New York, during one of the Hall of Fame weekends. When I posed my first question to him about the '54 Giants championship team's unusual dynamic for that time, in which the core players were composed of so many white players from the South and three blacks— Mays, Monte Irvin, and Hank Thompson—he quickly cut me off. "I ain't talkin' about race," Mays said. "I'll talk about anything else you want—the games, the World Series, Leo, whatever. But I don't ever talk about race."

As Monte Irvin told me, none of those Giants talked about race. It just wasn't an issue with them, even if baseball, seven years after Jackie's breakthrough, was still in its infancy when it came to integration, with half of the sixteen teams still without a black player at the end of the '53 season.

By contrast, Doby eagerly wanted to talk about it after holding back for so many years for fear of being portrayed as someone bitter toward baseball. When he was elected to the Hall of Fame in 1998, it was almost as though he'd been liberated. At that time he said, "I never thought I was overshadowed. Mr. Robinson was first, but he gave *me* the opportunity, so he should have gotten everything he got. I feel I've been rewarded for my merits, turning negatives into positives, as well as for my statistics."

In our subsequent conversations after that initial session in his house, Doby talked about the private pain of not being allowed to stay in the same hotel with his Indians' teammates during spring training, a policy that was changed in 1954, and the solitude on the road when none of his teammates invited him to play cards on the trains or simply hang out with them.

Race wasn't something that was talked about much in baseball in 1954. It was as though all the resistance to integration of the game and the accompanying taunts, slights, and verbal abuse toward black players from fans and other players and managers had mostly been played out in the first few years of Robinson's and Doby's lonely vigils. But whether baseball and America realized it, 1954 was the launching pad for a new era, when the dominant players in baseball were to be blacks and Hispanics. This was the essence of the book I'd envisioned. Besides Mays and Doby, Hank Aaron and Ernie Banks both made auspicious debuts in the major leagues in 1954, and even though they were ultimately not able to be factors in the pennant race, this book would have been very incomplete without their stories of their rookie seasons and how they got there.

The same goes for Roberto Clemente, who made his major league debut in 1955 and went on to become the first Hispanic player elected to the Hall of Fame. His story also began in 1954. I kind of stumbled across it in the summer of 1996 when I traveled to Waldoboro, Maine, to visit Clyde Sukeforth, the then-ninety-four-year-old former scout who'd signed Jackie Robinson for the Dodgers fifty years earlier. During the course of relating all the details of being sent to Chicago by Dodgers president Branch Rickey to look at Robinson and bring him back to Brooklyn, Sukeforth told of a similar assignment from Rickey in 1954, when both were working together again with the Pittsburgh Pirates. That assignment was to check out a pitcher on the Dodgers' Triple A team in Montreal, only instead, Sukeforth said with a wry grin, he discovered Clemente, whom the Dodgers were keeping under wraps because he was not protected on their forty-man roster and, thus, subject to the winter draft.

I regret that I never got to write Larry Doby's autobiography. We both got sidetracked after those initial interview sessions, and then, in 2002, he was stricken with cancer and too ill to work on a book. He passed away June 18, 2003. At Doby's memorial service six days later Joe Morgan, the African American Hall of Fame second baseman, delivered one of the eulogies. "Larry was never negative," Morgan said. "Without guys like Larry, what Jackie started would not have finished the way it has."

Although Doby never got to write his memoir, I would hope I was at least able to honor his memory by telling the best part of it in *1954*.

—*Bill Madden,*
November 8, 2013

PROLOGUE

ONE WEEK BEFORE THE START OF THE 1954 BASEBALL SEASON AND nearly seven months after the American League approved the transfer of the St. Louis Browns to Baltimore, the city's hotel operators met with Maryland governor Theodore B. McKeldin and his Commission on Interracial Problems to discuss segregation in Baltimore's hotels. It was a heated meeting, during which the governor fervently attempted to make his case that, with Baltimore having now officially become a "big league" city, it needed to adapt to the changing times in America. As the only city in the league holding firm to segregation in its hotels, McKeldin argued, Baltimore and the state of Maryland stood to become the target for "a lot of unfavorable nationwide publicity."

His plea fell on deaf ears. At the conclusion of the meeting the hotel operators refused to lift their restrictions against Negro patrons. Charles D. Harris, the attorney for the hotel operators, countered McKeldin's argument by stating, "The hotels are in the business of making a profit, which they stand to lose if they go along with public opinion."

Joe Durham, one of only two black players on that first Baltimore Orioles team—and the only one by the time he was called up from their Double A minor league team in San Antonio with two and a half weeks left in the season—remembered the strange experience of arriving in the big leagues and finding it not unlike the indignities that were part of life for the Negro in the minor league tank towns. As he stated in a 2013 interview:

> *I got in late at night from San Antonio and checked into the South-ern Hotel, which was the hotel the Orioles put all their players up. The next morning when I went downstairs to have breakfast, a black bellhop came up to me and asked: "How did you get in here?" When I told him, he quickly ushered me out the door to a house on Prestman Street in the black neighborhood, and I then got a room at the all-black York Hotel. I'm probably the first black person to stay in a segregated Baltimore hotel! Those three weeks at the York in September were a very lonely experience and I was grateful that one of my teammates, Don Larsen, would pick me up every day at the Casino nightclub, around the corner from the York, and drive me to and from the ballpark.*

Though he grew up in Newport News, Virginia, which was considered as much a "Jim Crow" city as Baltimore, Durham was amazed at just how intolerant the newest major league city still was toward blacks. "Even in Newport News they had done away with separate drinking fountains and the policy of not al-lowing blacks to try on clothes in the department stores," said Durham, who spent parts of three seasons in the big leagues and then went on to have a forty-year career with the Orioles as a batting practice pitcher, minor league instructor, and in their community relations department.

Desegregation would not come to Baltimore's hotels until 1957, when the Sheraton Belvedere in the historic Mount Vernon section of Baltimore became the first hotel in the city to admit black patrons. Meanwhile, for the first three years of the Orioles' existence Negro players on the visiting clubs were all obliged to stay either at the York or at the homes of friends of the black porters they knew from the trains.

Ironically, when, on May 17, 1954, the US Supreme Court issued its landmark decision in the *Brown vs. Board of Education* case, outlawing segregation of white and Negro children in public schools solely on the basis of race, Baltimore was the first southern city to integrate its schools. Change was in the wind in America, in which blacks and whites would now be able to attend the same schools and compete on the same athletic teams together, but as baseball had already vividly demonstrated, it would be slow in coming.

For now, seven years after Jackie Robinson broke the color line in baseball that had existed since the game's origin in 1876, half of the sixteen major league clubs—the New York Yankees, Pittsburgh Pirates, Boston Red Sox, Detroit Tigers, Cincinnati Reds, St. Louis Cardinals, Philadelphia Phillies, and Washington Senators—still had not integrated as of spring training 1954. In September of '53 the Chicago Cubs, owned by chewing gum magnate Phil Wrigley, finally broke their color line by signing Kansas City Monarchs shortstop Ernie Banks, generally acknowledged as the preeminent player in the Negro Leagues, and immediately bringing him to the big leagues, and the Philadelphia Athletics did likewise when they brought up Bob Trice, a twenty-four-year-old right-handed pitcher whom they'd signed as a pitcher/third baseman from the Homestead Grays of the Negro Leagues.

Both Banks and Trice expressed reservations about leaving the Negro Leagues and going into the mostly all-white majors, as neither of them had known anything else but playing with players of color. Were it not for the money, they both said, the major leagues had no special appeal. In 1954, however, their careers took drastic different turns. Years later Banks cited the fact that he was able to break in with Gene Baker, whom the Cubs had signed out of the Negro Leagues a few years earlier. As his second-base partner, roommate, and mentor, Baker had made it far more easy for him to perform to the superior ability he'd shown with the Monarchs. By contrast, Trice, after leading the International League in victories with the A's Triple A Ottawa farm team in '53, found life in the major leagues to be trying. Though pitching fairly well, with a 7–8 record for a seventh-place team, Trice, after a horrendous outing on July 11, when he was pounded for ten hits and nine runs in just three and a third innings, asked the A's to demote him back to Ottawa. In the beginning Trice was happy. The A's hired former Negro Leagues standout third baseman Judy Johnson as a spring training coach, assigned primarily to work and hang out with Trice. But Johnson was not retained once the season began, and Trice invariably found himself alone on the road and without a willing mentor and companion. Trice said,

> I planned to make this move anyway. I would've asked to be sent back to Ottawa even if I'd won. Everybody I've talked to says I'm crazy and maybe I am. I figure that in the long run this is what's best for me. I can't seem to win here in my present frame of mind and the team shouldn't miss me. Things are different in the minors where everybody's trying to improve himself. A fellow can go an hour or two early to the park and shag flies and work on ground balls. In Philadelphia I couldn't do that. With others using the field in the afternoon, everything has to be run according to schedule. In

games I found everything has to be done according to form and I was never much for form. It got to the point where I couldn't go into a game with the idea of getting the other side out. It just wasn't fun anymore. It was work.

Trice spent the rest of '54 at Ottawa, then returned to the majors briefly in '55, appearing in four games for the Athletics, before returning to the minors for good. He drifted to the Mexican League in 1956 and then retired, never fulfilling the great promise he'd shown at Ottawa in '53.

The number of integration holdout teams in the majors was reduced to five when the Pirates brought up second baseman Curt Roberts; the Reds added two outfielders, Chuck Harmon, an African American and Nino Escalera, a Negro Puerto Rican, to their '54 Opening Day roster; and the Cardinals promoted first baseman Tom Alston. The additions of Roberts, Harmon, Escalera, and Alston brought the total to twenty-seven black players, out of the 448 major leaguers, on the Opening Day rosters in 1954. Integration of baseball after Jackie Robinson's breakthrough with the Brooklyn Dodgers had been but a trickle as opposed to the initial projections of a steady flow from the Negro Leagues and the sandlots.

In particular, in that group there were four Latin players who would have been banned because of the color of their skin: Cubans Minnie Miñoso of the White Sox and Sandy Amoros of the Dodgers, and Puerto Ricans Vic Power of the Athletics and Rubén Gómez of the Giants. In a 2013 interview Orlando Cepeda, the Hall of Fame slugger and Puerto Rican native whose father, Perucho, was an iconic hitter in the Puerto Rican leagues from 1938 to '50 and a victim of the color line in Major League Baseball, told me, "The players who played with my father, who were my idols, like Minnie Miñoso, never knew why they couldn't play in the majors, they just knew they couldn't. And all the while I wondered, *Who were these people who decided they couldn't play? How did they make these distinctions who were and who weren't white enough to be in Major League Baseball?*"

For most of '54 the newly minted Baltimore Orioles, who, as the previous St. Louis Browns, were one of the first teams to integrate with the signing of infielder Hank Thompson and outfielder Willard Brown out of the Negro Leagues in 1947, remained all white. The Orioles' first black player, Jehosie "Jay" Heard, a diminutive (five feet seven, 145 pounds) thirty-four-year-old left-handed pitcher they'd signed out of the Negro Leagues in 1951, made his debut with them April 24, 1954, pitching one and a third innings of relief and retiring all four batters he faced in a game the Orioles were already trailing 10–0. He didn't pitch again until May 28, when he hurled two more innings of relief, giving up six hits and five runs. In early June the Orioles demoted Heard to Triple A Portland in the Pacific Coast League, and he was never to return to the majors. It wasn't until September 10, when they brought up Durham, that the Orioles had another black player. Durham wound up hitting .225 in forty at-bats that September as well as not only earning the distinction of being the first black player to homer for the Orioles but also, as he said, the first to stay in the segregated team hotel, if only briefly.

After their historic signing of Robinson from the Kansas City Monarchs of the Negro Leagues in 1946, the Dodgers, under the direction of their visionary general manager, Branch Rickey, were the most aggressive team in 1954 in bringing black players to the big leagues, with six: Robinson, catcher Roy Campanella, pitchers Don Newcombe and Joe Black, outfielder Sandy Amoros and second baseman Jim Gilliam. Next were the Cleveland Indians with five—center fielder Larry Doby, first baseman Luke Easter, pitcher Dave Hoskins, and outfielders Dave Pope and Al Smith—

and then the New York Giants with four: outfielders Willie Mays (who was returning from two years in the Army) and Monte Irvin, the aforementioned Hank Thompson (who had been subsequently released by the Browns) and Gómez, the Puerto Rican right-handed pitcher who the Yankees had previously released before he could reach the big leagues. It would also not be long into the '54 season when two other first-year black players, Banks of the Cubs and twenty-year-old Henry Aaron with the Milwaukee Braves, began establishing themselves as future stars with uncommon power.

But although there could be little argument about the impact the black players had had on those three teams—the Dodgers won four pennants and finished second the other three times with Robinson and company over those seven years; the Giants won the pennant in '51, Mays's rookie year, then slumped to second and fifth the next two years without him, and the Indians won the world championship in Doby's rookie year of 1948 and finished second behind the Yankees in '51, '52, and '53 as the All-Star center fielder came into his own—there was still staunch resistance from teams, especially in the American League, led by the Yankees, to integrate. In addition, seven years later after Robinson's breakthrough there remained an unspoken, unwritten quota—just like the color line itself—in baseball as to the number of black players clubs could have on their twenty-five-man roster, a quota that would have severe consequences for the Dodgers in 1954 regarding one of their top minor league prospects, Roberto Clemente.

By their sheer dominance—eighteen pennants and sixteen world championships from 1926 to '53—and a superior scouting staff who for over a quarter-century had mined an incomparable gallery of future Hall of Fame talent, from Lou Gehrig in their own backyard at Columbia to Joe DiMaggio and Tony Lazzeri in San Francisco, Bill Dickey in Little Rock, Arkansas, Yogi Berra in St. Louis, Mickey

Mantle in Oklahoma, and dozens of other perennial All-Stars, the Yankees did not see a need to drastically change course or their philosophy in the procuring of ballplayers. "We are not against bringing a Negro player to the major leagues," insisted Yankees' general manager, George Weiss, "but we won't be pressured into bringing up just any Negro player. It has to be the right one."

Meanwhile, during the summer of '54 a book that garnered more and more attention as the baseball season wore on, if only perhaps for its apparent prescience, was a novel by Douglass Wallop entitled *The Year the Yankees Lost the Pennant*, which, later in the year, was transformed into both a movie and a Broadway musical, retitled *Damn Yankees*. It was about a fictional 1958 season in which Joe Boyd, a middle-aged real estate salesman and lifelong fan of the perennial losers, the Washington Senators, sells his soul to the devil in order to keep the Yankees from winning their tenth straight AL pennant and world championship. Wallop, born in Washington in 1920, was himself a lifelong Senators devotee and clearly believed the Yankee streak of five straight world championships from 1949 to '53 was destined to go on interminably until or unless someone could find a way to stop them.

Little did he know, as his book moved steadily up the best-seller list, fueled no doubt by curiosity seekers not realizing it was fiction, the rise of the black superstars in baseball had already begun, eventually changing both Yankee attitudes and the game itself forever.

POWER TO THE (OTHER) PEOPLE

O N A COLD, SNOW-SPRINKLED AFTERNOON, DECEMBER 16, 1953, George Weiss, the New York Yankees imperial general man-ager, summoned the local media to the Yankee offices at 745 Fifth Avenue in midtown Manhattan to announce an eleven-player trade, a deal that had been in the works soon after the Yankees had completed their fifth straight world championship season by again defeating their cross-borough rivals, the Brooklyn Dodgers in the World Series. The fifty-eight-year-old Weiss, who in 1948 assumed the Yankees general manager position from his men-tor, legendary baseball executive Ed Barrow, had achieved the reputation of being one of the game's most coldly efficient op-eratives, combining the Yankees' superior scouting and player development system with hard-line, unsentimental judgments of his players' abilities and worth as well as a knack for prying the best players from the secondary teams in baseball through

judicious trades in which, invariably, the return sacrifice in players was largely inconsequential.

On the surface this appeared to be another of those deals.

"Today, the Yankees are announcing the largest trade in our
history, a deal involving 11 players with the Philadelphia Athletics, in which we are acquiring first baseman Eddie Robinson and
right-handed pitcher Harry Byrd," Weiss said to the gathering
of newspapermen from the dozen or so New York metropolitan–
area dailies and radio and TV reporters. Robinson was a strapping left-handed slugger whose twenty-two homers and 102 RBI
were both second on the seventh-place A's in '53, and the twenty-
eight-year-old Byrd was the 1952 AL Rookie of the Year who had
won fifteen and eleven games while logging a total of 465 innings
the previous two seasons. Weiss reported the Yankees were giving up two of their primary surplus players on the major league
roster, backup first baseman Don Bollweg and reserve outfielder
Bill Renna, along with four of their prize farmhands, including
Vic Power, a dark-skinned Puerto Rican whom Weiss described
as the "Negro first baseman with Kansas City, who may well go
on to become a great star."

At first Weiss glossed over the fact that the twenty-two-
year-old Power, who was capable of playing multiple positions,
had just led the Triple A American Association in batting (.349)
and hits (217) along with ten triples, sixteen homers, 115 runs,
and ninety-three RBI. But Weiss then noted how the trade
quickly filled the Yankees' two greatest needs: a power-hitting
first baseman to replace Johnny Mize, who retired after the '53
World Series, and a durable pitcher to bolster an aging starting rotation recently compromised when veteran "swing man"
Johnny Sain retired. "This will open the floodgates," Weiss proclaimed proudly. "The other clubs will now have to scramble. We
strengthened ourselves in the departments we needed help the

most, and the A's got a lot of good young players they need for their rebuilding."

Most of the assembled reporters seemed to agree it was a steal.

Once again, the Yankees plundering the weak sisters of their best players, was the general consensus in the room. *New York Times* columnist Arthur Daley wrote, "It looks like the biggest steal since the Brink's holdup. This was the perfect trade from the Yankees' standpoint. They got something for nothing—or virtually nothing."

And the esteemed Shirley Povich of the *Washington Post* added, "The Yankees' whopping trade with the Philadelphia Athletics yesterday was in the best tradition of the Yankee design for winning pennants, which has been foolproof for the last five years: Peel off some of your surplus players, let the other club gamble on your rookies, and make certain you get the solid guys you need. There were eleven players in this deal, but only two proven performers in the whole kit and kaboodle of 'em and, as usual, it was the Yankees who corralled them."

(Two days after the deal was announced the A's revealed they had turned down offers of both $200,000 from the Boston Red Sox and $50,000 plus four players from the Chicago White Sox for Byrd alone.)

But then a reporter posed a question to Weiss about the versatile, right-handed-hitting Power, who, along with catcher Elston Howard, had a couple of weeks earlier become the first black players to be promoted to the Yankees forty-man roster. "Wasn't he your top prospect?" the reporter asked. "Are you concerned about criticism that the Yankees have not promoted a Negro player to the big leagues?"

And as Povich added in his column, "The A's prize out of the swap could be Vic Power, the colored lad who batted .349 at the Yankees' Kansas City farm. As a consequence of the deal, though, the Yanks are apt to hear anew from the protest groups who, for years, have been picketing Yankee Stadium demanding the wherefor of no Negro players on the Yankee roster. . . . In shuffling Power off to the A's, the Yanks may again be vulnerable to the charge of deliberately drawing the color line."

Not surprisingly, such charges came fast and furious from the black *Chicago Defender* newspaper, which said that in trading Power, "The Yankees not only flaunted a chance to redeem themselves in the eyes of thousands of loyal Negro Yankee fans, but deliberately gave up one of the best prospects in the minor leagues."

"We did not want to lose Power," said Weiss, insisting that Power's color played no part in the trade. "But the Athletics would not make the deal without him being included. He was the first player they asked for."

(The day after the trade Power told reporters in Puerto Rico that he was thankful to the Yankees for sending him to the seventh-place Athletics "because I'll have a better chance to make the grade with them. I have read where the Athletics say nobody has a position assured. That suits me. That's why I think the change favors me.")

Upon further questioning about the Yankees being one of seven of the sixteen major league teams that had still not integrated since Jackie Robinson broke the color line in baseball with the Brooklyn Dodgers in 1947, Weiss grew a bit testy. "It would be weak to hold Power just because we were afraid of censure," he declared. "We've showed our good faith toward Negro players by bringing up Power and Howard [to the forty-man major league roster] and we will bring up others to the Yankees when they merit it."

To skeptics, that could well have been translated as: *To hell with all of you. We've won five straight world championships without a black player and in three of them beaten the Dodgers with Jackie Robinson. We'll integrate on our own timetable, not yours.*

Six years later, shortly after he was eased out as Yankees general manager because of his age, a still-defensive Weiss, in his first-ever in-depth interview, went out of his way to reiterate the Yankees' stance on integration to *Sports Illustrated*'s Robert Shaplen:

I want to say something about Negro players because we've been criticized in the past for allegedly dragging our heels on the issue. We may have been slow in coming up with the kind of Negro ballplayer we wanted, but there was never a question of bias. As a matter of fact, with the exception of Jackie Robinson, we were interested from the start in just about every Negro player who has come up to the majors. Going back to when Robinson was signed by Montreal in 1946, we assigned Paul Krichell and Joe Press, two top scouts, to canvass the Negro field. But we never believed in bringing up a Negro for the purpose of exploitation or to pep up attendance. Our first candidate for a Yankee job, Vic Power, did not turn out to be the man we wanted, even though, after we traded him, he developed into a fine player. We tried out plenty of Negroes through the years on our farm teams—at least 50 have been signed by the Yankee organization—but, with the exception of Power, none of them had what it takes until Elston Howard came along. . . . So even though we were once picketed, and received inquiries on our policy from the National Association of Colored People and others, this charge of bias is altogether unjustified, and I feel the record shows it.

Nevertheless, a 1949 letter to Krichell, the Yankees' legendary scouting director, from Press, a bird dog scout who operated the Yankees' Bushwick semipro team in Brooklyn, surfaced

during the 1974 Yankee Stadium renovation and certainly seems
to refute Weiss's assertions. In the letter, which was among the
cartons of papers and contracts tossed in the trash and salvaged
by memorabilia collectors during the stadium renovation, Press
appeals to his boss, Krichell, to take the wraps off in regard to
actively recruiting Negro players:

> *It is quite hard for me to understand your complete turn-around as
> far as the Negro baseball players are concerned. Within the past two
> years I have given you reports on practically every player, with the
> exception of a very few, who have since signed with other teams. A
> few of those I mentioned to you were Art Wilson and Orestes Miñoso
> and there are still more of these who, in my opinion, would fit in
> Organized Baseball without any trouble. They include Piper Davis,
> outfielder, and Mays, outfielder, both of the Birmingham Barons.*

In his interview with Shaplen, Weiss cited Artie Wilson as
a player the Yankees vigorously sought "but ran into rhubarbs
with the Negro Leagues or other big league teams." He didn't
specify what sort of rhubarbs and, of course, made no mention of
the Yankees scouting Willie Mays or dispatching any scouts to
Cuba to look at Orestes "Minnie" Miñoso, who signed with the
Cleveland Indians, one of the more aggressive teams in signing
black players, and went on to become a perennial AL All-Star.

Meanwhile, in 1960, Tom Greenwade, the renowned Yankee
scout who signed Mickey Mantle and Bobby Murcer among many
others, excoriated Power in an interview at his home in Willard,
Missouri with *New York Herald-Tribune* Yankee beat reporter
Harold Rosenthal. Like Weiss with Shaplen, Greenwade was ex-
tremely sensitive to the criticism the Yankees had taken over the
years about their slowness to integrate. But unlike Weiss, he made
no bones about why, when they finally did, it wasn't with Power:

The Yankees have never discriminated against Negroes. Our policy has always been: "When we find one good enough, we'll take him." Vic Power and Rubén Gómez [a notoriously high-strung dark-skinned Puerto Rican starting pitcher with the New York Giants who was originally signed by the Yankees but released after five seasons in their minor league system] *were not the right type. You had to know Power's reputation. He's a bad actor. Chases after white women and stirs up trouble. We had trouble with him in Kansas City* [the Yankees' Triple A farm team] *and we knew he wasn't going to the Yankees, so we got rid of him. Elston Howard, on the other hand, is a high type of Negro. He was the one we wanted.*

That would explain the treatment Power received after he was called up to the Yankees to undergo a physical at the end of the 1952 season. In a 1997 interview with the *New York Daily News*, Power, whose sweeping, one-hand style of catching balls at first base earned him the reputation of being too "flashy" and a "showboat," said that, even though he'd been placed on the forty-man roster, he was never allowed to actually don the Yankee pinstripes. "The Yankees never invited me to spring training. I never had a Yankee hat, never had a Yankee uniform," Power said. "They gave me a ticket for the [September 28, 1952] Yankees-Red Sox game that day—which turned out to be the second of Allie Reynolds' two no-hitters that season. I had a front row seat but they didn't invite me into the clubhouse for the celebration afterward."

But "Vic *was* a showboat," Howard's widow, Arlene, told me in a 2002 interview. "And later he had a very light-skinned wife, but then so was I. It was just the stupidity and prejudice of the times."

The "trouble" Greenwade referred to when discussing about Power in Kansas City in 1953 was a perceived lack of hustle. Even though Power was leading the league in batting at the time, Kansas City manager Harry Craft benched him for a left-handed hitter—against a left-handed pitcher—after he'd failed to chase a fly ball over his head in the outfield that went for a two-base hit. Power later explained that it had been a very hot day and that up to then he had played practically every day, all winter and summer. "I was in leftfield and they thought I didn't get back fast enough. I wasn't going to be able to catch the ball anyway and it would have still been a double," he said. "They couldn't have been too unhappy with me. I played 146 games last year."

In fact, Greenwade was actually the one who first discovered Power for the Yankees. Power was playing for an independent team in Caguas, Puerto Rico, for $100 a week in 1948 and caught Greenwade's eye when he was scouting on the island. Greenwade made a note about Power being a prospect the Yankees should follow. Two years later Power was playing for the Drummondville, Canada, team in the class C Provincial League, hitting well over .300, when the Yankees dispatched Johnny Neun, another of their top scouts, to take a look at him. Neun sent back a glowing report, citing Power's hitting skill, speed, and ability to play multiple positions. Then, in the last month of the season, during which Power hit .334 with fourteen homers, 105 RBI, and a league-leading ten triples, the Yankees purchased his contract for $7,000, of which the Drummondville owner reluctantly gave $2,000 to Power later. "I had to really nag him for what I was due," Power said. "He finally gave it to me in Canadian money, which at the time was worth 10 per cent less than American money." That winter the Yankees sent him a contract for their Triple A team in Kansas City for the 1951 season, which he quickly signed, only to be later informed he was being sent instead to Syracuse in the Triple A International League. "At first I didn't know why," he said, "but later I find out why—segregation—less of that in Syracuse than in Kansas City."

Elston Howard's entrance into Organized Baseball and his ascension with the Yankees was very similar to Power's. A four-sport star at the all-black Vashon High School in St. Louis, Howard dearly wanted to sign with his hometown team, the Cardinals. But after the Cardinals invited him to try out in the summer of 1947, Howard never heard back from them. A few days after that tryout George Sisler Jr., the Cardinals' assistant director of scouting, was having lunch with *St. Louis Globe-Democrat* sports columnist Robert L. Burnes and complained about his organization's racial policies. "I have been watching the best young prospect I've looked at in years—a big good looking kid just coming out of Vashon High," Sisler told Burnes. "I worked him out for two days and I'd stake my job on his ability to make it. But they won't let me sign him. I spent the whole morning pleading my case. I argued that now that the Dodgers have signed Robinson, everybody is going to fall into line. But I was turned down."

It wasn't until February of 1954, after Budweiser Beer baron August A. "Gussie" Busch had bought the team and ordered his scouts to start looking in earnest for black prospects, that the Cardinals "fell into line" as one of the last NL teams to employ a black player, by purchasing Tom Alston, a six-feet-five, 210-pound first baseman, from the San Diego Padres of the Triple A Pacific Coast League for $100,000 and four players, one of whom was Sisler's brother, Dick. Alston, a Navy veteran and college grad from North Carolina A&T, had hit .297 with 101 RBI while playing in all of the Padres' 180 games in 1953. He was listed as twenty-four years old but was, in fact, five years older than that, as the Padres owners had altered his birth certificate in order to extract a more lucrative compensation for his contract.

Alston made the Cardinals right out of spring training in 1954—some suggested because he was viewed as Gussie Busch's "pet project"—beating out the bulky six-feet-one, 230-pound incumbent, Steve Bilko, for the first-base job largely on the merits of his fielding. But the rest of Alston's brief major league career was both disappointing and tragic. On June 29, with his batting average at .245 with just four home runs, Alston was optioned by the Cardinals to Triple A Rochester to work on his hitting. There were those in the Cardinals organization who later said he needed work on all the aspects of his game and questioned why the club had paid such a price for him. Frank Lane, the Cardinals general manager in 1957, often referred to Alston as "a circus clown" who "couldn't play a lick"—harsh, to the say the least. Bob Broeg, the respected longtime baseball columnist for the *St. Louis Post-Dispatch*, was much kinder in his memory of Alston. "He looked like a real good athlete and was outstanding defensively," said Broeg. Early in that '57 season, however, Alston abruptly left the Cardinals, never to return. He'd suffered a nervous breakdown, and for the next twelve years spent time in two different mental hospitals. His final line in the majors: ninety-one games, .244 average, four homers, and thirty-six RBI.

As for Elston Howard, undaunted by his rejection from the Cardinals and determined to continue pursuing a professional baseball career, he decided to sign with Jackie Robinson's old Negro League team, the Kansas City Monarchs. After playing three years for the Monarchs, Howard's contract was sold in 1950 to the Yankees, who gave him a $2,500 bonus. Once again it was Tom Greenwade who recommended the signing. Greenwade's primary scouting territory for the Yankees was Missouri, Oklahoma, Kansas, and Colorado, and he had scouted the Monarchs extensively. Howard was Power's teammate at Kansas City in

1953, hitting .330 with twenty-two homers and 109 RBI while shifting back and forth from catching to the outfield.

With the trade of Power, Howard was now the Yankees' number-one prospect, on whom much of the media scrutiny was to be focused come spring training. But the *Chicago Defender*, among others, remained skeptical about when or if he would ever see the bright lights of Yankee Stadium. "Just how the Yankees hope to profit by retaining Elston Howard whom the big brass considers a 'far better prospect' than Power is the mystery," the *Defender* wrote. "An even bigger question is what now happens to Howard? Will he, too, be shunted off somewhere else before the training season opens to staining the color complex of the Yankees?"

As a matter of fact, Weiss did have a couple of more moves in hand that winter, and although they did not involve Howard, they served to upset the status quo of the all-white, five-time world champions far more than the eleven-player Vic Power trade had.

BILL VEECK LEAVES THE STAGE IN THE AMERICAN LEAGUE'S WINDS OF CHANGE

"Sometime, somewhere, there will be
a club no one really wants. And ole Will will
come wandering along to laugh some more.
Look for me under the arc-lights, boys. I'll be back."

—*VEECK AS IN WRECK*

I N THE SPRING OF 1953 BILL VEECK, THE ICONOCLASTIC OWNER OF the St. Louis Browns who had made a living of tweaking the noses of his fellow baseball lords, in particular George Weiss and Del Webb of the Yankees, was now feeling the squeeze from them. As owner of the Cleveland Indians from 1946 to 1949, Veeck had been the first to integrate in the American League when he signed center fielder Larry Doby in 1947. A year later, with Doby and fortysomething Negro Leagues pitching legend

Satchel Paige playing key roles, the Indians won their first world championship since 1920.

Although they had had a quick impact in the major leagues—Doby hit .301 with fourteen homers and sixty-six RBI in his rookie '48 season, then .318 with a homer and two RBI in the World Series against the Boston Braves, while Paige won six of his seven starts during the season with a 2.48 ERA—they were overshadowed insofar as fan appeal by their popular manager, 1948 AL Most Valuable Player shortstop, Lou Boudreau, and Bob Feller, the fireballing war hero, who led AL pitchers in strikeouts for the third straight year. The flamboyant Paige was well past his prime and, in fact, the Indians released him a year later. Conversely, Doby was introverted, often sullen, a loner who did not really become a fan favorite in Cleveland until 1952, the first year he led the AL in homers and drove in over a hundred runs. He also had a prickly relationship with Indians general manager Hank Greenberg, who, in '52, cut his salary from $25,000 to $19,000 because his batting average dropped off nineteen points from the year before.

But Veeck was now with the moribund Browns, who in the first two seasons of his stewardship had finished last and next-to-last with 192 losses. He found himself severely strapped financially and in a losing battle with his Sportsman Park tenants, the NL Cardinals, for fan support in St. Louis.

When Veeck and his syndicate bought the Browns for $1.75 million in 1951 he did so acknowledging privately that St. Louis could no longer support two major league teams. But even though the Cardinals had enjoyed a far more successful history than the perennially losing Browns, having won more pennants (nine) and World Series (six) than any other team in baseball except the Yankees, Veeck believed he had the means and the wherewithal to drive them out of town. What made Veeck confident he could prevail was the fact that (1) the Browns owned Sportsman Park where the two teams played and (2) the Cardinals' owner, Fred Saigh, was an attorney and not nearly as affluent as most of the other major league owners. Unfortunately for Veeck, both circumstances and his fellow owners conspired against him almost from the get-go in St. Louis.

Because he'd had to borrow over a million dollars to buy 33 percent of the team stock from his syndicate, he had left himself little working capital for operating expenses. A prime example of this, he later noted, was when his top scout, Bill Norman, whom he'd dispatched to the Negro Leagues in search of talent, reported back with great excitement about a shortstop with the Kansas City Monarchs named Ernie Banks. The owner of the Monarchs, Tom Baird, was a friend of Veeck's, but when Veeck called him about Banks, he was told the price was $35,000. Veeck pleaded with Baird to take $3,500 down "and the rest when you can catch me." Baird laughed. "That's the way I'm doing business myself," he said. "For Banks, I've got to get the whole $35,000 to pay my own bills." So, for lack of a few thousand dollars, Veeck lost out on one of the greatest players of all time, a rare power-hitting shortstop who could've been a franchise player for the Browns. Instead, determined to make sure an AL club didn't sign him, Veeck tipped off his friend, Phil Wrigley, owner of the Chicago Cubs, about Banks. Wrigley wound up paying the Monarchs $20,000 for Banks and a pitcher named Bill Dickey, and Banks went on to hit 512 homers in the big leagues as the franchise player for the Cubs.

Underfinanced as Veeck was, however, the biggest factor in his downfall in St. Louis was something completely out of his control. In April of 1952 Saigh was indicted on federal charges of having evaded $49,260 in income taxes between 1946 and 1949, and the following January, after pleading no contest to $19,000 in tax underpayments, he was sentenced to fifteen months in prison, and Baseball Commissioner Ford Frick ordered him to sell the Cardinals. All of this happened just as Veeck was seemingly winning his turf war with Saigh. After drawing only 293,790 in 1951, the Browns, thanks in large part to Veeck's promotions, drew 518,796 in 1952—more than they'd drawn in their only AL pennant season, 1944. For a while Saigh was unable to find any local buyers for the Cardinals, but as he engaged in talks with a group in Milwaukee and millionaire Texas oil magnate Clint Murchison, suddenly Gussie Busch, patriarch of the St. Louis–based Anheuser-Busch Brewery, stepped forward and bowled him over with an offer of $3.75 million for the Cardinals.

When that happened Veeck knew he was done in St. Louis. He would never be able to run the Cardinals out of town now, and his only recourse was to beat his own path out of St. Louis. His first choice was Milwaukee, where he'd operated the Triple A minor league Brewers in the American Association from 1941 to '45. Milwaukee was already building a new $5 million stadium, and the city fathers had been openly lobbying for a Major League Baseball team. The problem for Veeck was that local operators had recently sold the Milwaukee Triple A franchise to Lou Perini, owner of the Boston Braves, who were fighting their own losing battle with the Red Sox for fan support in a two-team city. Just three years removed from drawing 1,455,439 in 1948 when they faced Veeck's Indians in the World Series, the Braves had deteriorated into a 64–89 seventh-place team in 1952, with the lowest attendance—281,278—in baseball, and Perini claimed he'd lost $600,000.

In the days after Anheuser-Busch bought the Cardinals, Veeck engaged Perini feverishly about selling the Milwaukee franchise to him. When Perini continued to resist, Veeck knew the Braves' owner, despite his public denials, had decided to move his own team to Milwaukee in time for the 1953 season. Now Veeck had to scramble, and he quickly set his sights on Baltimore, which had a Triple A franchise in the International League and was also building a new stadium in hopes of luring a major league team. After lobbying the other AL owners, Veeck thought he had the necessary six votes to approve his move of the Browns to Baltimore, with only the Yankees sure to oppose him on general principle. But when he walked into the AL meeting at the Tampa Terrace Hotel in Tampa on March 16, 1953, he was stunned to hear the clubs, one by one, express their reservations about the Browns going to Baltimore. Unbeknownst to him, the Yankees had wielded their considerable influence with the other AL clubs and convinced the majority of them that, by turning down the Browns' transfer, they would succeed in ridding the game of Veeck, whose "revolutionary" ideas, like splitting gate receipts and sharing TV revenue, along with his often outrageous promotions—like sending a three-feet-seven midget, Eddie Gaedel, up to pinch hit in a game in 1951, or "Grandstand Managers Day," in which thousands of fans were able to vote on in-game strategic decisions by holding up placards—had made him an anathema to the staid baseball establishment. After the 6–2 vote against the Browns' shift, Veeck left the room. George Weiss, the Yankees general manager, then stood up and said, "Veeck is a lousy operator, we all know that. He owes the league money. The American League will be better off without him."

It was no secret why the ultraconservative stuffed-shirt Yankee high command regarded Veeck as an irritant and the league was better off without him. In addition to frowning on his zany promotions, the Yankees led the steadfast resistance to Veeck's various proposals at the league meetings designed to even the playing field for the less affluent clubs. In particular, he continually pushed for the visiting teams to be given a better break of the box office receipts and took that a step further by refusing to allow other teams to televise their home games against his Browns. The argument for that was, by televising home games, fewer fans would be attending the games in person, thus cutting into the box office receipts. The Yankees, however, successfully thwarted Veeck by getting the rest of the clubs to agree not to schedule any night games with the Browns, games that were their life blood. In his famous 1962 memoir, *Veeck as in Wreck*, Veeck summed up his relationship with the Yankees thusly: "Whenever I offered any plan that would give the other teams a fighting chance against them, they cried socialism, the first refuge of scoundrels."

Two days after the AL owners rejected Veeck, the National League met at the Vinoy Hotel in St. Petersburg, Florida, and voted unanimously to allow Perini to move the Braves from Boston to Milwaukee—the first franchise shift by either league in fifty years. By his refusal to sell the Milwaukee franchise to Veeck, thus preventing the Browns from moving there for 1953, Perini faced lawsuits and the prospect of a fan boycott if he waited another year, which explained the most hastily carried out franchise shift in baseball history. The Braves went to the 1953 spring training as a team from Boston and left it as a team in Milwaukee. And by their first thirteen home dates in '53, the Braves had drawn 302,667 fans, over 20,000 more than their entire 1952 season in Boston. By season's end Milwaukee had set an all-time NL attendance record of 1,826,397. They went over 2 million for each of the next four seasons.

All of this, it should be noted, was not lost on Brooklyn Dodgers owner Walter O'Malley, who was looking to replace his own ballpark, Ebbets Field, which was built in 1913 and becoming more and more decrepit. Ebbets Field's seating capacity was 32,000 compared to 36,011 at Milwaukee's new County Stadium, and when the Braves outdrew the NL champion Dodgers by 700,000 fans in 1953, alarm bells went off for O'Malley.

Now a lame duck in St. Louis for the 1953 season, Veeck, in order to pay his bills, was forced to sell his ranch in Arizona as well as Sportsman's Park to Gussie Busch for $1.1 million. Then, in June of '53, with another payroll in peril, Veeck had to sell his best pitcher, Virgil Trucks, to the Chicago White Sox for $95,000 in a transaction that was dressed up as a trade but was, in fact, a save-the-franchise cash deal. At the end of September Veeck made one more last-ditch effort at the AL owners meeting in New York to move the Browns to Baltimore, only to again be denied, this time by a vote of 4–4. Conceding defeat, Veeck was left no choice but to sell the Browns for $2.475 million to a Baltimore consortium headed up by a local attorney, Clarence W. Miles. It was Veeck who had enlisted Miles to be part of his original syndicate in order to satisfy the league requirement of having local ownership represented in his group. When the AL owners approved the sale, the only smiles wider than those of Miles and Baltimore mayor Thomas D'Alesandro were those of George Weiss and Yankee co-owner Del Webb.

A MONTH AFTER THE AL OWNERS' MEETING IN NEW YORK HAD succeeded in ridding baseball of Veeck for the time being, the Major League Rules Committee met in Manhattan and enacted two significant rules changes, the full impact of which would not be felt until the following spring. The first change regarded the sacrifice fly rule. The committee decreed that the sacrifice fly would now apply only when a runner was scored from third base on a fly to the outfield and that the batter would not be charged with a time at-bat. Committee chairman Jim Gallagher, the general manager of the Chicago Cubs, estimated that it would boost the average of long-ball hitters seven or eight points per season.

In addition, the nine-man committee adopted an amendment to Rule 3:16 that would now require all fielders to bring their gloves and other equipment from the field when they came in to the dugout for their team's time at bat.

From almost the beginning of time in baseball, fielders had been allowed to leave their gloves on the field when they came in to bat. Cleveland Indians general manager Hank Greenberg, a member of the committee, explained, "Aside from the possibility of hindering the play, gloves on the field look sloppy." Although it seemed like a logical change by the Rules Committee—and one that probably should've been made years earlier—it instead evoked howls of resistance from players, managers, and executives alike, especially in the American League, which voted 7–1 not to adhere to it. As teams began gathering for spring training in February of 1954, criticism of the rules change became more and more outspoken.

Clark Griffith, the eighty-four-year-old owner of the Washington Senators who had been in baseball since 1887, noted, "In 67 years I have only once seen a batted ball hit a glove lying out there, and that time it didn't affect the play. The ball was a single and ended up a single." Griffith further argued that there had never been a World Series game in which a batted ball struck a glove on the field and affected a play.

"This rule is driving us nuts," said Chicago White Sox manager Paul Richards. "My center fielder, Johnny Groth, is the third out for us three times the other day, and he winds up at second base after running out a fly ball. Then he has to come all the way back to the bench and get his glove before he can go to his position in center field."

"It's a silly rule," echoed Philadelphia Phillies center fielder Richie Ashburn. "I usually get on base 300 times a season. Since I score approximately 100 times, that means I'm stranded on base 200 times and have to make an extra trip to the dugout for my glove. If they want to make the field look tidier and prettier, they should plant flowers."

Apparently, in the early days of the rule change the players had not figured out that teammates could bring the gloves out to them after they were left on base at the end of innings.

Managers and general managers, meanwhile, saw the rule change as opening up loopholes for deliberately delaying games. "Suppose a situation prompted a club to stall, and some player held up a game with the statement that his glove had been mis-laid?" asked Boston Red Sox general manager Joe Cronin. "Could the umpire force that player to go into the field before that glove was 'found'?"

"What if you have a day when rain is threatening or it's started to rain?" asked Red Sox manager Lou Boudreau. "A manager or a player could stall, more or less legally. All you'd have to do is have your center fielder forget to take his glove out with him. Then he'd have to go back to the bench to find it. Same thing if you wanted to give your relief pitcher extra rest or warm-up pitches. It's like faking injuries on the football field."

And Giants manager Leo Durocher must have thought the rules change was directed at him. For years Durocher, who served as his own third base coach, had a superstitious ritual between innings of picking up the discarded glove of the opposing third baseman, pounding his fist into the pocket three times, then walking over to the third base bag and kicking it three times.

Nevertheless, after allowing everyone to air their gripes throughout spring training, Baseball Commissioner Ford Frick issued a five-paragraph bulletin to the sixteen clubs the day before the start of the season, demanding strict enforcement of the new gloves rule and threatening reprimands, fines, or even forfeiture of games if clubs and players failed to adhere to it. In pointing out this was "now a part of the official baseball rules,"

Frick decreed, "It cannot be changed by league or individual club action or league. League or club officials who attempt to make their own determination as to enforcement of the rule will be subject to such penalties as apply to other sections of the playing code."

Amazingly, that was the end of it. Just as there had been no specific incidents anyone could remember about the outcome of games previously being affected by batted balls striking gloves in the outfield or fielders tripping over gloves, there were no incidents of players forgetting their gloves or of games being delayed over the new rule in 1954. And ten years later it had been almost forgotten that, for the first seventy-five years of baseball, players had been allowed to leave their gloves on the field when they came in to bat.

LIKE THE BRAVES' SHIFT TO MILWAUKEE, THE BROWNS TRANSFER TO Baltimore as the reborn Orioles proved to be an instant box-office bonanza. On Opening Day in Baltimore, April 15, 1954, the Orioles drew a capacity crowd of 46,354 at the still-unfinished Memorial Stadium, after being greeted by twenty-two bands and thirty-three floats in a parade through the city streets that began at Camden Station, where they stepped off the train from Detroit. Fifty years later Duane Pillette, a pitcher on that '54 Orioles team, recalled it as "one of my most exciting times in baseball. I never had a big ego, but my heart and body kind of puffed up right there. During the parade I thought, 'Damn! We're pretty good!'"

Actually, they weren't any better than the Browns of the year before in St. Louis, finishing with the same dismal 54–100 record. Financially, however, they were a huge success, drawing 1,060,910 fans that first season in Baltimore and earning a net profit of $882,011 before taxes for Miles and his syndicate. Quite a turnaround from the $330,000 and $707,000 in losses Veeck had incurred the previous two seasons in St. Louis.

Indeed, the remarkable turnaround in fortune by both the Braves and Orioles in their new cities prompted the major league owners to begin serious discussions of expanding their horizons and, in particular, for the AL owners to focus on their other failing franchise in a two-city market, the Philadelphia Athletics. Under their ninety-one-year-old patriarch, Connie Mack, the A's, an original AL franchise in 1901, had enjoyed a proud history of two separate dynasties in Philadelphia, 1902–1914, when they won six pennants and three World Series, and 1929–1932, when they won three pennants and two more World Series. With Mack as their manager and general manager for the first fifty years, the Athletics signed and spawned eight future Hall of Famers in pitchers Chief Bender, Rube Waddell, Eddie Plank, and Lefty Grove; first baseman Jimmie Foxx; second baseman Eddie Collins; third baseman "Home Run" Baker; and outfielder Al Simmons; plus dozens of other standout major leaguers, including the 1952 AL Most Valuable Player, pitcher Bobby Shantz; nine-time hundred-RBI outfielder "Indian Bob" Johnson; thirties and forties outfield star Roger "Doc" Cramer; lifetime .307-hitting first baseman Stuffy McInnis; two-time batting champion Ferris Fain; and right-hander Ed Rommel, who twice led the AL in victories and then went on to a second career as an umpire.

But by 1954 the Athletics had fallen on bleak times. Since their last AL pennant-winning team in 1931, which Mack was forced to break up in order to secure enough working capital to keep the franchise solvent, they had had sixteen losing seasons, including ten last-place finishes. In 1950, at age eighty-eight, Mack was finally forced to give up the manager's reins while also turning the day-to-day operations of the club over to his two sons, Roy and Earle. Although they were still the owners of Connie Mack Stadium and the landlords of the NL Phillies, their tenants were routinely outdrawing them by more than two to one. In 1953 the third-place Phillies drew 853,644 to just 362,113 for the last-place A's. When the Athletics' turnstile pace failed to pick up in 1954, amid increasing financial distress and a burgeoning power rift between the Mack brothers, the AL owners sought to take measures to find a buyer for the team and relocate it. Enter Arnold M. Johnson, a forty-seven-year-old Chicago industrialist and friend of Yankees' co-owner Del Webb who, in December of 1953, had purchased Yankee Stadium from the Yankees for $6.5 million, along with Blues Stadium in Kansas City, the home of their Triple A minor league club. Before the sale of Blues Stadium to Johnson, Kansas City officials had sought to buy the park from the Yankees for the purposes of adding to its capacity and luring a major league team. Johnson, in turn, promised to continue working with them in that effort.

Sensing the American League's intentions, Philadelphia mayor Joseph Clark, on July 1, implored the Philadelphia citizenry to support the A's while also announcing the formation of a seventy-five-person "Save the A's" commission designed to drum up attendance for them. The commission was a failure, and in late July Roy Mack, who, with his brother, owned 52 percent of the team, insisted the A's would not be moved. At the same time, however, Roy Mack admitted both he and his brother had refused to sell their shares of the club to each other, leaving control of the failing franchise at a stalemate.

Despite reports of numerous Philadelphia groups expressing interest in purchasing the team from the Macks, only Johnson, buoyed by the approval of Kansas City citizens for a $2 million bond issue to purchase and enlarge Blues Stadium, had actually made an offer for the team.

Two days after the close of 1954 season the AL owners took up the Athletics issue in a rancorous six-hour meeting in New York in which Johnson's initial effort to buy the team was rebuffed after Connie and Earle Mack agreed to sell their shares, but Roy held out, asking for a two-week delay to find local investors. At this point the AL owners and Del Webb in particular were becoming exasperated with Roy Mack. Webb, it seemed, had a vested interest in Johnson getting the A's. The two had been partners in numerous businesses, one of them a large vending machine company, and in order to finance his purchases of Yankee Stadium and Blues Stadium in Kansas City, Johnson had taken out a $2.9 million mortgage against the properties with the Yankees co-owners, Webb, and Dan Topping. In addition, Johnson had promised the project of enlarging Blues Stadium to Webb's construction company. And though some owners thought it somewhat curious that Webb would be pushing so hard to relocate the Athletics in what would be the smallest market in baseball, Bill Veeck, for one, saw that as a ruse on the part of his mortal enemies, the Yankees.

After all, shortly after being forced out of baseball with the Browns, Veeck was given an option on the territorial rights to Los Angeles by Cubs owner Phil Wrigley, who owned the Triple A Pacific Coast League there. Armed with that option, Veeck attempted to enter the bidding for the A's with the idea of moving them to Los Angeles, which also happened to be the home base of Del Webb's construction company. Throughout the '54 season Webb had intimated to his high-rolling friends in Los Angeles, men like hotel magnate Conrad Hilton and real estate tycoon Henry Crown, his intentions of getting an AL franchise for the city. But he wasn't about to have the owner of that franchise be Veeck, who was never allowed to make a formal bid for the A's.

Rather, after two separate local groups offered to match Johnson's $3.375 million offer for the A's *and* keep the team in

Philadelphia, the AL owners held yet a third meeting on the issue in New York on October 28, at which they rejected an offer from a nine-man Philadelphia syndicate. Six days later the Macks agreed to sell the team to Johnson. The one notable condition of the sale approval was that Johnson had to sell Yankee Stadium—to avoid any conflict of interest with the Yankees, naturally. It was Veeck's conspiracy theory that Webb, believing that Kansas City would never be able to adequately support Major League Baseball, arranged with Johnson to have his friend be a "caretaker" there for a couple of years before moving the team again to Los Angeles.

No one will ever know, however, as Johnson died of a cerebral hemorrhage in March 1960 at the age of fifty-three. By the end of 1960 the A's attendance in Kansas City had plummeted to 774,944 from a record 1,393,054 that first season in '55. In that respect Webb had been prescient, although he was now perfectly happy just to have Johnson in the game, even if it was in Kansas City. For, in Johnson, Webb had himself a comrade in arms who, besides being someone he could count on in all the league votes, operated the A's like a Yankee farm team from 1955 to 1960, constantly replenishing their needs with a series of one-sided trades that sent one All-Star-caliber player after another— Roger Maris, Clete Boyer, Ryne Duren, Bobby Shantz, Ralph Terry, Héctor López—on the Kansas City shuttle to New York.

For Veeck, there was a last laugh, even if it was tinged with bitterness. In twice going to such lengths to keep him out of baseball in 1954, the American League, with the Yankees leading the way, managed to consign itself to two of the game's smallest market cities while leaving the door wide open for the National League to beat them to the West Coast with the shift of the Brooklyn Dodgers and New York Giants to Los Angeles and San Francisco, respectively, in 1957.

CHAPTER
3

WAITING FOR WILLIE

"I'm not sure what the hell charisma is,
but I get the feeling it's Willie Mays."

—TED KLUSZEWSKI

LATE IN THE AFTERNOON ON FEBRUARY 1, 1954, BOBBY THOMSON
returned home from the Richmond County Country Club, in
Staten Island, New York, where he went almost every day for a
round of golf and a run with his dog, up and down the rolling
hills of the course, when his wife, Elaine, greeted him at the door
and informed him that Chub Feeney had just called.

Beginning the day after the 1953 season had ended and
then all through the winter months of November, December,
and January, Thomson had anticipated getting this call from
the general manager of the New York Giants, mostly with a
sense of dread. From the time he was two years old, when his
father brought the family to America from Glasgow, Scotland,
where Bobby was born, he'd lived in Staten Island and had
gained iconic status there after seven years as a fixture in the

New York Giants' outfield, including one indelible moment, October 3, 1951, when he hit the most famous home run in baseball history. Thomson loved Staten Island, the only place he'd really ever known as home; loved New York and its worldly charm, and loved being a Giant, even if he went out of his way to shun the accompanying fame and popularity from having hit "the shot heard 'round the world" to beat the Brooklyn Dodgers in the momentous 1951 playoff game that climaxed New York's thirteen-and-a-half-game comeback to the NL pennant.

Two years after that "miracle" season the Giants had slipped to fifth place in the National League, 70–84, a record reflected by a pitching staff that also ranked fifth in the league in ERA in 1953. At season's end, Giants manager Leo Durocher could not help but look forward to 1954 and the return of Willie Mays from a year and a half in the Army. The wondrous twenty-two-year-old center fielder, whose hitting, fielding, and base-running élan was displayed over 121 games in his rookie season of 1951 and another 34 in '52, was drafted into the service. Mays had already been emphatically stamped by Durocher as a budding superstar. "Next year," Durocher told reporters after that last game, "we'll have Willie back, and this'll be a different team. Count on it."

Nobody knew that better than Bobby Thomson, who had done the outfield math—four into three didn't go—and read the papers all winter in which Durocher and Feeney were frequently quoted citing the Giants' most pressing need as an upgrade of the pitching staff. The thirty-year-old Thomson had had one of his best seasons in 1953, hitting .288, with a team-leading twenty-six homers and 106 RBI—probably too good a season to his reasoning. He was flanked in the outfield by twenty-six-year-old Don Mueller in right, who'd hit a career high .333 in '53, and Monte Irvin in left, coming off a .329 season with twenty-one homers and ninety-seven RBI. To get a quality pitcher, Thomson knew, the Giants were going to have to sacrifice a significant player, and with Mays coming back to assume duty in center field, he was the odd man out. They weren't going to trade Irvin, a thirty-four-year-old veteran of the Negro Leagues who had served as a kind of guardian for Mays, or Mueller, who, despite a lack of power, was Durocher's kind of player, with his superb defense, strong throwing arm, and knack for hitting in the clutch.

So when Thomson called Chub Feeney back, he knew what the general manager was going to tell him. The only thing he didn't know was where he was being traded. "We've made a deal with Milwaukee," Feeney said. "We're getting two good, young left-handed pitchers from the Braves, Johnny Antonelli and Don Liddle. I think you know, Bobby, you have been a very important part of the Giants franchise and given us seven very fine seasons. But we could not have made this trade without including you in it. The Braves insisted. You were the guy they wanted."

"I actually felt relief," Thomson recalled in an interview with me shortly before his death in 2010. "The Braves were a team that was clearly on the rise, having finished second in '53, their first year in Milwaukee, and Milwaukee had shown itself to be a baseball-crazy city. My one disappointment was that they'd had all winter to make this deal and waited until right before spring training. I barely had time to make all the travel and accommodation arrangements for my family. One thing was sure, though, I wasn't giving up my home in Staten Island."

Part of the reason the trade took so long was because the Braves' first priority that winter had been to acquire a second baseman, a mission they did not accomplish until the day after Christmas, when they sent thirty-five-year-old power-hitting left fielder Sid Gordon and two other players to the last-place Pittsburgh Pirates for twenty-six-year-old Danny O'Connell, who hit .294 in 149 games for Pittsburgh in '53. With Gordon gone, Braves general manager John Quinn now had a need for another power bat in left field, and he spent the month of January engaging Feeney on Thomson, all the while steadfastly trying to keep the twenty-three-year-old Antonelli out of the deal.

A native of upstate Rochester, New York, Antonelli was one of the original "bonus babies" of baseball, receiving $75,000 to sign with the Braves out of high school in 1948. Under the "bonus baby" rule, established in 1947, any amateur player receiving a bonus in excess of $4,000 had to be kept on the major league roster for two years before he could be assigned to the minors. Like so many fresh-out-of-high-school teenagers affected by the rule, Antonelli would have surely benefited from minor league seasoning and pitching regularly at the beginning of his professional career instead of pitching sporadically out of the bullpen for the Braves. Still, the youngster was able to hold his own in his first two seasons in the big leagues, 1949–1950, compiling a 5–10 record and 4.41 ERA before going into the military service for two years. When he returned to the Braves in '53, a much more polished pitcher for having pitched for the Third Infantry military team in Fort Myer, Virginia, against numerous other service teams stocked with major league players, he was inserted right into their starting rotation and was 12–12 with a 3.19 ERA, fifth best in the National League, along with 131 strikeouts in 175 innings. In midseason, however, Antonelli contracted pneumonia, which left him weakened much of the second half and probably deprived him of two to three extra wins.

In both cities the initial reaction to the trade was less than enthusiastic. Brave fans couldn't understand how Quinn could have given up on this promising young left-handed pitcher to whom they'd given so much money, whereas Giant fans were upset at seeing the popular Thomson sent out of town and questioned why he couldn't have simply been moved to third base to make room for Mays instead of exiled entirely.

In that regard Giants owner Horace Stoneham and manager Leo Durocher did their best to sell the trade to the fans as a potential pennant winner. "Bobby Thomson always played fine ball for us, and, of course, he'll always be remembered at the Polo Grounds as the hero of the 1951 season," said Stoneham. "But it has become evident that the Giants must strengthen their pitching staff for '54, and to get the men we wanted, Antonelli and Liddle, we had to include Thomson in the deal."

Echoing the owner, Durocher said, "We hated to lose Thomson, but we had to have pitching. Our club did all right with this deal."

Two weeks later Durocher greeted Antonelli, Liddle, and the rest of the Giants at spring training in Phoenix, Arizona. Antonelli was pleasantly surprised when the manager called him aside and informed him he was going to be the Giants' number-one starter. Then, in his opening address to the troops, Durocher spoke confidently about the season at hand and mostly about the guy who was not yet in camp.

"Gentlemen," Durocher said, "I'm sure you're all aware that this is a different team from the one that finished fifth last year. We've brought in some new players who are going to really help us, and in a couple of weeks our center fielder will be joining us from the Army. Those of you who were here in '51, when he came up as a twenty-year-old rookie, know what I mean when I say that he's that rare kind of player who can single-handedly lead us to the pennant. This is like getting us a twenty-game winner."

The player to whom Durocher was referring was, of course, Mays, who for the previous ten months had been stationed as a private in the Army at Fort Eustis, Virginia. Mays began his professional baseball career in 1948 at the age sixteen while he was still in high school in Birmingham, with the Birmingham Black Barons of the Negro American League. The Black Barons' manager, Piper Davis, was introduced to Mays by Willie's father, Cat, with whom Davis had been a teammate years earlier in the Alabama Industrial League. Davis was regarded as the premier second baseman in the Negro Leagues and was one of the players Brooklyn Dodgers general manager Branch Rickey was considering to break baseball's color line in 1946. But by then Davis was already thirty years old, and Rickey instead opted to sign Jackie Robinson, the shortstop for the Kansas City Monarchs of the Negro American League who was college educated and only twenty-seven.

Under the tutelage of Davis, Mays gradually became a complete player for the Monarchs. "He could hit and throw and really go get it in the outfield," Davis later recalled. "But he couldn't hit a curve ball. He also had to learn how to charge a ground ball that got through the infield and to throw the ball on one hop to the plate." Davis helped Mays master the curveball by having him straighten up more in his stance and getting him out of the habit of turning his front shoulder to the plate, which made it harder for him to see the ball.

"Piper was the one who had the most influence on me," Mays said, "because I wasn't old enough to understand all the things about the game all the older guys on the Barons knew. I was out there by myself, and Piper saw to it that I learned."

It took a couple of years with the Black Barons before Mays began to mature as a hitter commensurate to his defensive prowess. It was the latter who had scouts, like the Yankees' Joe Press, who recommended both him and Davis to his boss, Paul Krichell, to no avail, closely monitoring him. In 1949, when Mays became a .300 hitter for the first time, Davis got him a tryout with the Boston Red Sox as part of a working agreement the Red Sox had between their Class AA Southern Association affiliate, the Birmingham Barons, and the Black Barons. There are varying accounts about whether there was an actual tryout—apparently three straight days of rain postponed it—but what was confirmed was that Red Sox scout George Digby, who'd been watching the Black Barons, later raved to Boston general manager Joe Cronin that Mays was the "single greatest talent I have ever seen," only to have Cronin tell him the Red Sox had "no interest in the boy at this time."

In a January 2005 interview with Gordon Edes of the *Boston Globe*, the then-eighty-seven-year-old Digby related that the Black Barons' owner told him the Red Sox could have Mays for $4,500. When this was relayed to Cronin and Red Sox owner Tom Yawkey, the Red Sox sent another scout down to Birmingham to look at Mays. "But by then, Yawkey and Cronin already had made up their minds they weren't going to take on any black players," Digby said. "There was nothing I could do except imagine how we could have had Willie Mays and Ted Williams in the same outfield."

The next year the Red Sox did sign Davis to a $1,500 contract to play for their Class A Scranton team in the Eastern League, with the promise of another $1,500 if he was still on the roster by May 15. But on May 13, despite leading the Scranton team in batting, homers, RBI, and stolen bases, Davis was released for what the Red Sox cited as "economic reasons." And it was not until July 21, 1959, that the Red Sox became the last team in the major leagues to integrate when they promoted infielder Pumpsie Green from their Triple A Minneapolis affiliate. As for Davis, he never made it to the majors. After his curious release from the Red Sox he played eight more seasons in the Triple A

International and Pacific Coast Leagues and the Double A Texas League without ever getting another call.

Mays later said he was deeply disappointed the Red Sox did not offer him a contract. "I didn't care about the money," he told me in 2009. "I just wanted to play." But life is a series of fates, and although the Red Sox missed theirs with Willie, the Giants wound up beneficiaries of their apparent racially motivated snub—almost by accident. In May 1949 the Black Barons played a doubleheader in the Polo Grounds against the New York Cubans, who were owned and operated by Alex Pompez, a prominent sports promoter with numerous "side" occupations, including being an operator of the New York illegal lottery "numbers" game. His involvement with the racketeer Dutch Schultz's numbers operation led to his indictment by the New York district attorney in 1932, but he later became a star witness for the prosecution in their investigation. Despite his flamboyant and somewhat shady persona, Pompez was highly respected in Major League Baseball circles for his ability to recognize talent. Through the years Pompez sold a number of his New York Cuban players to the big leagues to keep the team going, and as co-tenants with the Giants at the Polo Grounds, he became good friends with Giants owner Horace Stoneham.

It was during that doubleheader, in which Mays was playing center field for the Black Barons, when Pompez got to talking with Giants' scouting and player development director Carl Hubbell, who was at the games to look at a couple of the Cuban players, third baseman Ray Dandridge and pitcher Ray Barnwell. However, when Hubbell saw Mays making a couple of effortless running catches in center field while hitting a half-dozen batting practice home runs into the Polo Grounds' farthest reaches in left and left-center field, he was bowled over and sought to sign him right there, only to have Piper Davis tell him of the promise he'd made to Mays' father not to allow Willie to sign with a major league team until he completed high school.

A year later Hubbell sent one of his top scouts, Eddie Montague, to Birmingham, purportedly to sign the Black Barons' first baseman Alonzo Perry. In fact, he'd instructed Montague to feign interest in Perry as a decoy for all the other scouts, with the Giants' real intention to sign Mays, who was now about to graduate from high school. During the year's interim Pompez, as a favor to Stoneham, had quietly brokered the deal for Mays with Barons' reclusive owner, Tom Hayes, who had an ardent distrust for major league operators and had continually put off overtures for Mays.

On the day he graduated from high school in June of 1950 Mays signed with the Giants for a $4,000 bonus and was assigned to their Trenton team in the Class B Interstate League, with Stoneham paying Hayes $10,000 for his contract. From there his rise to the majors was meteoric. He hit .353 in eighty-one games at Trenton in 1950 and was promoted all the way to Triple A Minneapolis for the 1951 season. He was hitting .477 in the first thirty-five games when Stoneham had him summoned to New York. However, the fan protest in Minneapolis over the quick call-up of the electrifying youngster was so strong that Stoneham was forced to take out full-page ads in the local newspapers explaining that New York needed Willie more and that it wouldn't be fair to him for the Giants to keep him in the minors.

When Willie went hitless in his first twelve at-bats for the Giants, however, he was bewildered, wondering whether he belonged in the big leagues. His teammates, Irvin especially, reassured him, and then, on May 28, in his fourth game, he got the first of what would be 3,283 major league hits, with a towering home run over the Polo Grounds' left field roof off Warren Spahn, the Boston Braves' wily left-hander and likewise future Hall of

Famer, whose wide arsenal of "out" pitches included, especially, a killer curveball. Afterward Spahn paid Mays the ultimate compliment: "I know the Army has taught a lot of fellows how to do a lot of things, but Willie's the only man the Army ever taught how to hit a curveball. He used to be a pushover for the curve before he went into the service."

Still, Mays' slump continued, and as the story goes, when it reached 1-for-26, Durocher found him crying in the clubhouse.

"What's this?" the manager asked.

"I'm sorry, Mr. Leo, but I can't help you," Mays reportedly said. "I just can't hit up here. I know you're gonna have to send me back to Minneapolis."

"Minneapolis?" Durocher responded. "You're not going back to Minneapolis, Willie. You're not going anywhere. You're going to be in the big leagues for a long, long time. I brought you up here to play center field, and as long as I'm the manager of this team, you're my center fielder."

And as Durocher asserted in that opening spring training address to the Giants in 1954, Mays' 1951 arrival with the Giants in fifth place at 17–19 coincided with their gradual ascension to second place by June 12 before staging their comeback from thirteen and a half games back on August 11 to the pennant. Mays recovered from that slow start with the bat to hit .274, with twenty homers and sixty-eight RBI in 121 games in '51. But it was his overall play—his speed and daring on the base paths and defensive prowess in center field—that quickly established him as the most exciting player in the game.

The play people felt most authenticated his other-worldly defensive ability was the catch he made off the Dodgers' Carl Furillo on August 15 in the midst of a sixteen-game Giants winning streak. With one out in the eighth inning, the score tied 1–1, and runners on first and third for the Dodgers, Furillo hit a fly ball to right-center that looked like an extra base hit and, even if caught, was deep enough to score Billy Cox from third with the go-ahead run. It turned out to be neither. Racing toward the right field foul line and away from home plate, Mays caught up with the ball and, without breaking stride, whirled, pivoted on the dead run, and fired a perfect belt-high strike to Giants catcher Wes Westrum, who tagged the stunned Cox out at the plate.

"That was the luckiest throw I ever saw in my life. He'll never make another throw like that one, the lucky slob," Furillo said bitterly afterward.

The normally effusive Dodgers manager Charlie Dressen expressed similar skepticism when asked for his assessment of the play. "That's the first time I ever saw an outfielder make that play," Dressen told reporters. "I have no other comment on it other than I'd like to see him do it again. If he does it again, then I'll say he's great."

Dressen wanted to see him do it again? Willie was only too willing to oblige. The following season, in the seventh inning of the Dodgers' home opener at Ebbets Field, Mays made what even he later considered to be his greatest catch ever when, with two out, he raced across the outfield to make a diving, sliding grab of a sinking liner hit by Brooklyn's Bobby Morgan at the foot of the wall in left-center field. After the making the catch, Mays lay motionless, face down, on the ground, prompting Durocher, third baseman Hank Thompson, the Giants trainer, and even the Dodgers' Jackie Robinson to rush to his aid. However, it soon became evident that Robinson had not run out there to see how Willie was. In an interview forty-five years later Mays described the catch and its aftermath: "I'm in the air, like parallel, I catch the ball, I hit the fence and knock myself out. When I woke up I see all these people around me, and I say to myself, 'What's

Jackie doing out here?' Damn, if he didn't come out just to see if I had the ball! Leo came out to see about me."

"I knew Willie was going to give us a lift," said Irvin. "Like Leo said, it was like getting us a twenty-game winner. I don't mean just those impossible catches, but the way he got everybody loose in the clubhouse and made us laugh and work up a spirit."

So it was no wonder then that Dressen and the Dodgers sang no sad songs when Mays went off to the Army a few weeks later.

IT WAS THE GIANTS GENERAL MANAGER, CHUB FEENEY, WHO LED THE growing wave of anticipation of Mays' arrival at the Giants' 1954 spring training camp by walking through the press room every morning warbling the daily countdown in song to the tune of "Old Black Joe": "In six more days . . . in five more days . . . in four more days . . . we're gonna have Willie Mays," until finally, on March 2, the big day arrived.

On an unseasonably cold Phoenix morning, the Giants players were playing catch and taking batting practice in preparation for an intrasquad game Durocher had scheduled for the afternoon. Earlier in the morning, Feeney was seen whimsically strolling through the clubhouse singing, "in C-sharp minor," as Roger Kahn of the *New York Herald-Tribune* reported, "In no more days, we're going to have Willie Mays."

After a nearly twenty-six-hour trip from Virginia, Mays, accompanied by traveling secretary Garry Schumacher, arrived at the Giants' clubhouse around noontime. Word of his arrival quickly spread out on the field—"the pennant is here"—and the players soon filed into the clubhouse, one by one sidling up to Mays' locker to welcome him back. After a few minutes Durocher came through the door, bounded across the room, and put a bear hug on Mays.

"Where you been?" Durocher gushed.

From that point on that spring, said Monte Irvin, it was as though Willie was Durocher's only player.

"Leo had all these friends in the clothes and jewelry business," Irvin said, "and Willie's locker was just full of stuff Leo got from them—shirts, ties, watches. He'd go up to Willie and ask, 'What do you want?' and Willie would say, 'What you got for me to-day?' Leo did all these things for Willie and forgot about all the rest of us. I remember Alvin Dark saying half-kidding one day, 'Hey, are we still part of this team?'"

But that was the thing. They *were* a team, with its unique blending of core players—shortstop Alvin Dark (Louisiana), first baseman Whitey Lockman (North Carolina), second baseman Davey Williams (Texas), outfielder Dusty Rhodes (Alabama), plus Irvin, third baseman Hank Thompson, and Mays—who were either sons of the South and products of a segregated environment or black. As Irvin noted, there was no jealousy of Mays; rather, Mays's effervescent personality and passion for the game endeared him to the southerners. He brought laughter to the clubhouse, and they had fun with him because he could also laugh at himself.

That was no better illustrated than the day, shortly after Mays had been called up from Minneapolis in 1951, when Earl Rapp, a lumbering six-foot-two, 220-pound reserve outfielder, offered to race him for $5. With all the Giants watching, Willie left Rapp in his tracks and easily won the race. But when he put out his hand to collect the $5, Rapp waved him off.

"No, no, Willie," Rapp said, to uproarious laughter from the other Giants players, "I offered to *run* you a race, not to *beat* you! You owe *me* the five dollars."

"We never, *never* talked about race or integration," Irvin said. "We truly had fun with each other. I think the key to the whole thing was the way Durocher handled us. Going all the way back to '51, when they brought Willie up from Minneapolis, Leo addressed us and said, 'I don't care what color you are, or what religion you are, or where you come from. I only care if you can help us win, and this kid Mays is going to really help us get to the World Series.'"

Durocher knew who his breadwinner was and knew exactly how to handle him. In that first intrasquad game he strategically held Mays out of both squads' starting lineup. Three, four innings went by as Mays paced and squirmed uneasily on the bench while Durocher allowed the anticipation within him to build. Finally, in the fifth inning Durocher called upon his protégé to pinch hit, and the overanxious Mays struck out swinging on three balls out of the strike zone. Once back in center field, however, he made a sensational diving catch of a sinking line drive the next inning and, then, the next time up, hit a tremendous 420-foot homer over the left field wall off a minor pitcher named Pete Modica. Durocher, coaching in the third base box, leapt in the air in exhilaration.

Finally, for his spring debut encore, the next inning Mays took off after a ball over his head, ran it down, turned, and unleashed a throw, some three hundred feet, back to first base to double off base runner Billy Gardner. He followed that up by racing fifty feet back in dead center to make an over-the-shoulder grab of a towering drive by reserve outfielder Bill Taylor. It was as though a bolt of lightning had struck and electrified the entire Giants' spring training complex.

Afterward reporters and photographers mobbed Mays in the clubhouse, as reports of his spectacular return were about to be the lead story in all the New York daily newspapers and even front-page news in some of them.

"Have you signed your contract yet, Willie?" a reporter asked.

"Nah, not yet, but I'll be easy to sign."

"What about the report you're going to ask for $30,000?"

"Thirty thousand?" Mays shrieked in his high-pitched voice. "I couldn't ask for that! Why if I asked The Man [Horace Stoneham] for $30,000, he'd shoot me. They won't have any trouble with me. I just want to play."

As it was, Mays signed a contract shortly thereafter for the same $13,000 he was making before he went into the Army.

That night Chub Feeney serenaded all the writers at dinner with his final version of his "Old Black Joe" parody song: "Gone are the days, when we didn't have Willie Mays."

IN 1954 THERE WERE ONLY FOUR MAJOR LEAGUE TEAMS TRAINING IN Arizona—the Giants, Cleveland Indians, Chicago Cubs, and Baltimore Orioles—constituting what was then the original Cactus League. As a result, the scheduling limitations brought about a whole lot of familiarity among the four clubs, and this would have repercussions six months later. The Giants and Indians played each other twenty-one times that spring, culminating with a cross-country barnstorming trip through Oklahoma, Texas, Louisiana, Alabama, Tennessee, and Indiana.

In a game in Dallas, on April 4, Tris Speaker, the Indians' Hall of Famer and lifetime .345 hitter then considered to be the greatest center fielder who ever lived, was celebrating his sixty-sixth birthday as a press box observer. Speaker had spent most of the spring with the Indians as a special spring training instructor whose interest had been particularly piqued by Mays and all the hype surrounding the kid. The day before, Mays went 4-for-4 against the Indians to raise his spring average to .420, and in this game he made one of his now-signature "run-catch-and-throw" defensive plays in center field in which he chased down a fly ball to center by the Indians' Al Rosen, made the catch, then whirled and threw out a base runner at third—on the fly—for a double play. When asked what he thought of the play, Speaker was pointedly reserved: "No one can find fault with an outfielder whose throw makes a double play," Speaker said, "but Willie's throw to third was on the fly. He should have bounced it so that if a 'cut-off' was needed, it could've been made." It seemed a very strange—and strained—criticism. Then, with a wink, Speaker added, "Let's wait awhile on Mays. At least until August."

Most of the southern venues on the barnstorming tour had never hosted games with integrated teams, but a primary motive for the Giants and Indians in making the trip was to hopefully help change attitudes in the South seven years after Jackie Robinson had broken baseball's color barrier. If there had been any incidents in the stands or racial epithets directed at the players, they went unreported.

However, on an earlier trip the two teams took to Las Vegas, March 19, there was an incident involving Mays that was deliberately not reported. The *Tribune*'s Roger Kahn was the only reporter to witness the incident, which took place in the gambling room of the Frontier Hotel, where the teams had had dinner and watched a show with Robert Merrill, the renowned Metropolitan Opera baritone singer. Mays was standing quietly by a craps table, watching the action, when Kahn approached him. They chatted briefly and Kahn walked away, only to be grabbed on the arm by a gruff, stocky man with a noticeable bulge on his left hip under his jacket. Pointing at Mays, the man asked Kahn, "Is that guy a friend of yours?"

When Kahn replied affirmatively, the man demanded, "Well get him away from the dice tables. We don't want him mixing with our guests."

"Do you know who he is?" Kahn asked incredulously.

"Yeah, I know who he is," the man replied, "and I want you to get that nigger away from the white guests."

At that point the appalled Kahn began to make a scene, indignantly shouting at the man about the hotel having invited Mays and the other players as guests. As the exchange between the two got more and more heated, Garry Schumacher, the Giants' publicity director, suddenly appeared on the scene to intervene.

"What's going on here?" Schumacher asked Kahn.

Momentarily cooling down, Kahn reached into his pocket for his press card, purposefully waving it in front of his unexpected antagonist, and declared, "Oh, it's okay. This joker here just gave me a helluva story for the *New York Herald-Tribune.*"

At that point, according to Kahn, the hood walked away, and Kahn went over to Monte Irvin, who was standing a few feet away, and reported to him what had just happened.

"I know how you feel, Roger," Irvin said, "but on this one I gotta ask you a favor and not write this."

Irvin then got a hold of Durocher and informed him of the incident.

"After I told Leo what happened, he told me, 'Have someone take you and Willie to the airport and wait for us there,'" Irvin related. "I was worried it would be embarrassing for Willie if this got into the papers. As far as race was concerned, Willie was an innocent. He was upset and didn't understand why we had to leave. 'Why would he say something like that?' he said of the guy who started it all. Years later I thanked Roger for not going with the story."

From Las Vegas the Giants and Indians went on to Los Angeles for two more scheduled exhibition games at Wrigley Field, the home of the Chicago Cubs' Pacific Coast League farm club. Excited as he was at having Mays back, Durocher remained bothered by all the various issues that contributed to the Giants' disappointing eighty-four game loss, fifth-place season in '53. At the winter meetings back in December Durocher admitted to reporters, "I did a bad job this year."

The pitching, Durocher was certain, was considerably improved with the additions of Antonelli and Liddle. After correcting a couple of minor flaws in Antonelli's mechanics and helping him perfect his changeup, Durocher's pitching coach, Frank Shellenback, expressed confidence the young lefty was ready to assume the admittedly daunting role of number-one starter for a new club. However, Durocher was perplexed at recurring reports that he and Bobby Thomson had not gotten along in '53 and that this was a factor in trading Thomson.

Durocher acknowledged there'd been disharmony on that '53 team—although not, to his knowledge, anything between him and Thomson—and now he privately vowed to resolve it. Specifically, there had been the decision early on in '53 to break in touted shortstop prospect Daryl Spencer, which meant moving Alvin Dark, the Giants' team captain and regular shortstop since 1950, to second base. Dark, a .297 lifetime hitter who'd been an All-Star in 1951 and led all NL shortstops in putouts in '51 and '52, did not take the decision kindly, and as the season wore on and he experienced some difficulty adjusting to shuttling back and forth from second to short and even third base, he and Durocher had some heated clashes. After Dark misplayed one ball at shortstop that wound up costing the Giants a game against the St. Louis Cardinals at the Polo Grounds, Durocher showed him up by sending Spencer down to the bullpen to warm up. Afterward Dark stormed into Durocher's office and demanded to be traded.

"You don't like the way I play short and you don't like the way I play second," Dark shouted, "so just get me out of here."

"You shoulda had that ball," Durocher shot back, "but you're not gonna be traded, and that's that."

Amid all the losing that year, it was as though Durocher lost sight of how much the Giants veterans—most notably the black players, Irvin, and third baseman Henry Thompson—respected Dark. This, despite the fact Dark had spent his entire adolescence in the Deep South and, until joining the Giants in 1950, had played exclusively on all-white teams as a great all-around athlete in high school, college, and in the minor leagues. At Lake Charles, Louisiana High School, Dark was an all-southern quarterback, earning himself a scholarship to Louisiana State, as well as a top flight basketball and baseball player, golfer, and a track star who broke ten seconds in the hundred-yard dash. Dark played in the same backfield at LSU with the legendary Steve Van Buren, who went on to lead the National Football League in rushing four times. But it was baseball where Dark's true passion lay, and after coming out of the Army after World War II, he turned down an offer from the Philadelphia Eagles of the National Football League to sign a $50,000 bonus with the Braves.

When the Giants acquired Dark from the Braves in 1949 along with second baseman Eddie Stanky, a longtime Durocher favorite from their days together with the Dodgers in the mid-forties, there was some concern about how he would feel playing alongside Thompson at third. What they didn't know was that, as youngster in Lake Charles, Dark's family lived a few blocks from the predominantly black area and that Dark frequently participated in neighborhood pickup games in which the blacks and whites mixed harmoniously. In fact, Irvin recalled an incident in the spring of 1954 that, in his opinion, summed up Dark's "color blindness." Dark, Mays, Thompson, and Irvin were working on an infield drill. Mays, who had been an infielder in the Army, was at second and Irvin was at first. "Afterward," Irvin said, "Alvin looked over to me and smiled and said, 'We Darkies did a pretty good job out there, didn't we?' I about cracked up!"

So when Spencer himself struggled in the field while his batting average hovered barely above .200 in '53, Durocher found
himself dealing with a dissension problem in his clubhouse,
something that seemed completely implausible just two years after the Giants' feel-good '51 season. Even before learning Spencer was being drafted into the Army that winter, Durocher had
done a lot of soul searching about what went wrong in '53, particularly his hard-line treatment of Dark, whom he himself had
made captain in 1952 after Stanky was traded to the Cardinals.
When Dark reported to camp in February Durocher immediately called him into his office. "I just want you to know," he said,
"you're my shortstop, no matter what."

When the Giants got to Los Angeles after their somewhat unsettling sojourn in Las Vegas, Durocher called the beat writers
together and made a point of showing them a letter he'd received
a few days earlier. In brief, the letter said, "Just a line to express
my appreciation for your wire. I also want you to know that it is
with great regret that I leave the Giant organization, although I
fully realize that trades are a part of baseball. I consider myself
fortunate to have played under you and I shall take along with
me many fond memories." It was signed, "Bobby Thomson."

"This," Durocher said to the writers, with an uncharacteristic
welling of emotion in his voice, "is the only down side of getting
Willie back."

DODGER BLUES

NINE DAYS AFTER THE NEW YORK YANKEES DEFEATED THEM FOR the second straight year in the World Series, the Brooklyn Dodgers called a press conference at their offices at 215 Montague Street on October 14, 1953, for what news reporters believed to be a routine announcement that Charlie Dressen was returning for his fourth season as Dodgers manager. There was, after all, no reason to think anything otherwise about Dressen's status with the team, and a few of the New York newspapers didn't even bother to cover the press conference at all.

Despite the disappointing World Series loss in six games to the Yankees, Dressen had led the Dodgers to two pennants and one near-miss in 1951, when they blew a thirteen-and-a-half game lead on August 11 and wound up losing a three-game playoff with their cross-borough rival New York Giants. What's more, in 1953 the Dodgers won a club record 105 games in out-distancing the second-place Milwaukee Braves by 13 games.

The peppery, five-foot-six, 168-pound Dressen was a bantam rooster of a man who never lacked for confidence in his own ability. The running joke among the Dodgers was that he was incapable of speaking a sentence without the word "I" in it. And there was an oft-told story about a game in which the Dodgers were trailing by a run in the sixth inning when they rushed off the bench to take the field, only to be stopped in their tracks by a shrill whistle from Dressen, who then hollered, "Just stay close to 'em, fellas, I'll think of something."

Much as Dressen's outsized ego may have grated on a lot of the Dodger players, there was no hint of any displeasure with him from team president Walter O'Malley. In fact, after the '53 Series loss to the Yankees—for which Dressen characteristically excused away by saying, "If I'd had Don Newcombe [the Dodger pitching ace who was in the Armed Services in 1953], I'd have beaten them"—O'Malley praised the Yankees for winning their fifth-straight world championship and went out of his way to say he found no fault with the job his manager had done. "We won 105 games, and that was quite an accomplishment in itself," O'Malley said.

Nevertheless, in the days leading up to the World Series and those immediately after it, O'Malley and Dressen found themselves engaged in a philosophical debate as to the length of a new contract. It was Dressen's belief that, after two straight NL pennants, he deserved some job security in the form of a three-year contract. Much of this could be attributed to the St. Louis Cardinals and Braves having just given three-year contracts to their respective managers, Eddie Stanky and Charlie Grimm, and the Giants, who, with Willie Mays also away in the service, had finished fifth in '53, had also just re-signed Dressen's archrival,

Leo Durocher, to a two-year new deal. O'Malley, however, had repeatedly reminded Dressen of the club policy in which all employees, including his immediate bosses, general manager Buzzie Bavasi and vice president of scouting and player development, Fresco Thompson, worked on one-year contracts. At the same time he was offering Dressen a substantial raise in salary, from $32,000 to $40,000.

Unbeknownst to the Dodger beat writers, the stalemate continued on until a week after the Series, when Dressen met with O'Malley at 215 Montague Street to state his case. Prior to the meeting Dressen discussed the situation with his wife, Ruth, and the two of them, with Ruth doing the typing, composed a letter to O'Malley, citing the Stanky, Grimm, and Durocher deals along with the fact that Charlie had been the only manager in the history of the Dodgers to win two consecutive NL pennants.

"Could I see the letter?" O'Malley asked Dressen.

"Sure," Dressen said, pulling it out of his jacket pocket.

For a tense minute and a half Dressen stood there as O'Malley read the letter. Smiling thinly, O'Malley placed the letter on his desk.

"That's a nice letter, Charlie," he said. "But there's one thing in there that's not quite right."

O'Malley never specified to Dressen what that "one thing" was, but a few days later, on October 13, Dressen was summoned back to the Dodger offices for another meeting with the Dodgers president, at which time O'Malley said, "We had a meeting with the board of directors today, and they all agreed with me that no one in the Dodger organization should get more than a one-year contract."

"Are you sure that's all you can do, Walter?" Dressen asked.

"I'm sure," O'Malley replied.

"Then I can't accept."

And that was that. Dressen and O'Malley had agreed to disagree, and neither was about to blink. O'Malley said there should
be a press conference called immediately, before the news leaked
out, to announce that Dressen would not be back. In assuring
O'Malley the news would not leak out from him, Dressen said
he wanted to be present at the press conference to give his side
of the story.

"I just want to know one thing," Dressen said, before depart-
ing O'Malley's office. "Is there anything else but club policy involved in your unwillingness to give me more than a one-year
contract?"

"Not a thing, Charlie," O'Malley said. "You've done a great
job, and we're well satisfied with your work."

At 10:30 the next morning, with all the reporters and photographers gathered at the Dodger offices, O'Malley strode to
the microphone and announced, "Charlie has resigned because he
asked for a three-year contract, and I have told him that I couldn't
see my way clear in breaking our policy of granting only one-year
documents to our employees." Then, brandishing the contract in
his hand, he added, "He can sign this one-year contract here right
now, and he will be our manager next year."

O'Malley then went on to say Dressen's salary would have
been more than any executive or player on the club.

"More than Red Barber?" a newsman asked, referring to the
legendary broadcaster who had recently resigned after fifteen
years as the Dodgers' number-one mike man to go to the Yankees.

"Yes, more than Red Barber," O'Malley said.

Wrote Arthur Daley in the *New York Times* the next day:
"Not since Durocher made his sudden switch from Ebbets Field
to the Polo Grounds in mid-season of 1948 has baseball had as
shocking a surprise as the non-signing of Charlie Dressen."

Dressen later revealed to *United Press International* baseball writer Milton Richman that, after he left the press conference to be with his wife, who was in a nearby hospital with a stomach ailment, Ruth Dressen had second thoughts about their decision.

"Don't you think it might be better to take the one-year contract?" Ruth asked.

"Do you know what you're saying, Ruth? Do you know what you're asking me to do?" Dressen replied indignantly. "You're asking me to go back on my word. As I said to you before when we went into this together and had plenty of time to think it over, when I say I'm gonna do something, I intend to keep my word."

Bill Roeder, the Dodger beat writer for the *New York World-Telegram & Sun*, perhaps best summed up the writers' reaction to the stunning developments. For, unlike the players, the writers had great affection for the voluble Dressen, who was always more than willing to fill their notebooks with colorful quotes of the Dodgers' triumphs and travails, not to mention his own managerial genius:

> *I've known Charlie Dressen eight years, and in my job as a baseball writer I can tell you what he likes for breakfast (eggs scrambled with cheese and chopped onions); I know what he thought of veteran players and what they thought of him. Being on the inside, I wasn't surprised when I heard Dressen had left the Dodgers. I was dumfounded. I never thought there would be an occasion for this. This whole business has shaken my faith in the merit of my own opinions, but I still have to believe Dressen came out a bad second and the front office was not a bit unhappy to see him go. . . . As a newspaperman I enjoyed covering Dressen. He'll occasionally backtrack when he thinks he said the wrong thing, for more than likely the*

front office tells him he said the wrong thing, but as a rule he'll state
his opinions on practically anything and let those opinions stand.

"I think by and large we took Charlie for what he was and that
was a good baseball man," said Carl Erskine, one of the Dodger
pitching staff leaders and the team player rep who won twenty
games in '53. "He was, if nothing else, totally into baseball. He'd
see guys going back to the clubhouse during games for a coke
or something and say, 'How can you guys think of anything else
but this game?'"

At the same time Erskine acknowledged Dressen's ego was
a detriment to him and, more than anything else, was probably
responsible for his divorce from the Dodgers. "Frequently you'd
hear some of the guys walking around the clubhouse singing
that Mexican song, 'aye, yi, aye, yi, yi . . . aye, yi, yi, yi, yi, yi!' [in
mock reference to Dressen always using the 'I' word]," Erskine
related. "But what you have to know about Dressen is that he
was paranoid about Leo. It went all the way back, I think, to
when he was a coach for Leo with the Dodgers [from 1939 to
1942]. I think Charlie was jealous of all the acclaim Leo got.
Anyway, when Leo got a two-year contract extension from
[Giants owner Horace] Stoneham after finishing fifth, Charlie
wasn't going to settle for anything less after he'd finished first."

A few days after his resignation Dressen got a phone call
from his old friend Brick Laws, owner of the Oakland Oaks in
the Triple A Pacific Coast League, for whom he had managed in
1949 and '50.

"What are you going to do now, Charlie?" Laws asked.

"I don't know," said Dressen, adding that he was going to
wait until his wife got out of the hospital and then go home.

"Would you manage for me out in Oakland again?" Laws
said. "I would be willing to pay you exactly what you were

making in Brooklyn, and you can manage for me for as long as you want."

Dressen didn't even have to think about it. "I'd love to, Brick. You got yourself a manager."

When word got back to O'Malley about Dressen's hiring in Oakland, the Dodgers president's response dripped with sarcasm. "I'm sure Mrs. Dressen will be very happy in Oakland," he said.

Once the Dressen resignation bombshell sunk in, speculation immediately began as to who would succeed him. The first name almost all the reporters bandied was that of Pee Wee Reese, the Dodgers' thirty-four-year-old captain and All-Star shortstop the previous nine seasons. Daley wrote in his *Times* column, "The logical man, of course, is that wonderful little guy from Kentucky, Pee Wee Reese. The captain of the Brooks shied away from the honor when Barney Shotton was relieved of his portfolio [in 1950] because he said he had too many playing years left and didn't want the burden at the time. This time, however, could be different. The Personality Kid from Louisville can almost see the end in sight—even though he didn't show it last season—and like Barkis, he's undoubtedly willin'.'"

And initially, Reese, like the character from Dickens's *David Copperfield*, sounded as though he was willing. "I always said before I wouldn't consider a manager's job while I still have some good playing years left," Reese told United Press International shortly after the Dressen resignation press conference. "But now this thing . . . I don't know . . . things look a little different now."

Reese's comments were followed by Dodger catcher Roy Campanella's endorsement of him for the job. Although admitting Dressen's resignation had "startled" him, Campanella said of Reese: "He'd be a very good successor. Pee Wee's our captain, and all the fellows on the club look up to him."

Five days later, on October 25, a story in the *New York Times* by veteran baseball writer John Drebinger under the headline, "Dodgers Expected to Name Reese as New Manager in Mid-November," reported that although "Walter O'Malley ostensibly is still sifting the qualifications of an endless array of applicants, it has been generally understood that the 34-year old Reese, the Brooks' field captain and top-ranking shortstop for more than a decade, was tabbed by O'Malley as Dressen's successor even before the club's differences with Chuck came to a head."

The inevitability of Reese continued for another two weeks until, finally, on November 5, Pee Wee suddenly told the Associated Press in Louisville that he had decided to eliminate himself from further consideration as the new manager of the Dodgers. "I still think I can play a couple of more years," Reese said. "Maybe I have made a mistake—I will know that in a couple of years. I think I have done the right thing. I know I'll never be sorry, no matter how things might turn out."

According to Buzzie Bavasi, Reese was indeed O'Malley's first choice. "He wanted someone the public could relate to," Bavasi told me in an interview years later. But Bavasi had what he felt was a better choice in Walter Alston, manager of the Dodgers' Triple A farm team in Montreal. What made Alston a better choice in Bavasi's eyes was his managerial experience: he'd managed thirteen seasons in the Dodger system, the last four at Montreal, the Dodgers' flagship Triple A farm team, where he'd finished first twice and second twice. Plus, he'd managed twenty-three players on the team's forty-man major league roster, including pitchers Erskine, Johnny Podres, and Clem Labine, outfielder George Shuba, and five of the Dodgers' six black players on the roster: Campanella, Newcombe, infielder Jim Gilliam, pitcher Joe Black, and reserve outfielder Sandy Amoros.

"I'll go down to Louisville and talk to Pee Wee," Bavasi told O'Malley, "but let's make a deal. If he doesn't want the job, we'll go for Walter Alston."

Bavasi later insisted that, contrary to reports, he didn't dissuade Reese from taking the job, but "I did not try to talk him out of his decision to refuse the offer either."

On November 24 the Dodgers announced the hiring of the forty-two-year-old Alston, "a career man in the Brooklyn farm system," to a one-year contract as their new manager. In introducing him, O'Malley took pains to say Alston had been the unanimous choice of his front office, Bavasi, and Thompson, and that he would be working on his tenth one-year contract with the Dodgers. That prompted one newspaperman to inquire sarcastically, "Suppose Alston wins the pennant and the World Series too? Will he be out next year?"

"That's something we'll have to take up in December," O'Malley said with a wink, "unless his wife writes a letter."

The selection of Alston was not greeted with a whole lot of enthusiasm from either the writers or the Dodger "flock," most of whom had hoped for either a "name" manager along the lines of the popular 1930s slugger, Lefty O'Doul, or Hall of Famers Frankie Frisch or Bill Terry, or former Dodger favorites, Cookie Lavagetto and Dixie Walker. The next day's headline in the *Daily News*, "Alston (Who He?) to Manage Dodgers," summarized the general view of the hiring. (Some forty-two years later the *Daily News* disparaged another new manager in town when it greeted the Yankees' hiring of Joe Torre to replace Buck Showalter in 1995 with the next-day headline, "Clueless Joe.")

In fact, Alston, whose total major league experience was one at-bat with the St. Louis Cardinals—a strikeout—in 1936, was the polar opposite of Dressen. Soft spoken, unassuming, and college educated (Miami of Ohio), Alston made it eminently clear from the get-go he wasn't going to be the quote machine Dressen was for the writers.

"I'm tickled to death to get the job," he said. "I will need help on a lot of things before we get into the season. . . . I guess I'm thrilled if you want to put it that way."

When asked about his theory for running a team, Alston, referring to his earlier profession as a high school biology and industrial arts teacher, said, "Teaching students is very much like managing baseball players. You've got to encourage some. You've got to drive others if you're going to get the best out of every individual."

"Alston was a teacher by trade," said Erskine. "On many occasions he'd be sitting in the dugout and turn to the player next to him and say, 'What would you do in this situation?' A lot of guys looked at that as a sign of weakness, that he didn't know what to do. But I think they were wrong. That was his way of testing them, to see whether they had their head in the game."

ONE OF THE LAST THINGS O'MALLEY SAID TO ALSTON AT THE NEW manager's introductory press conference was, "the job is yours. No one will be looking over your shoulder. You won't be fired for losing unless the team loses through your fault." And Charlie Dressen, when reached for reaction to the Dodgers' hiring of Alston, was quick to point out that his successor "will not only have all the horses I had, he'll have Don Newcombe back from the service and he won 20 games for me in 1951."

Leave it to Dressen to put all the pressure he could on his successor.

Nevertheless, Alston was not deluded about the challenge at hand for him as a first-year major league manager with no first-hand knowledge of the National League. Yes, the Dodgers had won a club record 105 games in 1953, and yes, Campanella was coming off a Most Valuable Player season in which he hit a major league record 41 homers for a catcher and led the National League with 142 RBI. And yes, Carl Furillo had won the NL batting crown at .344, while Erskine had won 20 games, and Duke Snider and Gil Hodges had driven in 126 and 122 runs, respectively.

Also, Dressen's decision in '53 to insert rookie Jim Gilliam at second base and the leadoff spot, which resulted in Jackie Robinson being shuttled around to third base and left field and the popular slick-fielding veteran third baseman Billy Cox losing a lot of playing time, proved to be inspired. Gilliam wound up hitting .278 with 125 runs scored while also breaking Eddie Stanky's NL rookie record of 92 walks with 100 walks. Further, the Dodgers set team records for homers (208), runs (955), RBI (887), slugging (.474), and total bases (2,545). No fewer than six Dodgers scored 100 or more runs in '53, tying a major league record. It was easy to see why they'd been acclaimed by many as "the greatest team in baseball history."

Yet for all those offensive "horses," the Dodgers had again been unable to beat the Yankees for baseball's big prize, and at the end of the '53 season that "greatest team in history" label had to be amended to the "greatest team in history never to win a World Series." Alston was not so naïve as to think the Dodgers' lineup, which almost to a man had had career seasons in '53, would be able to repeat those performances. For one thing, his two core players, Reese and Robinson, would both be turning thirty-five in 1954, and, unforeseen to him, Campanella was suffering a hand injury in spring training that would hamper him the entire '54 season.

But if there was one area of particular concern for Alston, it was the pitching. For, after Erskine (20–6, third in the NL in strikeouts with 187 in '53), the starting rotation was replete with question marks. Russ Meyer, whose fifteen wins were second to Erskine on the staff in '53, was talented but temperamental, and too often the latter trumped the former. From all Alston knew of Meyer, his 4.56 ERA in 1953 was far more indicative of his ability than his fifteen wins. They didn't call him the "Mad Monk" for nothing, as Meyer exasperated Dressen with his lapses of concentration after giving up an RBI base hit or not getting a call from the home plate umpire. The classic Meyer temper tantrum, for which he would be forever remembered, occurred May 24, 1953, when, pitching against the Philadelphia Phillies, he charged home plate umpire Augie Donatelli in the fourth inning in a rage over the arbiter's balls and strikes calls. After Roy Campanella intervened and ushered him back to the mound, Meyer picked up the resin bag and hurled it thirty feet into the air, whereupon Donatelli ejected him, but not before the resin bag came down and landed squarely on the Mad Monk's head! As he trudged to the dugout Meyer threw his glove in disgust, and the local TV cameras later caught him making an obscene gesture at Donatelli. Alston had been forewarned about the Mad Monk's unreliability, and despite those fifteen wins in '53, Alston wasn't counting on Meyer to be an integral part of his rotation in 1954.

From 1949 to '51 Preacher Roe had been the ace of the Dodger staff, winning fifteen, nineteen, and twenty-two games, respectively, but now the wily spit-baller and primary lefty in the rotation was thirty-seven and at the end of the line. Roe's record in 1953—11–3 for twenty-four starts—was almost identical to his 11–2 over twenty-five starts in '52. But his ERA of 4.30 in '53 was nearly a run and a half higher than the previous year, and even ol' Preach admitted it had gotten harder and harder to get his legs in shape for the long haul of a six-month season.

Then there was the curious downfall of Joe Black, the 1952 NL Rookie of the Year whose fifteen wins and fifteen saves as a long reliever and spot starter had stamped him as the Dodgers' most important pitcher that season. In '53, however, Black became an almost forgotten man on the Dodger staff, the victim of a mysterious loss of command and velocity. Most people around the Dodgers blamed Black's sharp decline on Dressen. Like everything else, cocky Charlie thought he was an expert on pitching, and in spring training '53 he decided Black needed to develop another pitch to go along with his average fastball and curveball.

It started with a slow curve, and when that didn't take with Black, Dressen had him start trying out a screwball. Then it was on to a forkball, again to no avail, and even so far as a knuckleball that Black just couldn't get to knuckle. One failed experiment after another. Whether it was frustration over not being able to remake the twenty-nine-year-old right-hander in his own image or just the reaffirmation of many that 1952 had been a fluke, Dressen used Black sparingly out of the bullpen—just four times in April—before giving him his first start of the '53 season, against the Giants, on May 21. This, following two straight rocky relief appearances in which he'd given up seven earned runs in five and a third innings. In the first inning, after Al Dark and Hank Thompson hit back-to-back one-out triples, Dressen lifted Black, and from then on, he used him in mostly mop-up relief situations with only two more starts. Black finished his sophomore season with a 6–3 record and 5.33 ERA and never again approached the fifteen-win brilliance of his Rookie of the Year '52 season.

So Black was another pitcher Alston had no reason to expect much from in 1954. Johnny Podres, the rookie left-hander who won nine games in '53, showed a lot of promise, having shot like a meteor through the Dodger organization from Class B ball to the majors in just two years, but he was still only twenty years old. There was also Clem Labine, who'd been 11–6 in '53 with a team-leading 2.77 ERA. In his three years in the big leagues Labine had shown ability to both start and relieve, but on the advice of the Dodger coaches and scouts, Alston viewed him as his best option for what constituted a closer in those days. Labine had a rubber arm with an excellent sinker and what was regarded as one of the most unhittable curveballs of any pitcher in the league.

Of course Newcombe would be coming back, but who knew how much rust had accumulated on that durable right arm after two years in the service or how long it would take for him to regain his 1951 form? Indeed, much as it may have seemed he'd been handed a team with no significant deficiencies, Alston could be justified at having concerns over the advancing age of his two key players, Reese and Robinson, and the fact that he had only one sure commodity, Erskine, in his starting rotation.

It probably never occurred to him the biggest problem he was going to have was his own reserved personality, in contrast to the laid-bare Dressen, and the culture shock this would be for the Dodger players, especially Jackie Robinson.

ERNIE AND HANK

A T THE SAME TIME THE GIANTS WERE WELCOMING WILLIE MAYS back to baseball in the spring of 1954, eighteen miles east of Phoenix, in the suburb of Mesa, the Chicago Cubs were embarking on a sort of "coming out" party for what they hoped would be baseball's first all-black shortstop-second base double-play combo. The Cubs had provided a hint of their plan at the tail end of the '53 season when, on September 17, they became the fourth NL team to integrate, bringing twenty-two-year-old shortstop Ernie Banks right to the major leagues after purchasing his contract from the Kansas City Monarchs of the Negro American League for $15,000. Three days later they teamed him up at second base with twenty-eight-year-old Gene Baker, a converted shortstop whom they had also bought from the Monarchs five years prior but had kept in the minors.

There are some who have suggested that Baker was the primary victim of the Cubs' dragging their feet on integration, as he was forced to play four seasons as the everyday All-Star shortstop for their Los Angeles farm team in the Triple A Pacific Coast League. Though Baker's stellar play with Los Angeles was surely worthy of promotion—rival Hollywood manager and former Brooklyn Dodger Bobby Bragan proclaimed him to be the best shortstop he'd seen since Pee Wee Reese broke into the majors in 1941—the Cubs stubbornly elected to stick with Roy Smalley, a weak hitter with below-average range and injury prone, as their primary shortstop during those four years.

Smalley became one of Cubs owner Phil Wrigley's favorite players after a career season in 1950 during which he played every game and hit twenty-one homers with eighty-five RBI. But the following season he broke his leg sliding into third base in late April, missing three months, and he was never the same. Plagued by injuries in '52 and '53, he hit just .222 and .249, respectively, and when he did play the Cub fans booed him unmercifully every time he made out or committed an error in the field, belying Wrigley Field's nickname, the "Friendly Confines." Still, it took their signing of Banks, universally regarded as one of the elite players in the Negro Leagues, to finally provide incentive for the Cubs to upgrade at shortstop.

On March 21 the Cubs announced they were trading Smalley to the Milwaukee Braves for a marginal middle relief pitcher, Dave Cole. To hear the way Wrigley explained it, though, it was a mercy trade:

We have decided to trade Roy Smalley to help him. He's an intelligent young man and I've always liked him. I believe he still has a chance to be an excellent ballplayer if he goes someplace else. Cub fans over the years have always shown fine sportsmanship, certainly better than most cities. However, they developed a strange quirk in the case of Smalley. They were brutal in their treatment of him. Roy could simply not do anything right for them. It was so cruel, it would almost bring tears to your eyes. He obviously became the scapegoat for the fans. They began to look upon him as the primary reason for the failures of the ball club these past few years. I have never felt as sorry for a ballplayer as I have for Smalley.

Unfortunately for Gene Baker, because of their sizeable invest-ment in Banks, the Cubs did not want to mess with the youngster's psyche by asking him to move to another position, so it was Baker who moved to second base to win his overdue promotion to the majors. By the time he finally got to the big leagues, Baker was well into his prime as a player. "I was so fortunate to have Gene there with the Cubs," Banks said in a 2012 interview with me. "He was a mentor to me. He taught me so many things about playing shortstop, positioning, cut-offs, relays—all of those things."

A supple six foot one, 180 pounds, Banks had already con-vinced the Cubs' brass in just his ten-game cameo in '54, when he hit .314 with two homers, both off St. Louis Cardinals right-hander Gerry Staley, that he was ready for the majors. On one of the first days of spring training Pants Rowland, the Cubs' seventy-four-year-old vice president who'd been around base-ball since 1915, was talking about Banks to a couple of Chicago newspapermen, saying,

When anyone ever talks about Cub shortstops, they bring up Joe Tinker, of Tinker-to-Evers-to-Chance fame. Well, I saw Joe Tinker and he was great. But Ernie Banks fields equally as well and has a much stronger bat. You can only guess at how Tinker would've handled today's "rabbit" ball. Banks handles it well. He plays those half-hops like ordinary grounders. His single failing, if

you could call it that, is throwing from deep in the hole. He has a
weak arm, but makes a light and accurate throw that the infielders
can handle. You have to be enthusiastic about Banks. He's just a
baby and already everyone is talking about him.

That may have been true, but Banks himself wasn't at all sure
what 1954 had in store for him. He had been surprised, though
not overwhelmed, when the Cubs brought him directly to the big
leagues after purchasing his contract from the Monarchs the previous September. After getting rave reports from all his scouts
on Banks, Cubs general manager Wid Matthews personally traveled to Kansas City to make the deal with Monarchs owner Tom
Baird, in which the Cubs would pay a total of $20,000 for Banks
and a pitcher named Bill Dickey. Once Banks and Dickey were
signed to contracts, they were on a bus to Chicago where Matthews met them at Wrigley Field. Banks remembered,

We didn't know where we were going. All the way from Kansas
City, Dickey and I talked about what we're gonna do that win-
ter. Then, all of a sudden, we look up and see this sign "Wrigley
Field"! When we got up to Wid Matthews' office he told Dickey
he was being sent to the minors and said to me, "You're going to be
with the Cubs." I went down to the clubhouse to get my uniform,
looked around and saw all these guys, Ralph Kiner, Hank Sauer,
and I'm saying, "Ho-ly! It's the major leagues!" But I'll be honest,
I was a little uncertain about being there. I wanted to stay with the
Monarchs. I was raised in Dallas in a time of segregation. I didn't
understand integration. This was a whole different world for me.
I had no fear—I learned that from the Bible. But I had lived in a
black community, went to a black school, played sports at a black
YMCA, played baseball for a black team with a black manager, and
that was all I'd ever known.

Prior to spring training '54 Cubs manager Phil Cavaretta invited Banks to his home in Dallas to get more formally acquainted. The two spent a day together, with Cavaretta, a lifetime .293 hitter in the majors, giving Banks some batting tips and discussing his plans for the coming season. As Banks remembered it in that same 2012 interview, his visit to Cavaretta's house had a special significance because at that time in Dallas "a Negro didn't often make social visits to a white man's house."

So in Cavaretta he felt he had a nurturing hand and a manager who was looking out for him. "But when I came to spring training, I still had no expectations," Banks said. "Actually, on the train ride from Dallas to Arizona, I missed Mesa and kept on going and had to get off at the next stop, Apache Junction, and work my way back."

As the spring moved along into the exhibition games, something else Banks needed to adjust to became increasingly apparent: a losing culture. Even though when Banks played for the Monarchs from 1950 to '53, the Negro Leagues were beginning a decline that would lead to eventual oblivion because of the breaking of the color barrier in the majors, the Monarchs were still regarded as a prestigious franchise, having employed at various times before him many of the greatest black players in history, including Satchel Paige, Cool Papa Bell, Bullet Joe Rogan, Turkey Stearnes, Willard Brown, and Jackie Robinson, all of whom were later elected to the Baseball Hall of Fame. In addition, their manager, Buck O'Neil, was highly respected for his baseball acumen, not only in the Negro Leagues but in major league circles as well.

Conversely, the Cubs had experienced six out of seven losing seasons since 1946, and prospects were not at all that bright for a reversal of that trend any time soon.

Nobody was more acutely aware of that than Cavaretta, who, after managing the Cubs to a .500 record in '52, saw them regress to an eighty-nine game loss, seventh-place team in '53. On March 28, with the Cubs fashioning a woeful 5–15 record in the Cactus League, a dis-spirited Cavaretta paid a visit to Wrigley in Phoenix. In brief, Cavaretta told Wrigley the Cubs did not have enough talent to compete for the pennant, and they especially needed help at first base, third base, and center field. This wasn't what the owner wanted to hear.

"I can't have a manager with such a defeatist attitude," Wrigley told Cavaretta.

The next day, with the team ironically in Dallas, his hometown, Cavaretta found himself an unwelcome footnote to history as the first manager ever fired during spring training. He was replaced by Stan Hack, the popular former Cubs third baseman who was managing their Triple A team in Los Angeles.

"This year he picked everyone but us to finish in the first division," Wrigley said of Cavaretta. "He was licked before he started. He said he didn't have the kind of ballplayers he wanted. He had given up on the boys, so to speak, feeling they were not pennant material. Well maybe not, but they could be, with the will to win."

"Cavaretta being let go like that in Dallas was very unsettling," Banks said. "I felt I had a kind of bond with him. But he made a statement that the Cubs were gonna finish last, and Mr. Wrigley didn't like that. I didn't really know Mr. Wrigley, but around that time I got a letter from him saying the coaches told him I wasn't trying. He asked to see me in his office. I went up there and I asked him, 'Why am I here?'"

"As I told you, the coaches seem to feel you're not trying, and where there's smoke there's fire," Wrigley said in an admonishing tone.

Bewildered as to what might have precipitated this, Banks stood up and looked the owner right in the eye. "Mr. Wrigley," he said, "I can assure you, I'm doing the best I can."

"That's just what I wanted to hear," said Wrigley.

It was the first and last time Banks ever had any kind of an issue with the Cubs' owner. Nevertheless, Wrigley questioning his work ethic was a rude awakening for the rookie shortstop. He was no longer in Kansas City, where his unquestioned talent and boyish zeal earned him the blanket admiration of his manager, O'Neil, and his teammates. Clearly there had been resentment in the Cubs clubhouse over all the attention and hype he'd been getting, something Banks couldn't understand. It never dawned on him that this criticism might have possibly been racially motivated, although it did bring him even closer to Baker, who slowly opened Banks's eyes to the ways and attitudes of America in the South in the 1950s—as well as newly integrated professional baseball. Banks said,

I was an innocent. I came out of a Dallas family of twelve, the first boy, who grew up in a segregated world. Gene was born in Davenport, Iowa, where things were different. He gave me a lesson on how envious and jealous people could be. When we barnstormed through the South in spring training we couldn't stay in the same hotel with the white players, and it was the same thing in St. Louis, that first year, where the Chase Hotel didn't allow blacks. One time, when we were in Mobile for a spring training game, the bus was stopped in town, and I got off to get some candy at a little store. As I approached the door a white guy came out and said, "You gotta go around the back." I didn't know what he was talking about. But after I got my candy and was walking back to the bus, Gene was waiting for me just laughing and laughing. "Why didn't you tell me about this?" I asked.

Another time in St. Louis, we wanted to go to a movie downtown, but as we went up to the ticket booth, the ticket taker started

waving us off. Gene turned to me and said, "I hope you enjoyed the
movie we're not going to be able to see."

After his first clubhouse meeting Hack called Banks aside
and told him that for the rest of the spring he planned to hit
him third in the lineup, ahead of Ralph Kiner and behind Hank
Sauer. Up until then Banks, who had missed a week earlier in the
spring after being hit in the head with a pitch, had been sharing the shortstop duties with Smalley and veteran Eddie Miksis,
who was also vying with Baker for the second base job, but as
Hack explained, "We want to get you as many extra at-bats as
possible."

A week later, after lashing out a bunch of hits and fielding
flawlessly as the Cubs' newly ordained regular shortstop, Edgar
Munzel, the Cubs beat writer for the *Chicago Sun-Times* wrote
this glowing report on Banks: "It's been a long time since the
Cubs have had a rookie who seems certain of stardom in his first
year and who stirs the imagination with the possibilities of his
greatness. But no longer. Personnel director Wid Matthews says
he can't miss and wherever the Cubs play this spring, rival managers and players line the dugout in fascination when the young
man is hitting."

Shortly after he penned that, however, Munzel found one rival manager, Jimmie Dykes of the Baltimore Orioles, to be less
than enthused with Banks's abilities. Dykes was an old school
hard-ass who'd been in the majors since 1918 as an All-Star-
caliber third baseman with the Philadelphia Athletics and Chicago White Sox for over twenty years and then as a manager of
both clubs before signing on with the Orioles for their maiden
season in Baltimore. After a Cubs-Orioles Cactus League game
in Yuma, Munzel approached Dykes to solicit his opinion on
the budding Cub shortstop and was stunned at the manager's

blunt assessment. "If you ask me," said Dykes, "he'll be out of the league by June."

"Why would you say that?" Munzel asked, aghast.

"I don't think he can hit .240," Dykes reiterated, "and that's why I believe he'll be out of the league by June."

According to Munzel in his dispatch from Yuma that day, Dykes then backed up his prediction by wagering a set of golf clubs on it with the *Sun-Times* scribe.

(Ironically, a few years later Dykes did a complete reversal on his opinion of Banks. As manager of the Cincinnati Reds in 1958, when Banks won the first of his back-to-back NL Most Valuable Player awards, Dykes said, "Without Ernie Banks, the Cubs would finish in Albuquerque.")

From all accounts Dykes was the lone Cactus League dissenter on Banks. Wid Matthews, as one might expect from the guy who signed him, was quick to refute Dykes's dire assessment of Banks's hitting, stating,

I'm not going to quote you batting figures or past performances on Banks. I know he hit .380 for the Monarchs in the Negro League last year. But the reason I believe he's a cinch .300 hitter is that he's the best batter against breaking stuff of any rookie I've ever seen come to the big leagues—and I'm not barring anybody.

That usually is a kid's weakness. Ninety-nine times out of a hundred when a rookie doesn't make it the reason is he can't hit the curve ball. How many times have you heard the story of the rookie writing home and saying, "I'll be home soon, Mom, they're starting to throw the curve balls." Well curve balls won't drive this young man home. On the contrary, they keep throwing him curve balls, and he'll be driving a lot of pitchers home! And you've got to like him for other reasons too. He can field, he can throw, he can run, and he's absolutely fearless at the plate.

A couple of weeks later Hack made it official: Banks and Baker would open the season as his shortstop–second base combo. (At the end of April the Cubs traded for a new first baseman, Steve Bilko, a trade that inspired a coin phrase by their veteran broadcaster, Bert Wilson, "Bingo to Bango to Bilko" on every double play executed by Banks and Baker.) Hack had managed Baker the previous two years at Los Angeles, so he knew all along what Baker could do even though he was converting to second base, but the day the Cubs broke camp the manager presented Banks with an engraved wristwatch as the outstanding rookie of the spring.

"Only then," said Banks, "did I feel like I'd finally become a major leaguer."

IF ERNIE BANKS CAME TO SPRING TRAINING IN 1954 WITH NO expectations, across the country twenty-year-old Hank Aaron arrived at the Milwaukee Braves spring training camp in Bradenton, Florida, with less than none. Although Aaron had nonetheless also received his share of hype after leading the Sally League in batting (.362), RBI (125), runs (115), and hits (208) the previous year, a jump to the majors all the way from Class A ball seemed out of the question. Making it even more daunting was the fact that Aaron was a second baseman, a position the Braves had moved to shore up over the winter with their acquisition of Danny O'Connell, a .294 hitter in '53, from the Pittsburgh Pirates. Between O'Connell and holdover Jack Dittmer, who'd hit .266 in 138 games for the Braves in '53 but led the National League with twenty-three errors, Milwaukee was pretty well fixed at second base. This is why when Aaron arrived at camp, manager Charlie Grimm told him to start breaking in an outfielder's glove and assigned coach Johnny Cooney to hit a hundred fly balls and grounders to him every day.

But even the switch to the outfield offered no extra opportunity for Aaron, as the Braves already had established outfielders in lifetime .290-hitting Andy Pafko in right and twenty-eight-year-old Billy Bruton, the NL stolen base leader as a rookie in '53 and first black player to make the majors without Negro League experience, in center. And over the winter, with their trade of pitchers Johnny Antonelli and Don Liddle to the Giants for Bobby Thomson, they'd addressed their biggest need—a right-handed hitting middle-of-the-order power hitter to complement left-handed-hitting third baseman Eddie Mathews, the NL home run leader in '53. In addition, they had Jim Pendleton, a .299 hitter in 120 games in '53, as their fourth outfielder. To Aaron's thinking there was no way the Braves would keep him on the major league roster to sit on the bench.

It did nothing for his psyche when he arrived at his locker on the first day only to discover his name over it misspelled *Arron*. Like Banks, Aaron quickly learned that perceptions overrode his press clippings. Over the winter the *Milwaukee Sentinel* had trumpeted his forthcoming arrival in spring training: "Not since Mickey Mantle was moved up to the Yankees has there been a player with as big a build-up as Aaron, a lithe, 19-year old Negro." But when Aaron began taking his outfield drills with Cooney, Grimm and the other coaches misinterpreted his smooth, loping style of running after balls as a bit of inherent laziness, even if they didn't really believe it. There is, after all, a difference—a big difference—between effortlessness and laziness, but in those days the former description more often than not was applied to white players like Joe DiMaggio: "Joe, in typical fashion, made his long run to catch the ball in deep left-center seem effortless."

In any case Grimm soon got to calling Aaron "Stepin Fetchit," a lighthearted (in his mind) but insensitive reference to the black film actor of the twenties and thirties whose character, "The Laziest Man in the World," was later condemned for being sadly illustrative of the negative stereotype of African Americans. And soon enough the *Milwaukee Sentinel* even picked up on it, describing him in a March '54 story: "He throws sidearm from the outfield and runs the bases like Stepin Fetchit with a hopped up motor."

"I never heard Charlie actually call me that to my face," Aaron told me in a 2012 interview. "I don't think he meant any harm with it. Unfortunately that was just the way it was back then. It wasn't thought of as any sort of bigotry. I didn't appreciate it, but I didn't pay much attention to it. I was more concerned with trying to make the ball club."

Nevertheless, those early misperceptions would still dog him years later after he'd reached his prime as one of the greatest players of all time. In 1957, when he was in the process of leading the Braves to the NL pennant and winning the Most Valuable Player award, a *Time* magazine feature on his "wrist hitting" ability referred to him as "the talented shuffler."

Aaron turned twenty a week before '54 spring training and, with barely one and a half seasons of experience in the lower minor leagues, came to camp, listed as a second baseman on the Triple A Toledo roster, as more of a curiosity than a potential major league–ready prospect. Grimm remembered how anxious all the Braves coaches and scouts were to see him take his first practice swings in the batting cage. For if there was one thing everyone had heard about Aaron, it was that he could flat-out hit. "The wrists," said the veteran scout, Rosy Ryan. "He's not a big guy—just six-one, 180—and doesn't look like a power hitter. But those wrists. I've never seen such quick wrists."

Ben Geraghty, Aaron's manager at Jacksonville in '53, prepared the Braves' high command for the gifted hitter they were about to see. "If Henry has a strike zone," said Geraghty, "it's from the top of his head to his ankles. In a year or so, he's going to make fans forget all about Jackie Robinson, and I'm not exaggerating."

Growing up in the poor section of Mobile, Alabama, Aaron picked cotton on a farm and delivered twenty-five-pound blocks of ice as a youth, jobs he later said possibly helped in greater strengthening his hands and wrists. At Central High School he was a two-sport star in baseball and football, and he turned down several football scholarships to pursue a career in baseball. He signed his first pro contract as a junior in high school with the Mobile Black Bears, an independent Negro League team. Then, in November of 1951 he signed with the Indianapolis Clowns of the Negro American League. In twenty-six games for the Clowns he hit .366, with five homers, thirty-three RBI, and nine stolen bases. The major league scouts took notice, a half dozen of them following the Clowns for the first part of the season. Two of them, Dewey Griggs of the Braves and Alex Pompez of the Giants, implored their teams to offer him contracts. As Aaron related, "I had the Giants' contract in my hand and was ready to sign it, but they wanted to give me an A-ball contract with a C-ball salary. Then the Braves came in with an offer starting me off in C ball but with B-ball salary. So for the difference of $100 a month, I could've been teammates with Willie Mays. Imagine that. I often wonder if the Giants had both me and Willie in their outfield if they'd ever have been able to move to San Francisco in 1957."

Aaron signed with the Braves on June 14, 1952. By then the Braves had been one of the more aggressive teams in acquiring black players. On April 18, 1950, they became the fourth major league team to integrate when they promoted Sam Jethroe, a speedy, switch-hitting thirty-three-year-old center fielder and Negro League standout in the forties whom they'd purchased from the Dodgers for $100,000 a year earlier. After the sale Dodgers president Branch Rickey conceded to *New York Herald-Tribune* sports editor Stanley Woodward, "This was the first time in my life I have sold a man who may be better than what I have." Rickey went on to tell Woodward he didn't think the Dodgers' ownership was ready for another black regular, that his progressive integration policy had hurt the team's scouting in the South. But by sending Jethroe to the Braves, Rickey added, "When more clubs have Negro players, it may be that we shall be able to overcome prejudice in those areas and reestablish our scouting advantages there."

Jethroe went on to lead the major leagues in stolen bases his first two seasons and was the oldest player ever to win NL Rookie of the Year honors when, in 1950, he batted .273 with eighteen homers and one hundred runs scored. "Jethroe was the fastest human being I've ever seen," said Dodgers fifties pitching ace Don Newcombe, who was himself the first black All-Star pitcher in the majors.

But after three years as the Braves' starting center fielder, Jethroe was sent to the minors, deemed to be past his prime. Jethroe's replacement in center field, Bruton, was almost a carbon copy of him. The Braves had signed Bruton off the sandlots in Birmingham, Alabama, in 1950 after he'd spent the previous two years in the Army. On the advice of Bill Yancey, the scout who signed him, Bruton told the Braves' hierarchy he was twenty-three instead of his real age, twenty-six, in order to get a more serious look from them. Much like Jethroe, Bruton led the National League in stolen bases his first three years in the majors.

Then, when Aaron came to spring training in '54, he was pleasantly surprised to see three other black players in camp—Bruton, Pendleton, and George Crowe, a six-foot-two, 210-pound bespectacled first baseman who'd won two minor league RBI titles and one batting title in four and a half seasons in the Braves' system. Before signing with the Braves, Crowe had been one of the greatest basketball players ever to come out of the state of Indiana, being named the state's first "Mr. Basketball" in 1939. After serving in the Army in World War II, he played baseball in the Negro Leagues and in the National Basketball League (the forerunner to the NBA) as well as with the Harlem Globetrotters.

With Bruton, Crowe, and Pendleton on their roster for the entire '53 season, the Braves ranked fourth behind the Dodgers, Giants, and Indians in terms of teams with the most black players in the majors. But for the thirty-one-year-old Crowe, that was a bittersweet experience.

The previous year, with the Braves still in Boston, he'd shared first-base duties with fellow left-handed hitter veteran Earl Torgeson through the first seventy games, only to be told in August he was being demoted to Triple A to help their Milwaukee farm club win the American Association pennant. At the time Crowe was hitting .258—second on the team and twenty points higher than Torgeson—and it was the only time in anyone's memory a major league team demoted a player purportedly to help a minor league team win a pennant. Crowe later said, "When I was in Boston Earl Torgeson wasn't that great a player, but he was high on the totem pole of politics. The Braves' manager, Tommy Holmes, had been his roommate when they were teammates on the Braves. Who do you think he was going to play?" Nevertheless, Crowe accepted the demotion without complaint and proceeded to hit .351 with six homers and twenty-nine RBI in Milwaukee's final twenty-seven games in '52.

But when he reported to spring training in '53 Crowe found himself displaced at first base by Joe Adcock, a hulking, six-foot-four right-handed power hitter whom the Braves acquired in a trade from the Cincinnati Reds over the winter. So Crowe spent the entire '53 season as a pinch hitter for the Braves and, in '54, found himself once again back in Triple A, where he hit .334 with thirty-four homers and a league-leading 128 RBI for Toledo.

Throughout the spring the four black players hung together, though Aaron became especially close to Bruton, whose contrasting gregarious, assertive personality along with the confidence of having been a regular for two years in the majors helped make for a much easier period of adjustment than it might have been for the twenty-year-old rookie in this still largely segregated environment. It was Bruton, enormously popular in Milwaukee, especially after hitting a tenth-inning homer against the Cardinals in Milwaukee's first-ever major league game, who took charge of all the arrangements the black players had to make—from finding restaurants on the road that would serve them to booking taxi cabs—and Aaron followed him around like a puppy all spring and throughout that first season. Despite the hype of the 1953 Sally League Most Valuable Player that accompanied him to camp, Aaron did his best to keep a low profile. In mid-March Red Thisted, the veteran beat writer for the *Milwaukee Sentinel* said of him: "Aaron hasn't spoken perhaps more than 100 words since he joined the Braves in spring training here."

But what is it they say about actions speaking louder than words? In a game against the Yankees in Bradenton Aaron hit a long fly ball to deep center field, over the head of Yankee center fielder Irv Noren, and it went for a triple. On Hank's next trip to the plate, Noren had stationed himself 415 feet from the plate, a distance reporters noted was 10 feet further than Milwaukee's center field fence.

Between his hitting and his fielding, Aaron, whether he knew it or not, had caused a dilemma for Grimm. "How can we send this boy out?" the manager asked general manager John Quinn. "He's as good a hitter as we have in camp, with the exception of Eddie Mathews, and while he's still learning in the outfield, that'll come fast with experience." Quinn agreed but wanted to reserve judgment.

Then, on March 13, the decision was made for them.

In the eighth inning of a game against the Yankees at Al Lang Field in St. Petersburg, Bobby Thomson was on first base when Pafko hit a ball sharply back to the box. Yankees pitcher Bob Wiesler, after knocking the ball down, quickly recovered it, pivoted, and threw to shortstop Woody Held, covering second, as Thomson slid into the bag. As soon as he hit the bag, Thomson began writhing in pain. His spikes had gotten caught in the loose turf, causing an awkward slide in which he suffered a triple fracture of his ankle bone.

"I started my slide too late," Thomson recalled in an interview years later. "I saw it coming when my foot caught in the loose dirt. It was just terrible bad luck. Grimm had told me before the inning that he was taking me out of the game as soon as the inning was over. But it was good luck for Henry. He never looked back."

In one horrifying instant the Braves' most celebrated off-season acquisition and key to their pennant aspirations was lost to them for the foreseeable future. Aaron had played earlier in the game and, after showering, was standing in a runway behind a fence on the third base side of the field when the play unfolded right in front of him.

"It was gruesome," he said. "Bobby was in terrible pain, and I just stood there, kind of frozen, watching him being carried off the field in a stretcher. It never occurred to me that this was going to be my opportunity to be the left fielder. Even then it might have been Pendleton, who'd been the primary backup outfielder the year before, except that Jim had been a holdout that spring and came to camp overweight and out of shape."

It was Bob Buhl, the Braves' number-three starter behind Warren Spahn and Lew Burdette, who enlightened Aaron about

his situation. That winter Buhl had been Aaron's teammate in
the Puerto Rican League, where the Braves had sent Hank to get
some experience in the outfield. He'd seen firsthand Aaron's hitting skills, and that whole spring he'd been Aaron's biggest ad-
vocate with Grimm and the coaches. "It's yours now, Hank," Buhl
said to him confidently the next morning before the team left for
Sarasota for a game against the Red Sox. And sure enough, a
short while later Grimm posted the lineup with Aaron in left
field, batting fifth. And to justify his manager's faith, Aaron hit
a home run off the Red Sox's Ike Delock, a monster blast hit so
hard over the trailers that bordered the left field fence that Ted
Williams was said to have run out of the Red Sox clubhouse just
to see who hit a ball that had such a distinctive crack.

"I really didn't know what was going to happen with me that
spring," Aaron said. "I had played some outfield in the Puerto Rican winter league, but I'd seen how a manager could bury a player,
like the Yankees did with Vic Power and Elston Howard. Howard
had a world of talent, but they didn't trust him to catch and moved
him to the outfield at first. The Yankees didn't even have black
players sitting on their bench, and if I'd have signed with them, it
would've taken me two to three extra years in the minors before I
got to the big leagues. So with all that in mind, I knew I had to get
off to a good start in spring training. Either way, I figured I was
destined to go back to Triple A no matter what I did."

The announcement two weeks later that the Braves had purchased Aaron's contract from Toledo was a mere formality. Beginning the day after Bobby Thomson broke his ankle in spring
training, Aaron became a permanent fixture in the middle of the
Braves lineup for the next twenty-one years, en route to surpassing Babe Ruth as baseball's all-time home run king. Thomson
was right—Hank would never look back.

CASEY'S SPRING OF DISCONTENT

"They voted Casey Stengel the greatest living manager.
That's a lot of bullshit. A joke. The only thing a
manager has to relate to is the players. Who did
Casey ever relate to? Nobody but himself."

—JACKIE ROBINSON, 1969

LONG BEFORE THE PULITZER PRIZE— AND TONY AWARD—WINNING
playwright Neil Simon created his *Odd Couple* of Felix Un-
ger, the fastidious neat freak, and his slovenly sportswriter
roommate, Oscar Madison, the New York Yankees had general
manager George Weiss and manager Casey Stengel. Each was a
baseball genius in his own right but with polar opposite personalities, demeanors, and style.

To the cold, laconic, and isolated Weiss, Stengel was warm
and effusive. Over a quarter-century in baseball as a front office
executive, Weiss had developed a reputation as a humorless, aloof,
bottom-line business operative, devoid of any sentiment when it
came to players, whereas Casey, who debuted in the majors in

1912, was more regarded as a clown—who once tipped his hat to the crowd and had a sparrow fly out of it—than for his .284 lifetime batting average in fourteen years as a player in the big leagues. Whereas Weiss regarded the writers a necessary inconvenience, almost never making himself available to them unless he had an announcement, the hard-drinking Stengel loved the newspapermen's camaraderie, staying up all night with them on the trains and in bars on the road. To him, they were always "my writers." Stengel knew their business and made a habit of providing the writers for the PM papers fresh angles for their stories from what he told the AM paper writers.

Add to that Stengel's eight out of nine losing seasons as manager of the Brooklyn Dodgers and Boston Braves, and it's a wonder what Weiss saw in this free spirit when he hired him to replace Bucky Harris as Yankees manager for 1949. Indeed, the day after the press conference Stengel's principal antagonist in Boston, Dave Egan, the notorious "poison pen" of the *Boston Record* wrote, "Well, sirs and ladies, the Yankees have now been mathematically eliminated from the 1949 race. They eliminated themselves when they engaged Perfesser Casey Stengel to mismanage them for the next ten years."

But Weiss knew Stengel, had even hired him once before—to manage the Yankees' Triple A farm team in Kansas City in 1945, a team that had been depleted of talent because of the war. Despite the Blues' seventh-place finish that year, he was impressed with Stengel's baseball acumen and the way he handled players. Just to be sure, however, Weiss tapped his two main West Coast scouts, Joe Devine and Bill Essick, for a report on Stengel, who had managed the Oakland Oaks of the Pacific Coast League from 1946 to 1948 and won the league championship in '48 with 114 victories. Both Devine and Essick told Weiss that Stengel was far and away the best manager in the PCL.

Now it was five years later, and much to the chagrin of Dave Egan—or the guy in Boston who sent Stengel a telegram his last year as manager of the Braves that read, "There's a train leaving Boston at 6 p.m. Be under it"—Stengel had achieved something no other manager in baseball history had ever achieved (and likely ever will): winning five straight world championships. Together, Weiss and Stengel were the most successful general manager–manager tandem ever, although as the 1954 season approached, there was a sense of uneasiness for both about the prospects for making it six straight.

In particular, the pitching was a major concern. The "Big Three" staff aces, Allie Reynolds, Vic Raschi, and Eddie Lopat, would all be thirty-seven, thirty-five, and thirty-six, respectively in '54, with Reynolds and Raschi both coming off "down" years in which they won just thirteen games apiece. In addition, Johnny Sain, who had gone 14–7 in '53 as a starter and reliever, had announced his retirement. "Some of our pitching is too old," Stengel said at a press gathering at the Yankee offices in New York in early February. "We need more pitching. If it's not on the farms, I don't know if we can win No. 6. Any club that wins too often gets careless. I said last fall we'd win six, seven, eight. Now I'm not so sure."

It was for that reason Weiss had moved quickly after the '53 World Series to make the eleven-player trade with the Athletics for twenty-nine-year-old workhorse starter Harry Byrd, whom a number of other teams had coveted. But aside from Whitey Ford, an eighteen-game winner in '53, the other pitchers Stengel was looking at to fill in the starting rotation—right-handers Tom Morgan, who was returning after a year in the service, and Jim McDonald, who had struggled somewhat as the fifth starter in '53, as well as diminutive (five feet eight, 160 pounds) soft-throwing rookie left-hander, Steve Kraly, the

Class A Eastern League pitcher of the year, with nineteen wins in '53—were all question marks.

Much as the pitching concerned Stengel, however, he became especially distressed upon learning he would be without the services in '54 of second baseman Billy Martin. The scrappy five-foot-eleven, 160-pound Martin had played for Stengel at Oakland in '47 and '48, when, as his pet project, the manager spent hours smoothing out his edges, working with him every day on the hitting and fielding fundamentals of baseball. In Martin, a street kid from Berkeley, California, and the product of a broken home, Stengel saw that rare kind of player who had the sheer desire and tenacity to rise above his own lesser talent. He loved Billy's hard-nosed style and his cockiness—"he's a fresh little kid, ain't he?"—and he believed that, more than Yogi Berra, Mickey Mantle, or Phil Rizzuto, Martin was the most important player in his lineup. His recurring term of affection for him—"my intangibles player"—was never more demonstrated than the '53 World Series when Martin was voted the Series' Most Valuable Player by batting .500 (12-for-24) with two triples, two homers, and eight RBI while setting a six-game record with twenty-three total bases in the Yankees' second-straight defeat of the Dodgers.

"Martin is the 135-pound home run champion of the major leagues," Stengel gushed afterward. "We have done a good job with him. When the season started, he was behind Bobby Avila and Nelson Fox among second basemen in the American League. Now, he is the No. 1 man at his position. He did it through fight and through gameness. It'll be harder than ever now to tell Martin he is not the long ball type."

But as it turned out, that would have to wait. On February 18, just a week before Stengel was to assemble the Yankees' pitchers and catchers at '54 spring training, it was announced that the military draft board in Berkeley had rejected Martin's appeal stating that he was his mother's primary source of support and was calling him back into the Army for the second time in less than three years. Fortunately for the Yankees, Jerry Coleman, the regular second baseman on Stengel's 1949, '50, and '51 world championship teams, had been released from Korea after his own second tour of duty as a Marine bomber pilot, in late September of '53 and, with a full spring training of baseball conditioning under his belt, would presumably be ready to take back his old job. Privately, though, Stengel wasn't so sure, although he did his best to downplay with reporters Martin's absence at spring training in St. Petersburg. "Don't forget," Stengel said, "it was Coleman's job that Martin took. When Coleman came back to us last year, he wasn't batting right. Those Reds in Korea didn't give him any time to get that hitch out of his swing."

No sooner had Stengel begun resigning himself to the loss of Martin than Weiss jolted him by jettisoning another of the cornerstone players of his five-straight championship teams. All winter Weiss had been engaged in an increasingly acrimonious contract dispute with Raschi, who, after winning twenty-one games in each of the '49, '50, and '51 seasons, tailed off to 16–6 in '52 and just 13–6 in '53. Bothered by periodic arm soreness in '53, Raschi also failed to log more than 200 innings (181) for the first time since 1947. It was Weiss's opinion Raschi was nearing the end of the line and throughout the contract negotiations with the erstwhile ace (who was also 5–3 with a 2.24 ERA in six World Series for the Yankees) remained adamant in offering him the maximum 25 percent pay cut from his $40,000 salary.

When the Yankee players filed into the clubhouse at Miller Huggins Field in St. Petersburg on the morning of February 23 they were stunned to see Raschi packing up all his belongings. Without warning, his Yankee career was over. In lieu of attempting any further negotiations to settle the contract dispute, Weiss had sold him to the St. Louis Cardinals for $85,000. Unlike his two fellow veteran aces—Reynolds, who was obtained in a 1946 trade with the Cleveland Indians for future Hall of Famer and second baseman Joe Gordon, and Lopat, a 1948 trade acquisition from the Chicago White Sox—Raschi, a native of West Springfield, Massachusetts (from where he gained the nickname the "Springfield Rifle"), was a homegrown Yankee, signing with them out of the College of William and Mary in 1941. It took nearly seven years, three of them in the service in World War II, before he finally joined the Yankees for good, and from there he went on to compile a sterling 120–50 record, with a 3.47 ERA from 1946 to 1953.

"Raschi's attitude was like so many other attitudes on this club," Weiss told C. C. Johnson Spink, editor of the *Sporting News* in St. Louis. "There are players among the Yankees who expect you to chase after them so they may take your money. There are players on this club who, through our string of five straight world championships, have become independently wealthy. We have developed a condition which is the enemy of hustle. We are not in a mood to stop winning, so we have taken steps to eradicate complacency. We will win without Raschi. We have some fine young pitchers who must get their opportunities for places on the team."

Weiss's harsh and insulting characterization of the respected elder statesman Raschi, one of the acknowledged fiercest competitors of all time, made for an even more uneasy clubhouse for Stengel. That morning the normally conversationalist Stengel had little to say to reporters. "Baseball's a funny game, ain't it?" he replied tersely when asked for comment on the trade, and then he walked away.

The Yankees players were keenly aware of the $6.5 million windfall the Yankees owners had reaped from the sale of Yankee

Stadium to Chicago industrialist Arnold Johnson over the winter, and there was widespread resentment at the general manager's suggestions that they had become greedy and complacent. From afar "Old Reliable" Tommy Henrich, the hard-hitting outfielder who'd been a vital part of six Yankee championship teams from 1937 to 1950, expressed his astonishment at the trade. "What? You're kidding?" Henrich said after reporters at the Auto Show in New York told him of the trade. "If there was only one game I had to win, the man I'd want out there on the mound for me would be Vic Raschi. That Weiss can sure be tough. Sure, the Supreme Court [in repeatedly upholding Baseball's antitrust exemption] ruled baseball is a sport. But let me tell you, Weiss and the Yankees are all business."

And in his Sports of the Times column the day after the trade, Arthur Daley wrote, "The Yankee players still haven't recovered from the shock of the brusque dismissal by the Yankee brass of Vic Raschi. There never has been anything soft or sentimental about the Yankee front office. It's populated with hard-boiled realists. The shipping of Raschi to the National League is mainly a cold, disciplinary measure, coldly calculated to whip into line all the other holdouts."

A few days later Stengel confided to the *New York Times'* Yankee beat reporter John Drebinger, "I could have stopped this, had I acted sooner. I knew George was getting pretty sore and I tried to get Raschi on the phone. Had I got them together I'm sure this would never have happened. Now I'm out a pitcher. Winning this one is gonna be mighty tough now. Losing Billy Martin is going to hurt. Our other guys are getting older, but in spite of all of this I say I still could breeze if I had Raschi."

At least Raschi didn't have to go far, as the Cardinals also trained in St. Petersburg, a few miles away from Miller Huggins Field. A few days later, at Al Lang Field, where both teams played their home spring training games, Raschi gave his side of the story:

> *Who ever figured this would happen to me? With George Weiss I had no chance, after all the years of service to the Yankees, to get what I wanted in the way of a contract. I had expected trouble with Weiss and I had tried to avoid it. He had warned me in the past and I got the impression that he was waiting for me to bog down and hit me hard. Had I been so useless in '53? I still don't know what complacency means. If it's determination to be paid what you are worth, then the Yankees have a lot of complacent players and Raschi was one of them. When a fellow wins 20 games, I felt he was entitled to a raise. Yet I always had to fight—and I mean fight—with them. Had I been so negligible a factor in the winning of a fifth straight pennant that Weiss was justified in trying to give me a full cut? I don't understand it, other than, with the Yankees, I obviously had no future.*

When Weiss made the big mid-December trade with the Athletics for Byrd and first baseman Eddie Robinson and proclaimed the rest of the AL clubs would now have to really scramble, he got no disagreement from Hank Greenberg, the general manager of the Cleveland Indians, who finished second to the Yankees in '51, '52, and '53. Greenberg, the Hall of Fame slugger who chased Babe Ruth's record of sixty homers with fifty-eight in 1938, was brought into the Indians' front office in 1948 by Bill Veeck and listed as a part owner even though he had invested zero money in the club. When Veeck sold out his shares a year later, Greenberg was elevated to the general manager's job by new Indians chairman, Ellis Ryan, but it didn't take long for him to alienate the entire Cleveland fan base.

It began with his decision to fire Lou Boudreau as Indians manager after the 1950 season and replace him with Al Lopez. After guiding the Indians to the 1948 world championship as a shortstop manager and winning AL Most Valuable Player honors by hitting .355 and driving in 106 runs, Boudreau was one of the most popular Indians ever. It did not matter that Lopez, who'd cut his managing teeth with one first-place finish and three seconds for the Pittsburgh Pirates' Triple A American Association farm team in Indianapolis after a nineteen-year career as one of the best catchers in the majors, soon proved to be a far superior manager to Boudreau. Boudreau had been a god in Cleveland, and Greenberg was forever a villain for having gotten rid of him.

After that a series of ill-conceived trades—he sent first baseman Mickey Vernon, who went on to win two batting titles, to the Washington Senators; outfielder Minnie Miñoso, who went on to become one of the most exciting players in the big leagues, to the Chicago White Sox; and third baseman Ray Boone, who went on to earn two All-Star honors, to Detroit—did not help Greenberg's cause with the fans either. All the while Greenberg's strong-willed opinions on everything from his disapproval of players getting married during their careers to his "heresy" proposals for expanding the majors and interleague play, served to portray him as arrogant and out of touch. Accordingly, despite averaging ninety-two wins over his five-year stewardship, the steadily declining Indians' attendance, from a record 2.6 million in '48 to just over a million in '53, was largely attributed to Greenberg's unpopularity.

It was therefore not surprising that, shortly after Weiss's preening over the Vic Power-for-Byrd-and-Robinson deal, Greenberg concurred, "Whether Byrd and Robinson will be able to do what the Yankees expect from them is a question, but for our part we must assume they will and that the trade has restored the Yanks to their 1953 strength. We'll do our utmost to improve our club as much as we can." In truth, though, Greenberg didn't see a need for any major changes with the Indians, who, in '53, had finished second in the American League in runs, first in homers, and with their pitchers fourth in ERA. In third baseman Al Rosen, the AL MVP in '53 who led the league in homers and RBI; center fielder Larry Doby, third in the AL in homers; and Bobby Avila, a .286 hitter who led all AL second basemen in fielding percentage, the Indians had three bona fide All-Stars, while in Bob Lemon, Early Wynn, and Mike Garcia, who combined for fifty-six wins in '53, they had a trio of top-of-the-rotation starters to more than rival the Yankees' Big Three. And behind them the great Bob Feller, though thirty-five and no longer the dominant fireballer of the forties, was still about the best number-four starter in all of baseball.

If anything, Greenberg felt, the Indians could use a little more offense, especially at first base, where Lopez had been dissatisfied with rookie Bill Glynn's paltry three homers and 30 RBI in '53, and the corner outfield spots, normally power positions, where veterans Dale Mitchell and Wally Westlake produced only twenty-two homers and 106 RBI between them in '53. It wasn't until February 10 that Greenberg made his first counter move to Weiss by sending a couple of so-so pitching prospects, Leroy Wheat and Bill Upton, to the Athletics for thirty-four-year-old corner outfielder Dave Philley, a .303-hitting All-Star in '53. Philley, who would go on to play another nine years in the big leagues and set a couple of pinch hitting records, was one of those players referred to in scouts' jargon as "a professional hitter."

"We got ourselves another solid outfielder who can be very helpful to us," Greenberg said.

AS THOUGH CASEY STENGEL DIDN'T HAVE ENOUGH PROBLEMS THAT spring of '54, other than Bob Grim, a twenty-four-year-old right-hander returning from two years in the service who'd impressed Stengel in the Yankees' pretraining minicamp, none of the young pitchers Weiss had touted to the writers had asserted themselves as bona fide replacements for the traded Raschi and the retired Johnny Sain in the starting rotation. Though he didn't say anything publicly about it, Stengel was also worried about his middle infield, where veteran shortstop Phil Rizzuto and returning second baseman Coleman were both struggling with the bat, and Willie Miranda, the slick-fielding shortstop they'd purchased from the St. Louis Browns the year before to spell Rizzuto, had been late reporting from his native Cuba. Even more concerning, there was Mickey Mantle's balky knee. The switch-hitting center fielder, who'd batted .295 with twenty-one homers and ninety-two RBI for the Yankees in '53, had been sidelined for most of March with a sore right knee that had been operated on over the winter and, doctors told Stengel, could preclude him from opening the season.

Then, just as the team was preparing to break camp, Stengel unwittingly found himself embroiled in a racial issue when Sam Lacy, the respected longtime sportswriter for the *Baltimore Afro-American*, accused him of being part of the conspiracy on the Yankees' part to keep Elston Howard out of the big leagues by asking him to convert to catching. In a scathing condemnation of the Yankees under the headline "Vicious Campaign Being Conducted," Lacy once again excoriated them over the Vic Power trade and the release of fellow Negro Puerto Rican, pitcher Rubén Gómez, from their Kansas City farm club in 1953 and then suggested strongly they were out to bury Howard as well. In the process Lacy accused some of the deans of the New York baseball writing fraternity of being co-conspirators in the Yankees' continued resistance to integrating.

Calling Howard "the most unfortunate young man in all of sportdom" and "the victim of a campaign calculated by a machine every bit as vicious as that waged by the rulers of boxing during the era of Jack Johnson and Joe Louis," Lacy declared Howard was a pawn in the hands of "operators who have no conscience." Noting how, after they'd gotten rid of Gómez and Power, they'd consciously leaked disparaging information about them to the press, Lacy in particular accused senior Yankee beat writer Dan Daniel of the *New York World-Telegram* as filling "his usual Yankee Yes-man role" by writing that Power was a "bad actor" with a "poor attitude" and *World-Telegram* columnist Joe Williams of doing likewise in describing Gómez as a boy "with poor attitude."

Lacy wrote, "That left Howard. Now something had to be done here. Inasmuch as their anti-Power campaign had built up Elston as the better ballplayer of the two, people might reasonably be expecting him to stick with the club this year. So how does Stengel and the Yankee brass handle this hot potato? Casey just converts him to catcher. Playing two years of organized ball and two years of service ball, Elston saw less than ten games behind the bat and those were voluntary assignments."

According to Lacy, Howard didn't like being asked to catch: "He knows his limitations in a strange position . . . and if he can't make the club as an outfielder, he'd rather get the experience he needs playing in the minors—at a position he feels he's best."

But Stengel had his reasons for wanting to make a catcher out of Howard, and although he was crude in articulating them, they were not racially motivated. For one thing, Howard lacked the speed Stengel thought necessary to play outfield. In discussing Howard with reporters, Stengel was alleged to have said, "They finally get me a nigger and he can't run." However, Stengel loved Howard's arm. "When you see this fellow catch in practice games," he told the writers, "you're gonna see one of the finest throwing arms any of us have seen in a long time."

It was fairly apparent Lacy had based his conspiracy theory on a private interview he'd had with Howard out by the gate in the parking lot, away from the Miller Huggins Field clubhouse. And with Yogi Berra, at twenty-nine, a five-time All-Star and winner of the 1951 Most Valuable Player award (he would go on to win two more, in '54 and '55), firmly entrenched as the Yankees' number-one catcher for the foreseeable future, Howard was certainly justified in wondering what kind of future he had with them if he was to catch. Because they also had a surplus of good catchers at Triple A Kansas City, including another top prospect, Gus Triandos, the Yankees elected to loan Howard to the independent Toronto Maple Leafs of the International League for the '54 season.

In continuing his assault on Stengel in the column, Lacy wrote,

There are other evidences of the "break-him-down" campaign [against Howard] in progress here, little things that can't be detected in the box score or in the writers' reports to the fans, like the other day when Elston caught the first five innings against Washington, his initial appearance in the Yankee lineup. Do you know how he was told he was going to start? [Yankee catching great] Bill Dickey, who is supposed to be making him into a catcher, and who would be expected to teach him confidence, waved to Howard from across the clubhouse and shouted: "You're catching today. Better slap some color in your face. You look scared already!"

"My only regret in writing this," Lacy concluded, "is that mine is but a small voice in a multitude of wolves.

Howard's wife, Arlene, had nothing but the fondest regard for Stengel, but she didn't trust Weiss's motives, often recalling how, at a cocktail party in 1952, others had reportedly overheard the general manager declaring, "I will never allow a black man to wear a Yankee uniform. Boxholders from Westchester don't want them. They would be offended to have to sit with niggers."

But Lee MacPhail, the Yankee farm director who made the deal with Tom Baird, the owner of the Kansas City Monarchs, to sign Howard, insisted Weiss was not a racist; rather, MacPhail said, he was "a conservative slow to embrace changes such as adding Negroes to the roster, but he did not look down upon them." MacPhail went on to say race had nothing to do with making Howard a catcher. "If anything," he said, "it made him more valuable."

For Stengel the one saving grace keeping Lacy's report from escalating into a full-blown racial controversy was that the *Baltimore Afro-American* was a small paper and the story didn't get widely circulated beyond the black media outlets. But friends made Howard aware of it, and he was livid, feeling betrayed by Lacy in what he thought had been a private, off-the-record conversation. Just before the Yankees announced that first baseman Bill Skowron and Bob Grim, the two most impressive rookies in camp, would be going north with the club while Howard was being reassigned to the minors, Howard confronted Lacy in the dugout at Huggins Field. "Why would you write that stuff, Sam? That's all bull and you know it," Howard shrieked. "From now on, stay away from me or I'll punch you in the nose!"

Howard then went on to hold a separate press conference with the same writers Lacy had essentially accused of being Yankee "house men," during which he insisted Stengel had treated him nothing but fairly and he was looking forward to working with Dickey further on his receiving skills. That, in turn, prompted an editorial in the *Chicago Black Defender* by the renowned black sportswriter Frank (Fay) Young, chastising him for renouncing Lacy. "All this praise that Howard gave old Casey, and the hell he tried to dish out to Lacy makes us laugh," the editorial said. "The 24-year old needs to learn to keep his mouth shut. . . . Facing Boss Stengel's white New York reporters, Howard back-tracked from what he'd told Sam Lacy, who is a sagacious sports reporter and editor. But all his bootlicking did was get him a train ride to Toronto. And the New York Yankees remain lily white. . . . A piece of advice to Howard. Never call a newspaperman a liar. It isn't a nice thing to do."

"The problem," Arlene told me in a 2002 interview at her home in Teaneck, New Jersey, "was that Elston simply wasn't a flaming crusader, and the black writers back then wanted him to be more like Jackie [Robinson]. All he wanted to do was to play baseball, and he wanted to play for the Yankees."

Arlene admitted she'd heard of that derogatory remark Casey had made about Elston's speed, but she chalked it up as being a product of his environment. Stengel was born in 1890 in Kansas City, a time and a place in America where casual use of the N-word wasn't regarded as bigotry but just blind indifference.

Elston told me how, during the World Series against the Dodgers, Casey would yell things at Jackie like "throw that nigger out!" and then he would catch himself, knowing Elston was there. But I think Casey was overly nice to Elston. He gave him his chance, and I never saw any overt prejudice from him.

That first spring with them was very hard for Elston. We had to stay in a boardinghouse because the team hotel in St. Petersburg didn't accept blacks. We couldn't even go on the beach or else we'd

*be arrested. When the Yankees had a big party at the St. Petersburg
Yacht Club, Elston wasn't allowed to go because the club didn't
accept blacks. I think it was then, when he didn't make a fuss about
it, that the black writers got upset with him.*

Stengel's trying spring, during which the Yankees' Grapefruit League record was an underwhelming 8–16 as the club
headed north on April 2, got a bit of a lift when Sain, the thirty-
five-year-old right-hander who'd announced his retirement earlier in the winter because he was tired of the travel and wanted
to devote his full time to an automobile dealership he'd recently
purchased back home in Walnut Ridge, Arkansas, announced he
was going to come back after all, once Weiss agreed to an $8,000
salary increase to $30,000. But even then there was skepticism
aplenty about the Yankees' ability to win a sixth straight world
championship.

From his hospital bed in Cambridge, Massachusetts, where he
was recovering from surgery for a broken collarbone, the great
Ted Williams of the Red Sox led the Yankee doomsayers' chorus by declaring, "I'm inclined to believe now that the Yankees
are going to have a tough time making it. Raschi was as good a
pitcher as they've had and they've sold him. They've lost Billy
Martin to the Army and nobody knows how much Mantle will
be able to play with that bum knee of his."

"The way the Yankees have been going in the Grapefruit
League cellar, they have not looked like first division, let alone
pennant winning stuff," wrote Daniel in the *World-Telegram*.
"That's why Johnny Sain has been induced to come out of retirement. When one defeat followed another, when adverse publicity
on top of bad press on the Raschi deal piled up, George Weiss
rushed his top Midwest scout Tom Greenwade out to Walnut
Ridge, Ark. to see Sain."

"They think nobody can beat them," co-owner Dan Topping warned on a visit to St. Petersburg at the end of March. "The five straight pennants have got them to thinking that way."

And that same day Hugh Bradley, the Yankee beat writer for the *New York Journal-American*, wrote ominously, "I believe the club suffers most from two things: There's been no positive proof anything important has been added to the squad this year, and so far the club lacks a 'take-charge' type guy like Joe DiMaggio."

Although Weiss would ordinarily be loathe to admit taking his lead from anything a sportswriter had to say, two days before Opening Day he pulled off another stunning trade, this one for Enos Slaughter, the ten-time All-Star outfielder with the St. Louis Cardinals. If ever there was a player who could be described as a "take charge" guy, it was the hustling old warhorse Enos "Country" Slaughter. This was essentially the Vic Raschi deal in reverse, as Slaughter, a lifetime .305 hitter whose "mad dash" from first base to home for the winning run in the seventh game of the 1946 World Series for the Cardinals had made him an icon in St. Louis. Even though Weiss was giving the Cardinals a top-notch center field prospect in twenty-two-year-old Bill Virdon as the key return player in the trade, fans in St. Louis were as incensed as Yankee fans had been when Weiss sold Raschi to the Cardinals a month earlier. Baseball people were both perplexed and shocked over the deal, none more so than the thirty-eight-year-old Slaughter, who thought he'd be a Cardinal for life. "This is the biggest shock of my life," Slaughter said in the Cardinals clubhouse in St. Petersburg, breaking into tears. "Something I never expected to happen. I've given my life to this organization, and they let you go when they think you're getting old."

"We have just traded one of the greatest baseball players in the history of the St. Louis Cardinals," admitted Cardinals owner Gussie Busch. "Enos has been 'Mr. Baseball' in St. Louis for almost 20 years. The word 'hustle' was practically invented for him. But the Cardinals are trying to build a young ballclub."

From the Yankees' standpoint there was only one way to explain the deal. Weiss, heeding Topping's warning words, wanted to shake the team out of its supposed complacency. Why else would they trade for another outfielder when Stengel already had two All-Stars in Mantle and right fielder Hank Bauer and a .300 hitter in left fielder Gene Woodling, plus Irv Noren, whom Casey called "the best No. 4 outfielder in the league"?

Having made a steady habit of beating the National League in the World Series, the Yankees didn't have a whole lot of regard for players from the other circuit. As such, they largely viewed Slaughter as an intruder, unequal to any of their outfielders with multiple rings.

"When the deal was announced, I told the writers I'd been 'slaughtered,'" Noren recalled years later. "None of us could figure it out. We thought we already had a pretty good outfield."

Stengel thought so too, and he wasn't about to take away playing time from the fellas who'd gotten him here, Bauer and Woodling, who'd been on all of his five-straight world championship teams, and Mantle, depending on his bum knee that had kept him out of much of the Grapefruit League and who, when healthy, was his best player. And Noren? Well, Casey had great affection for him too. He was the one who pushed Weiss to acquire the lefty-swinging Californian from the Washington Senators in '52, even though it meant sacrificing their best outfield prospect, Jackie Jensen.

"You'll be okay," Casey promised Noren. "You won't be sitting on the bench all year."

Sure enough, when the season began, Slaughter found himself mostly relegated to pinch-hitting duties by Stengel, and he didn't like it. He'd been a ten-year All-Star in the National League, for heaven sakes! But when he went to Stengel to complain about how little playing time he was getting, the manager cut him off. "My boy," he said, "you'll play when I want you to play, and you'll be here for a long time."

Slaughter had no way of knowing how unsettling the spring had been for Stengel, beginning with Weiss selling one of his ace pitchers from those five-straight world championship seasons and then losing his pet player to the Army. His team, with its idled center fielder and aging, slowed-down shortstop, had not played well throughout the Grapefruit League, prompting criticism from his bosses about complacency setting in with his veteran troops. Casey knew better, of course, just as he knew Sam Lacy's accusations of a racial conspiracy against Elston Howard was a trumped-up bunch of crap. But he was helpless to defend it and thankful at least that his infuriated writers chose not to fire back at Lacy publicly to turn it into a full-blown war of words, escalating the already-sensitive race issue with the Yankees.

The last thing Stengel needed was the new guy on the block, a guy he hadn't asked for, coming to him and asking for more playing time. There was another pennant to be won, and, with all those missing ingredients, nobody knew better than he did how daunting a task that figured to be.

LEO'S MIDAS TOUCH

"You and Durocher are on a raft.
A wave comes and knocks him into the ocean.
You dive in and save his life. A shark comes and takes
your leg. Next day, you and Leo start out even."

—DICK YOUNG

FOR A QUARTER CENTURY, DATING ALL THE WAY BACK TO HIS EARLY playing days with the Yankees where, legend has persisted, he stole Babe Ruth's watch, Leo Durocher had cultivated his mean image as baseball's most hated man.

Durocher also relished the celebrity life. He flaunted his friendships with Frank Sinatra, who in March of 1954 had culminated his big comeback with his Best Supporting Actor Academy Award as the doomed Private Maggio in *From Here to Eternity*, and Hollywood tough guy George Raft along with the assorted underworld figures always associated with them. And it also gave Durocher great private satisfaction knowing that his enemies, as much as they hated him, wondered how actress

Laraine Day, one of the most beautiful and classy women in Hollywood, could be married to such a confirmed scoundrel.

It was Durocher who, as manager of the Dodgers from 1939 to 1948—with the exception of '47, when he was suspended from baseball for his association with gamblers and underworld figures—became renowned for instructing his pitchers to be headhunters, most notably with the mild-mannered and gentlemanly legendary Dodger killer Stan Musial. In fact, it was during a game in 1943, after two consecutive Durocher-ordered knockdown pitches by a mediocre Dodger right-hander named Les Webber, that Musial had to be restrained from charging the mound—the only time in his career "The Man" ever attempted to go after an opposing pitcher. In the case of Ruth's pilfered watch in 1929, there have been varying accounts through the years as to whether Durocher was actually the thief. What is not in dispute, however, is that Ruth despised the cocky and abrasive five-foot-ten, 160-pound Durocher and never hesitated to call him a liar and a thief, almost to the Bambino's dying day in 1948.

Durocher loved being hated. Upsetting the opposition, he felt, always gave him the edge. The classic example of that was the brawl he initiated, when he was manager of the Giants, against the Dodgers on September 6, 1953. The Giants were in fifth place, twenty-nine games behind the front-running Dodgers, and losing again to them, 2–1, in the second inning at the Polo Grounds when Brooklyn right fielder Carl Furillo, one of Durocher's favorite targets through the years, was struck on the right hand by a pitch from Giants rookie right-hander Rubén Gómez. The hot-tempered Furillo, whose feud with Durocher went back to 1949 when he was—in his mind, deliberately—beaned by a pitch from another Giant right-hander, Sheldon "Available" Jones, and sent to the hospital overnight, yelled a few

obscenities at Gómez on his way to first base. But once at the
bag he redirected his venom at the Giants' dugout and at Durocher in particular. Durocher didn't hesitate to meet Furillo's
challenge, charging out of the dugout. As the two quickly began tussling, they fell to the ground, with both benches empty-
ing. After a wild scramble of players and coaches, Furillo, who
was leading the National League in batting with a .344 average,
emerged with a broken hand.

"He [Durocher] dared me to come after him," Furillo said. "I
looked into the dugout and he's glaring at me, with his mouth
moving, and then he started wriggling his index finger."

"He's a goddamn liar," Durocher shot back. "I'm looking at
him and he's pointing at me and the next thing I know he was
coming at me. So I went out to meet him. Maybe I should've let
him come into the dugout."

"The Giants aren't gonna jump in for him," Furillo retorted.
"They hate his guts. If he knew the half of it. . . . "

"I don't know what Carl was talking about," Monte Irvin said
years later. "He'd killed us that year—heck, he'd killed everyone
that year—and he knew Leo's style. Leo would do anything to
win, and if that meant knocking down a guy who was hurting
us, then that was it. We were all on board with that. Look what
he did to Musial! Stan was one of the best guys who ever played
the game, but he killed Leo when Leo was in Brooklyn, and he
killed the Giants, and Leo was always ordering his pitchers to
flatten him.

"I have to believe Leo was the only guy Stan ever had no use
for. I just know that when Stan and I were on the [Hall of Fame]
Veterans Committee together, Leo was the one guy Stan ever
said he couldn't vote for."

In his office later, Durocher merely smiled at the turn of
events. His Giants may have been hopelessly out of the race, but

he'd gotten his measure of satisfaction in that Furillo was lost to the Dodgers for the rest of the season. The next day Dick Young, the *New York Daily News* Dodger beat writer, summed up how once again, even in defeat, Durocher was able to use his "bad guy" image to his favor and come out looking like a winner: "The Giants, fightingest corpse in the history of medical science, lost to the Brooks yesterday for the last possible time this season, but spilled a bit of blood on the way down. They got Carl Furillo out of action . . . with a broken metacarpal in the left hand—the mysterious result of a non-punch brawl with Giants manager Leo Durocher."

Even the quote that was forever associated with him, "Nice guys finish last," you have to believe Durocher calculated to encourage and rile up more antagonists. He allegedly made it—or rather a variation of it—on June 6, 1946, while manager of the Dodgers, putting down the Giants and, in particular, their manager, Mel Ott, during batting practice at the Polo Grounds. He was talking to Frank Graham, the legendary baseball writer for the *New York Journal-American*, and Dodger broadcaster Red Barber, who asked Durocher, "Why can't you be a nice guy for a change, Leo?" According to Graham's column the next day Durocher pointed over to the Giants' dugout and replied, "Nice guys! Look over there. Do you know a nicer guy than Mel Ott? Or any of those other Giants? Why they're the nicest guys in the world. And where are they? In seventh place! Nice guys! I'm not a nice guy and I'm in first place. The nice guys are all over there, in seventh place." Later, in his own book, which he titled *Nice Guys Finish Last*, Durocher revised Graham's account of the incident, writing, "I called off Ott's players as they came marching up the steps with him, Walker Cooper, [Johnny] Mize, [Willard] Marshall, [Buddy] Kerr, [Sid] Gordon . . .

and said, 'take a look at them. All nice guys. They'll finish last. Nice guys. Finish last.'"

"ISN'T IT A LOVELY DAY?" DUROCHER SAID TO A GATHERING OF newspapermen in the Giants' dugout before the Opening Day game against the Dodgers at the Polo Grounds on April 13, 1954. "[Giants owner] Horace Stoneham was telling me that this was the first time in six years that we've had decent weather for a home opener. That's why I find it so hard to believe. I've been so amazed at everything I've seen this spring that I keep warning myself that things can't be that good—our pitching, our hitting, our fielding, and now our weather. Yet I'm sure they're not optical illusions."

For his Opening Day starter Durocher chose grizzled, thirty-seven-year-old right-hander Sal "The Barber" Maglie, the erstwhile Giants' ace who led the National League with twenty-three wins in their pennant-winning season of 1951 and won eighteen in '52 but, hampered by a bad back, slumped to 8–9 in '53 while finishing only nine of twenty-four starts. Over the winter Maglie had determined he was either going to find a remedy for his persistently aching back or retire. He went to a chiropractor in Buffalo, New York, who suggested he try wearing a three-quarter-inch lift in his right shoe to compensate for a slight curvature in his spine, which the doc diagnosed as the source of his discomfort the previous two years. As spring training went along and Maglie demonstrated exceptional control and increased velocity, Durocher was certain Maglie was back in form.

Over on the other side of the field the defending NL champion Dodgers were in an equally cheerful mood after a somewhat uneasy spring training under their new manager, Walter Alston.

Carl Erskine, Alston's designated Opening Day starting pitcher, was shuffling through the bat rack when he turned to Junior Gilliam, the Dodgers' second-year second baseman, and mused, "We need a new bat, Junior. This one's splintered."

"Why don't pitchers have their own bats?" interjected Jackie Robinson.

"Let me answer that," said Pee Wee Reese, wandering into the conversation, "How would you feel if you accidentally picked up a bat and discovered it was a Preacher Roe model?"

Roe, the Arkansas hillbilly, was in the twilight of a highly successful career—aided considerably, foes maintained, by having been a master practitioner of the spitball—as the Dodgers' top lefty on their 1949, '52, and '53 championship clubs. He was also destined to go down as one of the worst hitting pitchers (.110 with one homer and twenty-eight RBI in 722 career plate appearances) in the history of baseball.

"Aw, hey boys," Preach countered, "I do have one home run!"

Soon, however, Durocher's hopes that all the good things he'd seen in his club would be reaffirmed as real and not optical illusions, beginning with the opening game. Though Maglie was touched up for a couple of solo homers by Roy Campanella in the second and fourth, he was the beneficiary of three Giant homers off Erskine—a two-run blast by Alvin Dark in the third, a solo shot by Hank Thompson in the fifth, and a tie-breaking solo shot by Mays in the sixth. And Marv Grissom, the thirty-six-year-old right-handed reliever the Giants had picked up from waivers from the Red Sox in July the year before, shut the Dodgers down on one hit over the final two and two-thirds innings to preserve the 4–3 win. Mays's deciding homer was a tremendous blast, high into the upper deck in left over the 414-foot sign. It was hit so hard that press box observers estimated it would have traveled over 600 feet had the seats not impeded it.

Thus, in one momentous swing of the bat, all the spring training hype had been realized. Willie Mays was back, and Durocher's bold predictions that his twenty-two-year-old wunderkind center fielder would be the catalyst in transforming a fifth-place outfit in '53 into a champion in '54 suddenly didn't sound like a lot of typical Leo false bravado.

"We knew it wasn't," said Erskine. "There was never any question in our minds they were a different club with Willie. We'd seen it in '51 when he first came up and put a charge into them, and we'd seen it in '52 when they were in first place [25–8] when he left them [May 28] and then fell out of it a few days later and never really challenged us the rest of the way."

By the start of the '54 season Mays had already made the transition from rural Alabama country boy to quintessential New York street kid. When he was discharged from the Army the Giants found him a rooming house on St. Nicholas Place and 155th Street, a short walk from the Polo Grounds. And after Giants' games he could be frequently found playing stickball with the kids in Harlem. As legend has it, he would cheerfully greet the youngsters, shouting, "Say Hey." Barney Kremenko, the *New York Journal-American* Giants beat writer, later said the "Say Hey" was also Mays's way of announcing his arrival in the clubhouse every day. "So, in my paper, I started calling him the 'Say Hey Kid,' and it stuck," Kremenko said. (And how it stuck! Before the '54 season was over there would be no fewer than three records released saluting Mays, all of them referring to him as the "Say Hey Kid.")

The Dodgers achieved a split of the opening series with a 6–4 win the next day as Don Newcombe, making his first start in three years after spending '52 and '53 in the military service, pitched a six-hitter. The next day the Giants embarked on a brief two-game road trip to Philadelphia and Brooklyn that they again split. But in the game in Philly, which was called by rain after seven innings, with the Giants declared 2–0 victors, the debut of Johnny Antonelli, the twenty-four-year-old lefty who'd been the principal return in the February 1 Bobby Thomson deal with the Braves, particularly impressed Durocher. Most everyone agreed that, after fashioning a 12–12 record and 3.19 ERA in twenty-six starts in '53, Antonelli was on the verge of fulfilling the promise the Braves held for him when they signed him to a $52,000 bonus out of Jefferson High in Rochester, New York, in 1948 and brought him directly to the big leagues. Still, there were a few kinks in his mechanics and approach he would need to get worked out that spring with Durocher's pitching coach, Frank Shellenback. After an intrasquad game, during which Antonelli was roughed up for a bunch of runs in five innings, Shellenback approached him, saying, among other things, he was overstriding. Throughout the spring Shellenback fine-tuned Antonelli's mechanics while continuing to build him up mentally.

"Shelly was a great psychiatrist," Antonelli later said. "He never stopped telling me what a great pitcher I was. After awhile I came to believe it."

In that first game against the Phillies Antonelli limited them to three hits and one earned run over six innings, striking out five. But it was not his fault the Giants weren't able to muster any runs off Murry Dickson, the wily thirty-seven-year-old Phillie right-hander, before the rains came and shortened it to a six-inning affair. Antonelli's next start was a complete game, a 6–2 win over the Pirates, on April 20. Then, five days later, Antonelli hurled a three-hit, 3–0 shutout over the Phillies to complete a Sunday doubleheader sweep that lifted the Giants over .500 (6–5) for the first time since Opening Day.

"I have the confidence I can do the job for the Giants," he said. "I know I can go nine innings—no doubt about that. I know I have enough stuff with a good fastball, curve and changeup. Last year with Milwaukee we had a lot of good pitchers and we had to worry about work. The Giants traded for me because they needed me. I would like to keep starting every fourth day, if that's all right, but I'm willing to relieve between starts if needed."

As far as Durocher was concerned, with a bullpen in the capable hands of Grissom and knuckleballer Hoyt Wilhelm as well as Don Liddle, the little lefty craftsman who'd come over in the Thomson trade with him, Antonelli's promise of being able to "go nine every time" out was sufficient.

The Giants finished April, 8–6, in second place, a half-game behind the Dodgers, and then went on to lose five of their next six, dropping into the familiar territory of fifth place. Their lone win during that spell was a 9–7 triumph over the Cardinals in the second game of a May 2 doubleheader during which they very uncharacteristically scored eight runs in the fourth inning. The key blow in the rally came when Cardinals manager Eddie Stanky removed his righty starter, Joe Presko, with runners at first and second and one run already in, and replaced him with lefty Royce Lint. Durocher, in turn, called back lefty-swinging Bill Taylor, whom he'd sent up to hit for his pitcher, Liddle, and replaced him with right-handed-hitting utility infielder Bobby Hofman. In what turned out to be the first in a record number of Durocher "magic wand" pinch-hitting strokes in '54, Hofman connected for a three-run homer.

The first such big inning all season for the Giants, it led to salvaging the last game of the three-game series in St. Louis, but it was of little consolation to Durocher, who had held out Antonelli for a week specifically so he'd have his best lefty to counter the Cards' Stan Musial. The strategy, as it almost always did for Durocher when it came to Musial, backfired miserably. Stan the Man went 4-for-4 with six RBI in the first game on Sunday, slamming three homers, two of them off the rusty Antonelli, who lasted just four innings in the 10–6 Cardinals' romp. In the second game Musial slugged two more homers for three more RBI. His five homers in a doubleheader were a major league record, and afterward Musial's bat was sent to the Hall of Fame in Cooperstown.

"I can't believe it," Musial said. "You mean real sluggers like Babe Ruth, Lou Gehrig, Ralph Kiner—men like them—never hit five homers in a doubleheader?"

Characteristically, Musial refrained from outwardly expressing any personal delight and satisfaction at achieving this record-setting home run explosion against a Durocher-managed team.

For the first month the Giants really struggled for runs, with only right-fielder Don Mueller hitting over .300 and Mays mired below .230. As Joe King, the Giant beat writer for the *New York World-Telegram*, observed critically, "It is clear the Giants will have to make their bid on pitching, which seems competent if it is only organized by Durocher soon."

Indeed, for the first few weeks the only Giant who was really hitting was the lefty-swinging twenty-seven-year-old Mueller. Picking up from where he left off in 1953, when he hit over .400 in September to lift his average from .326 to a season-end .333, Mueller's average stood at .387 after going 5-for-5 with a triple to left-center, a double to left, and singles to center, left, and right-center, in that May 2 nightcap triumph against the Cardinals. That had become his mantra: put the ball in play—wherever—and hit them where the fielders weren't. In doing so in such prolific fashion he earned the nickname "Mandrake the Magician," after the popular syndicated comic book hero of the time. After managing just forty-two homers in his first two thousand at-bats in the majors, Mueller resignedly concluded coming into the '54 season that he simply was never going to be a power hitter, despite his lanky six-foot, 185-pound frame. But, he said, he could be just as valuable to the Giants by hitting for high average:

In my best homer season, 1951, even with a lucky streak of five homers in two days, I hit only sixteen. There are lots of players who can hit ten to fifteen homers but few who can top .300. Certainly it would be better for the team if I hit the way I know best and stop trying to do something which hardly can pay off. I am going to have a much better chance to score a run with a single or a double than I would trying to put power on the ball, which I don't have. I was brought up to meet the ball. All my minor league teaching was that way. Why not stick to that and take the homers as they come?

In time Durocher came to agree. For the first three months of '54 he'd been batting Mueller fifth or sixth in the lineup, but on July 7 he inserted him into the number-three hole, conventionally reserved for the best power-and-average hitters in the game, like Musial, Duke Snider, "Big Klu" Ted Kluszewski of the Cincinnati Reds, and Larry Doby over in the American League.

"That's where it looks like he's going to stay," said Leo. "It's the ideal spot for him because he moves runners into scoring position. You can bet on him. He never misses a signal on the hit-and-run, he plays the kind of game I like, and with a runner like Al Dark ahead of him, he is just right hitting third. Maybe he doesn't have a lot of power, but he fits right in there at number three."

Mueller took to hitting third like a hummingbird to a honeysuckle bush. The very next day the soft-spoken Missourian went 4-for-5 with a double in the Giants' 11–2 rout of the Dodgers, and three days after that, on July 11, he hit for the cycle with four

RBI in a 13–7 win over the Pirates—the only player in baseball to accomplish that feat in '54.

On May 6 the Giants arrived in the visiting clubhouse at Crosley Field in Cincinnati to the news that Roger Bannister, a twenty-five-year-old British medical student, had become the first man in history to run a mile in under four minutes. With the aid of two "pacemakers," fellow students Chris Brasher and Chris Chataway, Bannister had completed his history-making journey in 3:59.4 at the Iffley Road track in Oxford, England, in front of nearly three thousand chilly spectators.

"Even though we weren't really into track and field, it was such big news that day, everyone was talking about it," Monte Irvin recalled. "Primarily we were talking about as to how it related to us—that once you're able to do something in your mind mentally, you're able to do it physically. I think that was a big part of our '54 club. We went into that season already mentally believing we could do it."

Just the same, the Giants had gotten off to a plodding start, and after losing two more games in Cincinnati to fall to 3–6 on an eleven-game road trip, they found themselves in seventh place. And whether Durocher knew it or not, storm clouds were already forming around him. A few days after the Giants got home from the trip Joe Reichler, the senior baseball writer for the Associated Press, approached Dark at the Polo Grounds and confided to him that Giants owner Horace Stoneham was becoming more and more disenchanted with his manager.

"I'm just asking, Alvin, do you like Leo?" Reichler said.

Despite the differences they'd had in '53 over his fielding at shortstop, Dark had the utmost respect for Durocher. Reichler's question seemed a little ominous to him. "Sure I like Leo," the captain replied. "He's a great manager who gets more out of his players than anyone. Why would you ask, Joe?"

"Well, if that's the case, you better do something," said Reichler, "because Stoneham says if you're not on top by the All-Star break, Durocher's through."

Dark was both incredulous and alarmed—the season was barely a month old. But he knew Reichler to be a diligent and honest reporter and not one to stir up shit for his own purposes. He'd clearly gotten this directly from Stoneham. Later that day Dark called a players-only meeting in the clubhouse, at which he relayed to his teammates what Reichler had told him. "From now on, we have to praise Leo every chance we get," Dark implored. "Whenever we go on the radio with [Giants broadcaster] Russ Hodges, or the TV pre-game show with [Durocher's wife] Laraine [Day] we have to make sure to say Leo's doing a great job."

Looking over at first baseman Whitey Lockman, who'd had his share of verbal dust-ups with Durocher through the years, Dark said, "Whitey, you know Leo's been on you many times, even though you're having a great year, well, he's been on me too. But it's always in the clubhouse. Publicly, he's behind all of us. So it's time we start telling everyone what a great manager he is and how we wouldn't be the team we are without him."

In a 2012 interview Dark recalled that clubhouse meeting and why he felt compelled to call it. "My loyalty was to my manager," he said. "We were playing for this manager, and whatever he told us, we had to do. He was a very, very demanding man, and you had to do it his way. But Leo was one of the greatest baseball men I ever knew. I think the problem was someone up there didn't like him."

"Stoneham resented Leo because of all the movie stars he hung around with," said Monte Irvin. "He was jealous of him, and he couldn't stand the fact that Leo was constantly in the papers with all his celebrity friends and with Laraine. In a lot of ways Horace was very insecure."

Although Dark's plea to his teammates to start publicly giving their manager props whenever the opportunity availed itself was well meaning, what was really needed to quell the owner's threat was for the Giants to start picking up their game. Coincidental or not, shortly after that meeting Mays began making his move on what would be the defining season of his career.

Following the back-to-back losses in Cincinnati the Giants moved on to Pittsburgh, where the losing stopped and a six-game winning streak began. Before the first game against the Pirates, Durocher, perhaps sensing Stoneham's unrest, dressed down his troops for their uninspired play thus far and shook up his lineup, the most surprising element of it being his move of light-hitting second baseman Davey Williams, whose terrible start had his batting average hovering under .150, into the leadoff spot. The result: Williams went 2-for-5 and drove in only his second run of the season; Antonelli, rebounding from his four-inning kayo in St. Louis six days earlier, pitched a five-hitter, and Mays hit a solo homer to give the Giants their first night-game triumph of the season, 2–1, before a crowd of just 7,147 at Forbes Field.

Four days later, against the Reds at the Polo Grounds, Antonelli pitched his second-straight one-run complete game, lowering his ERA to 1.96. On May 14 the winning streak hit six, with a 9–6 win over the Cubs that lifted the Giants into a tie for first place with the Phillies. It was a short stay there, as five out of six losses followed, the only win being Antonelli's third-straight complete game, 9–2, over Milwaukee in the second game of the May 16 doubleheader.

"We didn't get really going until late May, when Willie started really heating up," said Irvin.

Beginning on May 22 the Giants, who'd been wallowing at .500, went on a 41–11 tear-up to the July 11 All-Star break. Over that span Mays hit twenty-three homers, one fewer than he hit in his entire first 155 games in '51 and '52. Rubén Gómez, who'd been battling a recurrent sinus condition and struggled—2–3, 6.00 ERA—in his first six starts, took the ball that Saturday in Philadelphia and tossed a nifty six-hit, 5–0 shutout over the Phillies. It was the start of a six-game winning streak that included three shutouts for the twenty-six-year-old Puerto Rican who had earned a place in Durocher's rotation by winning thirteen games and logging 204 innings as a rookie the year before. Durocher liked the fact that Gómez was a bit of a hot head. Although the young righty's wildness—he had almost as many walks as strike-outs in '53 and '54—was enough to exasperate any manager, Leo felt the fear factor among opposing batters that, on any given pitch, this wild man might unleash one in their ear, helped compensate for that.

Originally the property of the Yankees, Gómez wound up with the Giants almost by accident. Playing winter ball in Puerto Rico as a teenager, Gómez developed a reputation for being hot tempered and eager to fight at the slightest provocation, and it followed him throughout his minor league journey in the independent leagues. When the St. Jean, Quebec, team sold him to the Yankees' Triple A farm in Kansas City in 1952, Gómez found himself languishing in the bullpen with no work. The Yankees said it was because he was temperamental and the other players were afraid of him. Gómez wondered whether maybe it was something else—like the color of his skin. There was, after all, only one other player of color on the Blues that year, and that was his Puerto Rican country-mate, Vic Power, whom the Yankees had themselves signed but were clearly in no hurry to promote beyond Triple A despite his showing as a dominant hitter in the league. In any case, Gómez paid $5,000 to buy out his own contract in Kansas City and then got Giant scout Tom Sheehan to meet his terms for a $10,000 bonus and a berth in the majors at once. "If I don't produce after a year," he told Sheehan, "you can send me down to the lowest farm team you've got."

The day after Gómez's shutout over the Phillies Mays began his tear, during which he went 23-for-40 with eight homers and twenty-one RBI over the next ten games, lifting his average from .260 to .337, while the Giants climbed to second place, two games behind the front-running Dodgers. On June 9, in Milwaukee, Antonelli pitched them into a temporary tie for first by throwing a 4–0 shutout against the Braves and their ace, Warren Spahn. The next day Durocher once again dug into his magic bag to pull out a 1–0 win over the Braves. Gómez and the Braves' 6–8 righty Gene Conley had dueled to a 0–0 stalemate into the tenth inning when, with one out and nobody on, Durocher called upon Bill Taylor, the hulking six-foot-three, 212-pound lefty-swinging spare outfielder, to pinch hit for second baseman Billy Gardner, his roommate on the road. "Lose one, and I'll give you a hundred bucks!" Durocher shouted to the rookie as he strode to the plate. With that, Taylor hit Conley's first pitch high and far over County Stadium's right-center field fence, for his first home run in the big leagues.

"I told Billy, who was always pinch running for me, that this one time I was getting him out of the game, but that I had to hit one out for my roomie," Taylor said afterward. Meanwhile, a beaming Durocher vowed to the writers he would absolutely pay off to Taylor, but he was quick to add, "This is not a standing offer."

It was just the way the season was going now. The starting pitchers, Antonelli, Maglie, and Gómez, were all consistently turning in strong outings, and Mays was at or near the top of all the Triple Crown categories. Mueller was hitting over .330 out of the number-three slot, and Durocher was making all the right moves. On the night of June 15, at the Polo Grounds, the Giants took sole possession of first place when Hank Thompson hit a two-out, three-run, game-winning homer off Cincinnati lefty reliever Jackie Collum for a 5–3 triumph over the Reds.

A month earlier the Giants had claimed thirty-three-year-old Hoot Evers for the $10,000 waiver price from the Red Sox in the hopes that the former two-time All-Star outfielder could provide some added pop off the bench. But Evers was 0-for-3, with two strikeouts in his first three pinch-hitting appearances for them when, on June 19, Durocher sent him up to hit for relief pitcher Hoyt Wilhelm with one out, two on, and the score tied 2–2 against the Cardinals in the ninth inning. On a 2–2 pitch from Cardinals righty Joe Presko, Evers connected for a game-winning three-run homer. It was his only hit in eleven at-bats for them when he was released a month later. In Durocher's mind the game-winning homer, which came after the only loss in a streak of ten wins out of eleven, was well worth the ten grand.

Cardinals manager Eddie "The Brat" Stanky, who'd been Durocher's favorite player, with the Dodgers in the forties and on his '51 Giants pennant-winning team, thought he had the next day's game salted away with a 6–3 lead behind Vic Raschi in the sixth only to once again be trumped by Leo's managerial genius. For this day's magic, with one out and Mays at first in the sixth, Durocher sent up Hofman to hit for Gardner, and the twenty-eight-year old all-purpose man, on cue, delivered his third pinch-hit homer of the season to make it a 6–5 game. Giants catcher Wes Westrum, batting just .150, followed with another homer to kayo Raschi and tie the score. When Stanky brought in righty Cot Deal to replace Raschi, Durocher looked down his bench again and summoned lefty-hitting Dusty Rhodes, who broke the tie and sent the Giants off to victory with yet another pinch-hit homer. The Giants had earlier broken the Dodgers' twenty-two-year major league record of seven pinch-hit homers in a season, and Rhodes's blow made it nine. They would add one more when Whitey Lockman hit a grand slam on September 11 against the Reds. Of the ten pinch blasts, eight of them turned defeats into victories.

It was easy to see why Durocher loved Rhodes, a free spirit who never knew a curfew he couldn't break but who was immune to pressure. Just the same, the Alabama country boy's lack of concentration on the field and discipline off it began to exasperate Durocher. Such was the case before 51,464 at the Polo Grounds on June 29, when the Giants were locked in a tense thirteen-inning struggle with the Dodgers, who were only one game behind them in the standings at the time. Third baseman Don Hoak had put the Dodgers ahead, 3–2, with a homer off Grissom in the top of thirteenth, when the Giants loaded the bases with two out in the bottom of the inning and Durocher sent Rhodes up to pinch hit for catcher Ray Katt. Rhodes looked at the first two pitches from Dodger righty Billy Loes and became incensed when home plate umpire Frank Secory called them both strikes. As he began heatedly protesting to Secory, Durocher rushed from the dugout and grabbed him before he got himself ejected.

"Dammit, Dusty, get a hold of yourself," Durocher screamed. "You can't do anything about those two pitches. They're gone. So just go back in there, forget about 'em, and get us the hit we need." Shrugging, Dusty got back into the box, looked at yet another Loes delivery, this one in the dirt, and calmly whacked a breaking pitch into center field for the game-winning two-run single.

Durocher admitted to never ceasing his amazement at Rhodes's ability to come through with big hits, oftentimes after only a few hours of sleep. At the end of the 1953 season Durocher went to Giants owner Horace Stoneham and complained, "You've got to get rid of this guy. He's the worst fielder I ever saw. Granted, he can hit a little and with power, but his glove is useless." Stoneham merely smiled and said he'd think about it. Then the Giants went on a goodwill tour in Japan, during which Rhodes routinely showed up for the team bus in a disheveled state, much to Durocher's further dismay. On one of the last days of the trip Durocher went up to Stoneham's hotel suite in Tokyo to once again demand that Rhodes be traded, sold, or released when the team got back home, only to find the owner sharing a bottle of bourbon with Dusty. Furious, Durocher screamed at the bemused Stoneham, "I'm serious about this, Horace, it's either Durocher or Rhodes! I don't want him on this club!"

But three months into the '54 season, of course, Durocher had a whole different opinion of Rhodes. In an interview years later Durocher said, "Dusty was the one guy I didn't have any training rules or curfews with. Hell, I'd often take *him* out to the bars! He never took any of the other players with him. He never caused any trouble. He never lied to me, and he always showed up the next day ready to play."

"It was unbelievable how all Leo's moves kept working out," said Irvin. "It was as if every time he needed a home run or a game-winning hit, he'd just order one up off the bench, and we were all eager to oblige. He just had a Midas touch that year."

All through June and into July the Giants kept winning and winning, 34–8 from June 3 to the July 11 All-Star break, and five of them—Antonelli, Mays, Mueller, Dark, and Grissom— were named to the All-Star team. Antonelli was 13–2 with a 2.12 ERA at the break, whereas the veteran Grissom had eleven saves and a 1.97 ERA, and Mueller, at .356, was running second in the batting race to the Dodgers' Duke Snider's .368. In their three-game sweep of the Dodgers at Ebbets Field on July 6–8, during which they outscored them 26–6 and increased their

National League lead to six and a half games over their bitter interborough rivals, Mays went 5-for-11, with four homers and nine RBI, to raise his average to .333.

Mays was having such an impact on the '54 season in general and the Dodgers in particular that on June 26, when he hit his sixth homer in five days, Dodgers owner Walter O'Malley instructed Ebbets Field public address announcer Tex Rickards to announce over the loudspeaker to the Dodger fans that Willie had just hit another home run in Chicago. Ever the promoter, O'Malley recognized the common appeal of the exciting Mays, even to Dodger fans.

Meanwhile, for a couple of days it appeared Dark might be denied a place on the All-Star team when tabulators for the fan balloting in Lake Charles, Louisiana, discovered a curious irregularity. It seemed they'd received an envelope containing fifteen ballots, all of them marked for Dark, a native of Lake Charles, with the return address: Memorial Park Cemetery. Unfortunately, Dark was informed, they could not accept votes from dead people.

That was fine with Dark, who would have just as soon looked forward to the three-day break as an opportunity to hone up on his golf game. Besides, the Giants were in first place at the All-Star break, a comfortable five and a half games ahead of the Dodgers, and this meant his manager's job was now safe.

INDIAN SUMMER

WHEN HE ARRIVED AT 1954 SPRING TRAINING IN TUCSON FOR his fourth season as manager of the Cleveland Indians, Al Lopez was feeling uncharacteristically restive. The normally easygoing Senor, as friends and baseball associates commonly and affectionately referred to him, had almost resigned after his third-straight second-place finish behind the Yankees. That was the problem: despite a sizeable core of All-Star players—pitchers Bob Lemon, Early Wynn, Bob Feller, Mike Garcia; center fielder Larry Doby; catcher Jim Hegan; second baseman Bobby Avila; and third baseman Al Rosen, the 1953 AL Most Valuable Player—the fans of Cleveland had clearly demonstrated with a steadily decreasing season attendance a growing indifference to Lopez's perennial also-rans. In '53 the 1,069,176 attendance was the lowest for the Indians since 1946, and it was more than a 50 percent drop-off from their 1948 and '49 seasons, when they drew well over 2 million.

Lopez had heard the criticism. The Indians might be good, if only not quite as good as the Yankees, but they were dull and methodical, and that, the critics said, was a reflection of Lopez's laid-back style of managing. "I know what they've said," Lopez told a writer early in the '54 spring, "but it just isn't true. Nobody in the league was involved in more exciting games than we were last year. All those close ones, whether we won or lost, damn near killed me. We were in every game, right to the last out, because our pitchers just wouldn't let the other club get a big lead. And don't forget, even the pre-War Indians and the club that won the world championship in 1948, were never known for their speed."

Lopez, to be sure, was just as tired of finishing second to the Yankees as the fans were. On top of that, Lopez had grown increasingly intolerant of his boss, Hank Greenberg, who frequently meddled in the on-field baseball matters. Indian fans never forgave Greenberg for firing the popular Lou Boudreau as manager in 1950 and replacing him with Lopez. Greenberg was accustomed to fan abuse. As one of the few Jewish players in the major leagues in the thirties, he was subjected to constant anti-Semitic bench jockeying and slurs from the fans. His Detroit Tigers teammate Birdie Tebbetts said, "There is nobody in the history of the game who took more abuse than Greenberg unless it was Jackie Robinson. I was there when it happened. I heard it." Perhaps because of a result of that, Greenberg was one of the first players to offer encouragement to Robinson in his rookie season of 1947, and the two formed a close bond.

The night after his hiring was announced, Lopez was with Greenberg at a banquet of the Associated Grocery Manufacturers in Cleveland, and when Greenberg got up to speak, a chorus of "Bou-dreau! Bou-dreau! Bou-dreau!" greeted him.

The howls continued when Greenberg introduced Lopez, but it was the Senor who deftly neutralized them. "Lou Boudreau is one of the finest fellows I've ever met in baseball," Lopez told the crowd. "I know I'm following a tough act. But it's good to be in a town where the fans are capable of such affection for a manager. I hope I can earn some of it myself." Suddenly the "Boudreau" catcalls dissipated into loud applause. At the end of the banquet Greenberg confided to Lopez how relieved he was that his new manager had—at least temporarily—been able to quell the storm around them.

But as the '53 season moved into its waning days and it had become increasingly certain the Indians were once again not going to catch Casey Stengel's front-running Yankees, Lopez sensed a strain in his relationship with Greenberg and wondered whether his boss was starting to believe the fan criticism that he was too laid back. At the end of September Lopez went to Greenberg and offered to resign, only to be reassured he had his boss's full support. That was reiterated by the Indians' board of directors, who, to a man, insisted Lopez stay on and then gave him a two-year contract extension.

Still, the job security did not lessen Lopez's concerns during those early days in Tucson nor do anything for his chronic insomnia. Ordinarily the insomnia, which he first began to suffer from when he was a catcher for the Dodgers in the thirties and that doctors told him was the product of a nervous stomach, wouldn't kick up until the games began for real. But this spring, in addition to still feeling uneasy about his relationship with Greenberg, Lopez wondered, too, whether his boss had done enough to address what the Senor felt were the key points of difference between the Indians and the Yankees—first base, the corner outfield spots, and the infield defense. Right before spring training Greenberg traded for outfielder Dave Philley, a proven hitter with more range and power than either of Lopez's corner outfielders in '53, Dale Mitchell and Wally Westlake. Lopez said he was also anxious to get a long look this spring at "the two Negro kids," righty-hitting Al Smith and lefty-swinging Dave Pope, both of whom had hit for average in the minors and could cover a lot of ground in the outfield. It was Greenberg's hope, too, that one of them would emerge to claim the other corner outfield spot, to flank Doby in center, with the switch-hitting Philley.

Once Lopez installed George Strickland as his shortstop a month into the previous season the infield defense began to stabilize, although he still felt Strickland and Avila needed more playing time together to be a more cohesive keystone unit. That spring Lopez also made no secret of his dismay with Avila and some of the other Indian players for leaving their "games" in winter ball. "They feel they're in shape and therefore can take it easy when they get to camp," Lopez said, careful not to single anyone out, although the writers all knew who he was talking about. "The worst possible thing a player can do is give the impression that he's lazy. And that's exactly what some of those who played winter ball are now doing."

Then there was first base, perhaps the main source of Lopez's premature spring insomnia. During his first two seasons as Indians manager Lopez's first baseman had been the big, strapping Luscious "Luke" Easter, a fun-loving but woefully slow-footed six-foot-four, 240-pound mountain of a man who was already thirty-three years old when the previous Indians owner, Bill Veeck, signed him from the Kansas City Monarchs of Negro Leagues in 1949. Despite severely limited speed and range—the result of a recurring left knee problem and a severe automobile accident near his hometown of St. Louis that resulted in both his legs being broken at the ankles—Easter had prodigious power. On June 23, 1950, he hit the longest home run ever at Cleveland's cavernous Municipal Stadium, a 477-foot shot into the upper-deck stands in right field, and he accounted for eighty-six homers and 307 RBI from '50 to '52. With that kind of production, Lopez was able to live with Easter's base-path clogging and defensive limitations at first base as well as his concentration lapses. (On more than one occasion the Senor would glance down the bench to see Easter dozing off after a late night of playing cards and drinking beer.) But in '53 a broken foot limited Easter to just sixty-eight games, and it was as though Big Luke suddenly got old or just realized his age. He was back in camp in '54, but in Lopez's mind he was done. Unfortunately, the Senor's first base alternatives had limitations of their own.

Bill Glynn, the twenty-seven-year-old second-year man who took over for Easter in '53, had impressed Lopez with his defensive acumen at first base, but his .243 average, with just three homers and 30 RBI in 411 at-bats, were unacceptable. As a result, to compete with Glynn, right after the season the Indians made a trade with the Dodgers for Rocky Nelson, a left-handed slugger who'd failed in two previous big league trials with the Cardinals and Cubs but who led the International League with 136 RBI at Montreal in '53. At the outset of spring training Greenberg conceded to Lopez that first base was still a major trouble spot and assured him he was continuing to work on a trade to rectify it. In the meantime Greenberg announced he was also inviting thirty-two-year-old left-hander Hal Newhouser to camp. Newhouser had once been one of the premier pitchers in the American League, winning back-to-back Most Valuable Player awards for the Detroit Tigers in the war years, 1944 to 1945. But a sore arm had prompted the Tigers to give him his unconditional release in July of '53, and he was prepared to stay retired until Greenberg, who'd been his forties teammate in Detroit, called and urged him to give it one more shot. Newhouser agreed and went to Bradenton, Florida, for the winter to try to work his arm back in shape. "I haven't signed a contract," New-houser said upon reporting to Tucson. "I won't until I'm certain I can help the Indians. Right now my arm feels fine and didn't have any trouble while I was in Florida."

Throughout the spring and all those games in the Cactus League against the Giants, including their barnstorming trip across the South on the way back home, one player particularly stood out for Lopez—an effervescent twenty-three-year-old rookie named Rudy Regalado. A Los Angeles native of Mexican descent who was signed by the Indians out of the University of Southern California in 1953, Regalado was invited to camp after hitting a combined .320 with eighty RBI at Class A Reading and AAA Indianapolis his first year of pro ball. Though primar-ily a third baseman, Regalado impressed Lopez with his ability to play multiple positions that spring, all the while hitting up a storm. At one point, when Avila came down with a stomach ailment, Lopez installed Regalado at second. After four games, during which Regalado had multiple hits, Avila suddenly an-nounced he was feeling better. "What's the matter, Bobby, you worried?" chided one of the writers.

Regalado's hot hitting throughout the spring—he hit close to .500 and led the club in homers and RBI—got Lopez to thinking maybe Regalado could even be the answer at first base if Nelson didn't work out. As the Opening Day cut down to twenty-eight players neared, Lopez assured Regalado he was going to make the team. "If he keeps on hitting, he's going to play somewhere on this club," Lopez said.

"THIS COULD BE THE BEST CLUB I'VE EVER MANAGED," LOPEZ SAID after the Indians launched the season with an 8–2 complete-game victory for Early Wynn over the White Sox, in which Avila went

4-for-6 out of the leadoff spot and Strickland 3-for-4 with a homer and two RBI. "Spring training proved to me that we have
strengthened ourselves. Our outfield is better because of Dave
Philley. Our infield is better because Bobby Avila and George
Strickland now know each other's habits, and Hal Newhouser is
going to help our pitching staff. But mainly we're better because
we have some terrific kids on the squad this year—kids like Rudy
Regalado, Dave Pope, and Ray Narleski and Don Mossi in the
bullpen. They all have talent and great desire."

So would he care to make a prediction, a writer asked?

"I'm just hoping we finish a notch higher than last year," Lopez said with a wink.

Lopez's initial optimism was quickly tempered, however, by
a string of six losses in seven games after their first two wins.
On April 25 he decided to take drastic measures before the early
slump snowballed. Until then Lopez had been able to get only
one at-bat for Regalado. He had also decided that neither Glynn
nor Nelson was going to be able to provide the kind of offensive
production he needed at first base. So, in order to rectify this, he
turned to his best player. Al Rosen, who, after coming within one
batting average percentage point of winning the Triple Crown,
had been the first unanimous AL MVP in 1953. Lopez knew
Rosen was the one guy he could count on to put team ahead of
ego, although as the All-Star third baseman recalled later, he
was initially shocked at his manager's request, especially since
Glynn was leading the league in batting with a .400 average at
the time. Rosen said,

> *Lopez came to me and said he wanted me to move over to first base,*
> *even though I'd only ever played a few games there in the minors*
> *at San Diego in 1949. Easter was through, he didn't think either*
> *Glynn or Nelson was going to do what was needed there and he*

wanted to get Regalado, whose best position was third base, into the lineup. He told me it was only going to be temporary, that Green-berg was working on a trade for a first baseman. What could I do? We couldn't keep going on the way we were playing. I had so much respect for Al, I couldn't say no.

Meeting with the writers in the visiting clubhouse at Detroit's Briggs Stadium that morning, Lopez explained he'd been think-ing about the move for a while. He also lied to either them or Rosen in saying he hoped it would be permanent. As for benching Glynn, who seemed to be blossoming at least as a high-average hitter, Lopez said, "Glynn was doing a fine job, it's true. But when you're losing, a manager sometimes will bench even a .600 hitter to shake things up."

Rosen's misgivings notwithstanding, the controversial move proved to be an instant success. That first game the Indians outslugged the Tigers, 10–9, as Regalado went 3-for-5, with a walk and two runs scored, and Rosen went 3-for-5, with a pair of doubles, a sac fly, and three RBI. It was the start of a stretch of nine wins out of ten for the Indians that moved them to a half-game from first place. After losing two of three to the Yankees, May 10–12, in the second series of the year between the two archrivals, the Indians moved into first place on May 16 amid an eleven-game winning streak. That was snapped on May 25, when the White Sox dealt Bob Lemon his first loss of the sea-son, 4–2. In the fifth inning of that game, however, they suffered a more serious setback to Lopez's great experiment, even if it didn't initially seem so, when Rosen broke his right index finger stopping a hard smash to first base from Chicago's Jim Rivera.

In a 2010 interview at his home in Rancho Mirage, California, Rosen, then eighty-six, waved a grotesquely crooked finger in front of a reporter's face. "Would you look at this?" he said. "It's been like this for fifty-six years. This is the way it healed, and now it's arthritically permanent like this."

As much as it hurt, Rosen wasn't about to come out of the lineup, not when he was hitting .372 and coming off a hot streak of eight homers in nine games. As he explained further in that 2010 interview, this was 1954, a far different time, when players played with broken bones and muscle pulls, and surgery was only a last-resort option.

In today's world you come out of the lineup and sit until it gets well. I was a player who was leading the league in everything. It soothed my ego every day to be able to go out there and hit. After the inning, I went into the trainer's room and just taped it up real good and kept playing. I had to learn to throw with my middle fingers, and I couldn't wrap it around the bat. I don't think the Indians ever even took an X-ray of the finger. As you can see, it never recovered. In retrospect, Lopez should've just put Regalado at first base.

The day after he broke the finger Rosen went 2-for-4 with a homer and two RBI and scored two of the Indians' runs in their 5–4 loss to the White Sox. Two days later, May 28, he hit another homer to help them beat the Tigers, 3–0, behind Wynn's two-hitter. And that's when it stopped. Over the next six games Rosen failed to get an RBI, and his batting average dropped forty points. But he was determined to stay in the lineup for the three-game series against the Yankees, June 2–4, and wound up going 2-for-12 with no extra base hits or RBI as the Indians again dropped two of three to fall into a temporary first-place tie with the Chicago White Sox. After the third game it was apparent Rosen's makeshift "tape" cast hadn't worked. That night, the eve of a three-game series against the Athletics in Philadelphia, Rosen and Bob Lemon were staying with friends in Norristown,

Pennsylvania, when the finger swelled to twice its normal size. The next morning he had Lemon drive him to Montgomery Hospital, where the doctors X-rayed the finger and found a chip fracture on the external side of the knuckle. There was no more pushing it now. The Indians sent Rosen back to Cleveland to have the finger examined and treated by their own physician, who told him he could rest it for a week to ten days and let it heal on its own.

"It was a bad decision on my part to try and keep playing with it," Rosen said, "because it was the end of my career. I was never the same hitter again, and I even had to learn a whole new grip on my golf clubs."

At least, if nothing else, Rosen's injury brought a new sense of urgency to Hank Greenberg's efforts to trade for a first baseman, and on June 1 the Indians announced the acquisition of twenty-nine-year-old Vic Wertz from the Baltimore Orioles. Though Wertz was an outfielder by trade, Greenberg had been trying to obtain him since the winter, always with the idea of moving him to first base. Having been an outfield/first base "swingman" himself in his playing days, Greenberg did not believe the transition would pose much of a problem for Wertz. Defense, however, had never been Wertz's strong point, and in that respect, after a couple of weeks of working his way into a first baseman, he proved to be barely adequate. Nevertheless, it was Wertz's bat for which Lopez and Greenberg wanted Wertz. A somewhat paunchy, six-foot, 200-pound left-handed hitter, Wertz had hit twenty, twenty-seven, twenty-seven, twenty-three, and nineteen homers over the previous five seasons for the Tigers and St. Louis Browns, but when the Browns moved to Baltimore and its spacious Memorial Stadium for 1954, his power suddenly dissipated. Because Wertz was hitting only .202, with one homer in twenty-nine games at the time of the trade, Greenberg was able to get him for a second-line pitcher, Bob Chakales, instead of Art Houtteman, his number-five starter, whom Orioles GM Art Ehlers had been holding out for. "The hugeness of the Baltimore ballpark demoralized me," Wertz admitted. "I can't complain about getting a chance at some World Series loot, though. I only hope I'll be able to play regularly for the Indians."

At the same time Rosen was going on the disabled list, the Indians lost their other top hitter, Avila, to a chipped thumb, suffered when the Yankees' Hank Bauer slid hard into him on a tag play at second base on June 2. Avila, likewise, didn't want to come out of the lineup. He was off to the best season of his career, leading the American League in batting at .392, and he didn't deem the injury serious enough to forsake this rarified hitting zone he was in, even for a couple of days. He played five more games, going 5-for-18 against the Yankees and A's, before finally deciding to have the thumb X-rayed, where the chip fracture was revealed. In Avila's case the doctors put a splint on the thumb and advised him to keep off the field for at least a week.

Avila, the twenty-eight-year-old Mexican, was regarded as a bit of a loner by his Indians' teammates because, due to the language barrier, he felt uncomfortable hanging out with them on the road. Although he tried overcoming this handicap by purchasing an English-Spanish dictionary and studying it constantly in his hotel room and on the team busses, his traditional late arrivals at spring training from playing winter ball in Mexico, where he was a national hero, did not sit particularly well with his mates or his manager. Lopez admired Avila's keen batting eye—he'd averaged nearly .300 in four-plus seasons with the Indians and seldom struck out—but his defense was an issue. In '52 Avila led AL second basemen in errors, with twenty-eight, only to cut that total to just eleven in '53 after Lopez teamed him up with Strickland at short.

A much-acclaimed high school baseball player in Vera Cruz, Avila turned pro at sixteen and played five years in the Mexican League, with steadily rising batting averages. While playing third base in winter ball in Cuba in 1947 he came to the attention of the Dodgers, who had been playing a series of exhibition games in Havana. Then-Dodgers manager Leo Durocher liked Avila so much he offered him $10,000 to sign with them. Shortly thereafter, however, Commissioner Happy Chandler suspended Durocher from baseball for consorting with gamblers, and the Dodger offer was never finalized. At the same time Bill Veeck, the maverick owner of the Indians, who was preparing to break the AL color line by signing Larry Doby, ordered his scouts that spring to find him "winning ballplayers, irrespective of race, color or nationality."

Veeck had gotten a tip on Avila from one of his bird dog scouts in Mexico, Yamo Ornelas, who reported, "Avila can do everything except speak English." That was enough for Veeck to send his top scout, Cy Slapnicka, down to Mexico. "Follow Avila around the Mexican League, and if you like him, sign him," Veeck told Slapnicka.

Avila was immediately impressed when Slapnicka told him how he'd signed three of the Indians' greatest players, Bob Feller, outfielder Hal Trosky, and third baseman Ken Keltner. "When he tell me that," Avila recalled years later, "I forgot to ask, 'How much?'" Instead, Slapnicka asked Avila how much it would take to sign him. Avila thought about it for a moment, and replied, "I take $17,500." Slapnicka, who, with Veeck's direction, was prepared to go much higher, stuck out his hand and said, "You got it."

It wasn't until three years later when Joe Gordon, the Indians' mainstay second baseman and future Hall of Famer, retired that Avila got to start making good on Slapnicka's confidence in him. He'd batted just .220 for the Indians' Triple A farm team in Baltimore in 1948, learning only later he'd played the whole season with a hernia. The following season, because of the rule requiring clubs to keep "bonus players" on their twenty-five-man roster, he was able to get into just thirty-one games, mostly as a pinch runner. But once he became the Indians' regular second baseman, Avila quickly demonstrated his hitting prowess, batting .299 in 1950, .305 in '51, and .300 with a league-leading eleven triples in '52. Early in the '54 season Dizzy Dean, the Hall of Fame former St. Louis Cardinals pitcher, was in Cleveland in his capacity as a broadcaster for the ABC TV *Game of the Week*. Observing Avila at the plate, Dean commented, "If any modern-day hitter can make .400, it'll be Avila. The kid is a smart hitter. He can do everything—hit to all fields, bunt, hit-and-run, and, for a little guy, he's even got enough power to worry the pitcher." When told of Dean's praise afterward, Avila said, "If I ever hit .400, they make me president of Mexico."

The thumb injury sidelined Avila for two weeks. He was back in the lineup June 23, but he did not really get his stroke back until July 5, when he went 8-for-18 over the next four games to raise his average back up to .356 and stir up speculation about winning the batting title. Noting how Rosen had missed by one percentage winning the batting crown in '53 and was recognized as the Indians' best pure hitter, Avila said, "Rosie will be glad to be one-two with me, and I be glad to be two-one with Rosie on top. If we both are high I think it mean the pennant."

Even before the acquisition of Wertz, Lopez's mind was spinning as to what his lineup was going to be after Rosen and Avila returned. The Senor had privately conceded it'd been a mistake to ask his best player to move to first base, and then, when Regalado's inexperience, both at-bat and in the field at third base, began to show up, Lopez benched him on June 25 and brought in the rookie Al Smith from left field.

The twenty-six-year-old Smith, a star high school baseball, football, and boxing athlete in St. Louis whom Veeck signed as a shortstop from the Negro Leagues' Cleveland Buckeyes in 1948, had been the most pleasant surprise of the '54 season for Lopez after winning the left field job in spring training and hitting a solid .280 into late June. "Smith has been such an eye opener as a fielder, hitter, base runner and his versatility that I've had to make room for him in my regular lineup," Lopez said when explaining his plan to move Smith back to left field when Rosen returned to third base.

(Smith's return to the outfield allowed the Indians to make a little bit of history a month and a half later, on August 6, when Lopez started the other rookie Dave Pope in left along with Doby in center and Smith in right against the Athletics. It marked the first time an all-Black outfield had started in the major leagues.)

It was not until after the Indians lost two of three to the Yankees in Cleveland on June 25–27, having their first-place lead trimmed to one and a half games over the White Sox and three over third-place New York, that Lopez made the lineup moves official. Rosen was reinstated at third, and Wertz, despite his lack of mobility, was now deemed his everyday first baseman.

"We'll have better defense at third and Wertz will give us more power in the lineup," the Senor said.

Rosen expressed his gratitude for being returned to third, where he felt "100 per cent more comfortable," but he was angry about a report in one of the New York newspapers that said he would refuse a bid to the All-Star Game in Cleveland because of his injured finger. "I never made any such statement to anybody," Rosen said. "I don't know how anyone could write such a thing without asking me. I would be greatly honored to be elected to the All-Star Game and I would be proud to play in it. That New York story could cause me to lose votes now. If I got elected, I'd want to play no matter how badly hurt I was."

The three-game series against the Yankees had indeed been a little unsettling for Lopez, not just because it had given the third-place Yankees, now only three games behind, renewed faith that the Indians could be had by them—as always—but also because it resulted in yet another injury to one of his key players. In the Sunday finale Bob Lemon, his staff ace who won twenty or more games in five of the previous six seasons and led the American League in innings pitched in '48, '50, '52, and '53, tore a rib muscle on his left side while batting in the third inning and had to leave the game with one out in the bottom of the inning. Lopez was at least heartened by the six innings of four-hit emergency relief by the veteran Hal Newhouser, who had pitched a third of an inning of relief the night before, that enabled the Indians to salvage the game, 4–3.

After the game Newhouser went up to Indians pitching coach Mel Harder and explained why he'd started out every inning pitching sidearm. "I have to, Mel," he said, pointing to his left shoulder. "If I went overhand right away, I'd rip these muscles. That's where I had trouble before. I start out sidearm until I stretch 'em. Six innings today? That's the longest for me in two whole years!"

Nevertheless, Yankees manager Casey Stengel was not at all down after losing the finale, instead taking the opportunity to poke a few jibes at the Indians. "In this series, the Indians showed me that they had lost something," the ever-calculating Stengel needled. "I don't know just where to put my finger in the search for clues. But Lopez' pitching had gone down, Rosen showed his inexperience around first base, and their third base problem has not been solved. The drive and the pep the Indians had shown have abated. Too bad we could not take the last game. That really would have put those Indians on the anxious seat."

Such was the way of Stengel, who loved the daily banter with the newspapermen, even at the risk of providing bulletin-board

fodder for opposing teams. A month earlier, in answer to a ran-
dom question about the second-place White Sox, he'd chosen to
go into a long discourse to take a shot at his longtime nemesis,
Frank Lane, the equally outspoken Chicago general manager,
who had been gloating over his pickup of five-time All-Star third
baseman George Kell from the Red Sox:

> *The sale of Kell to the White Sox makes no difference to me or to
> the Yankees. How many third basemen has Lane bought in the last
> few years? Now I think this here Kell is a nice feller and I hope
> he likes Chicago, which is a fine city. They have the best defense
> in the league and if Kell lives up to what Frank Lane expects, the
> pennant is in Chicago's Comiskey Park right now and we ought
> to call off the race. Yes, Chicago has the defense and Cleveland has
> the hitting and it would be a dirty trick if, at the end, we had the
> pennant again.*

It was not until July 1 that Stengel's Yankees were finally
able to surpass the stubborn White Sox into second place behind the Indians. But thanks to another stretch of eleven wins
in twelve games, beginning with that Newhouser victory over
the Yankees, the Indians were able to maintain their first-place
lead without the services of Lemon, their leading winner at 9–4,
when he went down with the rib cage injury. In Lemon's absence
during that streak the back end of Lopez's rotation stepped up
with Newhouser, Houtteman, and the thirty-five-year-old Feller
each winning two games. Then, with the All-Star Game in Cleveland approaching, the Indians suffered a four-game sweep at the
hands of the White Sox in Chicago, July 9–11, the only time all
year they would lose more than three games in a row. Meanwhile
the Yankees were mounting another charge, winning eleven of

twelve, from July 1 to the break. In losing both ends of the first-half finale Sunday doubleheader, the Indians managed just two runs against the Sox's two top starters, Billy Pierce and Virgil Trucks. Pierce's shutout in the first game ran the Indians' score-less streak to twenty-eight innings, and frustrations boiled over when Lemon and pitching coach Mel Harder were both thrown out of the second game for protesting pitches with home plate umpire Frank Umont.

Suddenly the large first-place lead the Indians had held since June 12 was down to a scant half-game over the venerable Yankees as the season hit the halfway mark.

"What we need is a little vacation," Lopez said after the sweep from the White Sox. "The All-Star Game could not come at a better time for us."

Not for all of them, though. It turned out the New York story about him planning to turn down the All-Star Game didn't hurt Rosen in the least. He was the top vote-getter in the fan balloting and was joined on the AL team by Avila, Lemon, and Doby, who started the season slowly but homered in five consecutive games from June 30 to July 4. And despite their nagging injuries, Rosen, Avila, and Lemon all accepted—and played. Lopez later revealed that Rosen had come to him and suggested they might want to inform AL manager Stengel how much the finger was affecting his hitting and that his presence in the lineup might, therefore, be a handicap. But after talking to the Indians' team doctor, who told him Rosen's finger might stay swollen all year, Lopez decided not to say anything to Stengel.

"Again," said Rosen, "it was a different time. You got selected to the All-Star Game, it was an honor. And back then there was real league pride. You wanted to play with your peers from the other teams, and you played all out, to win. The All-Star Game to us was kind of like a midseason World Series."

And what an All-Star Game it was, with Cleveland already the focal city in the country for another vastly different sensational event. On July 4 Cleveland was thrust into the nation's headlines when Marilyn Sheppard, the pregnant wife of a prominent osteopathic physician in the suburb of Bay Village, was brutally murdered in the bedroom of their home. Her husband, Dr. Sam Sheppard, was convicted of second-degree murder and sentenced to life in prison, though he was acquitted in 1966 and to his death, maintained his innocence.

Under the backdrop of the sensational Sheppard murder case gripping the city's consciousness, 68,751 baseball fans— the second-largest crowd in All-Star Game history—poured through the gates of the mammoth, three-tiered Municipal Stadium for the twenty-first "Midsummer Classic" on July 13. Prior to the game the press box fraternity was saddened by the news out of New York that Grantland Rice, dean of the nation's sportswriters, had died of a stroke at age seventy-three while working on his column, "The Sportlight," in his Manhattan apartment.

The game, however, was a fans' delight, with the American League breaking a four-game losing streak and prevailing in an 11–9 slugfest that featured a record six homers. Afterward Arch Ward, the former Chicago newspaperman who founded the All-Star Game in 1933, termed it "the best one ever."

It certainly was for the Cleveland fans, who saw their heroes, Rosen, Avila, and Doby, dominate the game. Whereas the fans had voted Rosen and Avila onto the team, Stengel had selected Doby, saying, in praise of the Indian center fielder, "I'd much rather have that fella with me, than against me. If I had him with the Yankees, our sixth pennant would be a cinch." And though

Rosen's finger was healed, it was still swollen, and before the game he went to Stengel and told him, "You have my permission not to play me if you think I might hurt our chances." Stengel talked it over with Baseball Commissioner Ford Frick and decided to play Rosen anyway. "After your first time up, if you want to come out, let me know," he told Rosen.

Rosen's first at-bat resulted in a strikeout, but as he said, "Then my pride took over. I couldn't come out after doing that."

Instead, after getting a tip from Ted Williams, who suggested he slide his hand up the bat a couple of inches to compensate for the injured finger, Rosen hit two homers and drove in five runs. "Anything the Thumper says about hitting is like word from above," Rosen said. "I thanked him afterward." At the same time Avila reported that his thumb was still tender but nonetheless went 3-for-3 with two RBI. And Doby, pinch hitting in the eighth inning, hit a solo homer to tie the score, 9–9. Following Doby's homer, singles by the Yankees' Mickey Mantle and Yogi Berra and a walk to Rosen loaded the bases, and one out later, the White Sox's pesky little second baseman, Nellie Fox, hit a soft blooper into shallow center field for the game-winning, two-run single.

It was thus no wonder Stengel was in a buoyant mood as he left Cleveland for New York, where the Yankees opened up the second half with a three-game series against the last-place Baltimore Orioles. Upon sweeping the Orioles the Yankees ran their winning streak to thirteen when the principal in the Vic Power trade, Harry Byrd, a major disappointment up to that point, shut out the Tigers on five hits in the first game of a July 18 doubleheader to even his record at 5–5. The Yankee winning streak ended with the Byrd shutout, but after winning the finale of the three-game series, with Detroit behind another three-hit shutout by the aging but still game Allie Reynolds, who upped his record to 10–1, they defeated the White Sox, 4–1, on July 20 to move into a first-place tie with the Indians.

Of particular satisfaction for Stengel during this Yankee hot streak was the hitting of Irv Noren, the reserve outfielder who, two years earlier, Casey had urged GM George Weiss to acquire from the Washington Senators. Weiss had to sacrifice one of the Yankees' top outfield prospects, Jackie Jensen, along with pitcher Frank "Spec" Shea, a fourteen-game winner as a rookie in 1947, in the deal, and he was none too happy when Noren had a very ordinary '53 season, batting .267 with just six homers in 109 games. This was part of the reason Weiss, without consulting Stengel, reached out and acquired Enos Slaughter from the Cardinals in spring training.

But on June 4 Slaughter fractured his wrist running into a fence in Cleveland in pursuit of a fly ball, enabling Stengel to start giving the twenty-nine-year-old Noren more playing time. During the thirteen-game winning streak Noren went 27-for-64, with six homers and seventeen RBI, lifting his average from .323 to what would have been a league-leading .359 had he not been shy the necessary plate appearances. Noren took over the AL batting lead in early July, prompting Stengel to name him to the All-Star team. Suddenly a star had been born in the Bronx, to the point at which the *New York Daily Mirror* assigned their Yankee beat writer, Ben Epstein, to do a three-part series on Noren. Harold Rosenthal, the Yankee beat writer for the *Herald-Tribune*, said,

Nobody knew anything about Noren as he'd been kind of buried in the Yankee outfield behind Mantle, Bauer and Woodling. When he

BABY HAMMER: Hank Aaron made the jump all the way from Class A ball to the major leagues in 1954. In his rookie season for the Milwaukee Braves, he wore No. 5. The next year he changed to No. 44 and began making his "Hammerin' Hank" legend—surpassing Babe Ruth as baseball's all-time home run champ with 755 and being elected to the Hall of Fame in 1982. (NEW YORK DAILY NEWS)

GARRULOUS YANKEES ICONS: Yankees manager Casey Stengel (left) who loved to talk . . . and talk . . . and talk, and the longtime "Voice of the Yankees," the legendary Mel Allen (right), conversing in the dugout at Yankee Stadium prior to a game in 1954. (NEW YORK DAILY NEWS)

BRING IT ON: Cleveland Indians star sluggers Larry Doby (left) and Al Rosen (right) arrive at New York's Grand Central Station for the start of the 1954 World Series. (NEW YORK DAILY NEWS)

HERO AND BEAUTY: Willie Mays, hero of the 1954 Giants' world championship season, chats with actress Laraine Day, wife of Giants manager Leo Durocher, prior to a game at the Polo Grounds in 1954. (NEW YORK DAILY NEWS)

INSTANT ACE: Johnny Antonelli, acquired by the New' York Giants from the Milwaukee Braves on Feb. 1, 1954, would have surely been the National League Cy Young winner in '54 had the award existed. For his new team, Antonelli led the NL in winning pct. (21–7, .750), ERA (2.30), and fewest hits/9 innings (7.27). Here he celebrates his 21st win after hurling a 1–0, five-hit shutout over the St. Louis Cardinals, September 13. (NEW YORK DAILY NEWS)

HISTORIC KEYSTONE COMBO: In 1954, Chicago Cubs rookies, Ernie Banks (left) and Gene Baker (right), formed Major League Baseball's first all-black shortstop-second base combo. They remained together until 1957 when Baker was traded to the Pittsburgh Pirates. Banks went on to win two National League MVP awards, hit 512 homers, and was elected to the Hall of Fame in 1977. (NATIONAL BASEBALL HALL OF FAME)

MANAGER AND CAPTAIN: In 1954, career minor league player and manager Walter Alston (left) was named to manage the Dodgers after much initial speculation that Pee Wee Reese (right), the popular longtime Dodger shortstop and team captain, was ownership's first choice for the job. (NEW YORK DAILY NEWS)

CASUALTY CAMPY: Brooklyn Dodgers catcher Roy Campanella (right), who was the National League MVP in 1953, shows his injured left hand to his son. Campanella injured the hand sliding into a base in spring training and finally had to undergo surgery. He was never right the whole '54 season, batting a career-low .219. (NEW YORK DAILY NEWS)

INDIAN BRAINTRUST: Hank Greenberg (left), the general manager of the 1954 Cleveland Indians, who hired Al Lopez as manager and acquired many of the key players on their 111-win team, and former owner Bill Veeck (right) who, in 1947, signed Larry Doby as the first black player in the American League. (CLEVELAND ST.-MICHAEL SCHWARTZ LIBRARY)

CUBA VS. MEXICO: For much of the first three months of the '54 season, Minnie Miñoso (left), the Chicago White Sox's "Cuban Comet" who was the first black Hispanic in the major leagues, led the American League in batting until being overtaken by Indians' second baseman Bobby Avila (right), of Mexico, who won the batting title with a .341 average. Miñoso finished second at .320. (CLEVELAND ST.-MICHAEL SCHWARTZ LIBRARY)

CENTER FIELD KINGS: In 1954, Tris Speaker (left), a lifetime .345 batter with 3,514 hits, was considered the greatest center fielder in baseball history. That spring, however, Speaker, who was in the Cleveland Indians' camp as an advisor, conceded that the Giants' sensational Willie Mays (right) might one day challenge his place on that throne. (CLEVELAND ST.-MICHAEL SCHWARTZ LIBRARY)

YANKEE KILLERS: On July 23, 1954, the first-place Indians beat the Yankees, 8–2, to go one and a half games up on their rivals as Early Wynn (center) scattered 14 hits. Al Smith (left) had a homer, a double, and five RBI, and Larry Doby (right) hit a pair of homers. The Yankees never got any closer to first place after that. (CLEVELAND ST.-MICHAEL SCHWARTZ LIBRARY)

UNINTENDED GLOVEMAN: Cleveland Indians' Al Rosen, a multi-All-Star and 1953 American League Most Valuable Player at third base, displays both his third base glove and a first base glove, where he was asked to play at the beginning of the '54 season. Rosen sustained a broken finger fielding a ball at first base and, despite moving back to third, was never the same hitter. (NEW YORK DAILY NEWS)

BIG CHIEFS: Cleveland Indians' manager Al Lopez (left), who silenced his critics in 1954 by finally beating the Yankees for the pennant while winning an American League record 111 games, confers with his mound ace, Bob Lemon (right), who tied teammate Early Wynn for the league lead in victories with 23. Lemon, Wynn, and Lopez are all in the Hall of Fame. (NEW YORK DAILY NEWS)

TWO FOR THE TITLE: Along with the Dodgers' Duke Snider, Giants' team-mates Don Mueller (left) and Willie Mays (right) waged a three-way battle for the National League batting title in 1954. On the last day of the season, Mays went 3-for-4 to edge out Mueller, .345–.342. (NEW YORK DAILY NEWS)

SOUL OF THE GIANTS: Monte Irvin was the quiet Giants' clubhouse leader who was assigned by manager Leo Durocher to serve as a sort of guardian for Willie Mays. A lifetime .293 for eight seasons, Irvin left most of his best years in the Negro Leagues. He was elected to the Hall of Fame in 1973. (NEW YORK DAILY NEWS)

PHIL TRIES SPECS: The 1954 season was the worst of Hall-of-Fame Yankee shortstop Phil Rizzuto's career. The 1950 American League MVP (above) hit just .195 in '54 and found himself periodically benched and pinch-hit for by manager Casey Stengel. In desperation, Rizzuto (below) resorted to wearing glasses in late August but ditched them after a couple of weeks. (NEW YORK DAILY NEWS, BASEBALL HALL OF FAME)

SURPRISE YANKEE STAR: Irv Noren had been an unsung fourth outfielder for the Yankees his first two seasons with the team, 1952–1953. But after an injury to Enos Slaughter, Noren began getting regular playing time in '54 and wound up leading the Yankees in hitting with a .319 average while contending for the batting crown down to the last couple of weeks of the season. (BASEBALL HALL OF FAME)

BIRTHDAY GUY: Enos Slaughter (second from left) has help celebrating his 38th birthday from Yankees manager Casey Stengel (left), pitcher Bob Grim (second from right), and Mickey Mantle (right). The veteran outfielder Slaughter was acquired by the Yankees from the St. Louis Cardinals just prior to Opening Day 1954 in a trade that was not greeted with a lot of enthusiasm in the New York clubhouse. (NEW YORK DAILY NEWS)

DEM GINTS: New York Giants' starting lineup for Game 1 of the 1954 World Series: (from left to right) Whitey Lockman, Davey Williams, Hank Thompson, Alvin Dark, Don Mueller, Willie Mays, Monte Irvin, and Wes Westrum. (NEW YORK DAILY NEWS)

HEADLINE HEROES: *New York Daily News* front page after the hometown Giants completed their four-game 1954 World Series sweep of the Cleveland Indians. (NEW YORK DAILY NEWS)

WONDROUS WILLIE: Willie Mays made countless catches like this, none, of course, more famous than his one off Vic Wertz in Game 1 of the '54 World Series. This one was almost as famous, a leaping one-handed grab of Duke Snider's long drive high above the center field exit gate in Ebbets Field, Aug. 15, 1954.
(NEW YORK DAILY NEWS)

THE CATCH: *New York Daily News'* Pulitzer Prize–winning photographer Frank Hurley's famous "sequence" shot of Willie Mays's saving catch off Cleveland's Vic Wertz in the eighth inning of Game 1 of the '54 World Series. Hurley took this sequence with his new high-speed Hulcher 70 camera that he was using for the first time that day.

(NEW YORK DAILY NEWS)

HOW CLOSE IT REALLY WAS: Cleveland Indians right fielder Dave Pope leaps high in vain to catch Dusty Rhodes's 260-foot three-run 10th-inning homer off Bob Lemon that barely cleared the Polo Grounds' right field wall and gave the Giants a 5–2 win in Game 1 of the '54 World Series. The shot later ignited a huge controversy when sportswriters, evoking a politically incorrect term of the time, called it a "Chinese" homer. (NEW YORK DAILY NEWS)

KISSING IT GOODBYE: Giants' pinch hitter extraordinaire Dusty Rhodes kisses the bat he used to hit the three-run "sudden death" 10th-inning homer that beat the Indians, 5–2, in the first game of the 1954 World Series. (NEW YORK DAILY NEWS)

WAIT 'TIL NEXT YEAR: Brooklyn Dodgers owner Walter O'Malley (left) offers a congratulatory handshake to Giants owner Horace Stoneham (right) for winning the 1954 National League pennant. Victorious Giants manager Leo Durocher (second from left) and Dodgers manager Walter Alston (second from right) look on. (NEW YORK DAILY NEWS)

LIONS IN WINTER: Jackie Robinson (left) and New York Daily News sportswriter Dick Young (right), two longtime "friendly" antagonists when it came to the debate on race and social issues, share a laugh as white-haired "seniors," at the 1972 Reds–A's World Series in Cincinnati. Nine days later, Robinson died of a heart attack at age 53 at his home in Stamford, CT. (NEW YORK DAILY NEWS)

started hitting and carrying the Yankees like he did, there was this mad journalistic rush on all the writers' part to stretch Noren's background story. It was a funny situation in New York, as Willie Mays was driving the fans wild over at the Polo Grounds; Duke Snider was pounding the ball to a pulp in Brooklyn, and the distinguished Yankees had to vie for space in the newspapers with a player whose own previous stock of clippings would have to be stretched somewhat to fill a five-and-ten notebook.

Once they started digging, however, the writers discovered Noren had a fairly impressive dossier. The son of a baker from Pasadena, California, Noren was a star left-handed pitcher at Pasadena Junior College and then a first baseman in the Army at Fort Ord in California. Upon being discharged from the Army, the Brooklyn Dodgers signed him to a $5,000 bonus. In the Dodger farm system he was converted to a center fielder and was named Most Valuable Player of both the Texas League in 1948 when he hit .323 at Fort Worth and the Pacific Coast League in 1949, when he hit .330 with 130 RBI for Hollywood. It was after his big season at Hollywood when Dodgers president Branch Rickey sold Noren to the Senators for $65,000.

"Brooklyn made a mistake with Noren," Stengel was saying at Yankee Stadium in mid-July to a group of reporters, who were seeking more information on the budding outfielder. "They had Snider in center and [Carl] Furillo in right and I guess they felt Irv couldn't play leftfield too good on account he was left-handed and that he couldn't pull the ball real good. He had a habit of hitting over second to left-center."

With the Yankees, hitting coach Bill Dickey worked with Noren's stance, keeping his arms away from his chest so he was able to handle the high pitches better. There were no problems, however, about his outfield defense. "He plays the ball like an infielder," said Stengel, who had a well-documented disdain for outfielders who "play it safe and think things out."

"So has Noren moved into the 'untouchable' category as Mantle and Yogi Berra?" a reporter asked.

"Oh, I'd trade him," Stengel said, "if someone offered me a house or something like that. But not for anything else."

Stengel's raised spirits at how the season now seemed to be turning were somewhat dampened when the Indians came into New York and took two out of three from the Yankees the weekend of July 23–25 to move back to a one-and-a-half-game lead in first place. Going into the series Doby had seventeen homers, three behind the AL leader, Mickey Mantle. In the two Indians wins, Friday and Saturday, Doby went 4-for-8, with three homers and five RBI, prompting Al Lopez to remark to the writers, "This is the first year I've seen him enjoying play-ing so much. He's played in every game and he's much more relaxed and that's helped him cut down on his strikeouts. After two strikes—usually two good swings—he changes his stance and dares the pitcher to fool him. He's made a big difference in our club."

"This is a friendly team," Doby said. "We're all trying to help each other."

But it hadn't always been a friendly team for Doby.

While he was with the Navy on a lonely Pacific island in Oc-tober 1945, Doby recalled "having the greatest feeling of my life." His buddies were all huddled around a radio when the news came that the Dodgers had just signed Jackie Robinson to a contract. Prior to joining the Navy for duty in World War II, Doby, a star four-sport athlete at Eastside High School in Paterson, New Jer-sey, had decided he was going to pursue a professional baseball ca-reer, although he was resigned to the fact it would be in the Negro Leagues. "When I heard the news of Jackie's signing, I knew then

I had a chance to play major league baseball," Doby recalled years later. "I'll never forget the tingling sensation I felt inside."

Upon being discharged that December, Doby came home to Paterson and sought out his friend Monte Irvin, who was a standout outfielder with the Negro Leagues' Newark Eagles. With Irvin's help, Doby got a contract from the Eagles, signing with them as a second baseman, and in '46 he batted .341 and was named to the Negro League All-Star team. He was worried, however, when no offers were forthcoming from any major league clubs. It wasn't until July 3 the following year that Bill Veeck, the owner of the Indians, signed Doby, batting .458 for the Eagles, telling him to report two days later to Comiskey Park in Chicago, where the Indians were playing a series with the White Sox.

As Doby further recalled, his welcome to the big leagues as the first black player in the American League was anything but warm and congenial. "Unlike Jackie, who'd been warned by Branch Rickey [about] the kind of things . . . indignities . . . racial taunts . . . he could expect, no one told me anything about those things," Doby said in a 1995 interview. "I was only twenty-two years old, and while the Indian players treated me the way they probably treated any rookie, no one tried to make friends with me either. On the trains no one invited me to play cards or talked over the ballgames with me, and I roomed alone on the road, in separate Negroes-only hotels in a lot of cases."

Veeck informed Doby, with Joe Gordon, a seven-time All-Star entrenched as the Indians' second baseman, that initially the plan was to start him out at first base and as a backup at second and short for the rest of '47.

But when Doby, who had never played first base, asked to borrow a glove from Eddie Robinson, one of the Indians' two incumbent first basemen, Robinson refused. Doby saw it as a racial slight, later quoting the Texas-born Robinson as saying he "wasn't gonna let no nigger use his glove." In fact, Robinson threatened to quit baseball when Doby joined the team, although in his 2011 memoir he insisted it was never about any inherent prejudice against blacks but rather his outrage at possibly losing his job to someone who had never played in the majors—after Indians coach Bill McKechnie had assured him a few weeks earlier that he was the Indians' everyday first baseman. "I was so mad, I told Les Fleming, our other first baseman, that 'if they put Doby at first, let's quit,'" Robinson said. "McKechnie later came into the clubhouse and told me I was making a big mistake; that they're going to say I didn't want Doby to play because he was black. Years later, Larry and I became friends and I think he realized I threatened to quit because I was mad at [Indians manager Lou] Boudreau for giving my job to someone who had never even played the position, not because he was a black guy coming in."

When the July 5 game started, the lefty-hitting Doby found himself on the bench, alone at the far end of the dugout. It was not until the seventh inning, with the Indians trailing the White Sox 5–1, that he was summoned to pinch hit for Indians pitcher Bryan Stephens against Earl Harrist, a right-handed reliever who had just come into the game for Chicago. After swinging wildly and missing on the first pitch and watching a called strike two on the second pitch, Doby watched the next two Harrist deliveries for balls and then swung and missed again on a pitch outside for strike three. Devastated at such an embarrassing debut, he skulked back to the dugout and slumped at the end of the bench, his head in his hands. A long-standing myth, perpetuated by Veeck, was that Gordon, seeing Doby in his despair, walked down to the end of the dugout and put his head in his hands after also striking out. In fact, Gordon was on third base at the time of Doby's first at-bat, but he did go out of his way to play catch with Doby before games—when no one else would—and offered counsel to him on the ways of the big leagues. Doby said,

Joe Gordon was the only player who tried to help me. Joe was the regular second baseman, and I worked out in batting practice at his position. He told me a lot of things I hadn't known about playing second, and then he gave me a lesson in hitting. But nothing seemed to help me. I had jitters in the field, and I hit only .156 in twenty-nine games that year. I thought I was through before I even got started. Then, on the last day, Bill McKechnie came over to me and said, "Go home and get a good rest, and when you come back in spring training, we're going to make you into an outfielder."

To that end the Indians provided Doby with the finest outfield instructor he could've ever wanted, Hall of Famer Tris Speaker, who was universally regarded as the greatest center fielder ever to play the game.

"Speaker was the perfect teacher for me," said Doby. "He drilled me on every aspect of outfielding, and Hank Greenberg dropped in to give me some tips on batting that spring. Everything would've been perfect except I couldn't stay with the team at the Santa Rita Hotel in Tucson. A ballplayer should spend twenty-four hours a day with the squad. Playing winning ball means getting into the spirit of things, being a member of the team, not an individual."

"Doby was a helluva player," said Rosen. "But he had a tendency to get down on himself, and he was a bit of a loner. He was a man of moods, a kind of dual personality. Looking back, I can understand that now. He went through a lot those early years with us. I saw a great deal of prejudice toward him, and Doby didn't do anything to exacerbate it. I always said Doby had a tougher time than Jackie did because nobody prepared him for what he was in store for. Jackie had an outer shell of people that Doby didn't have."

Even though, as a Jew, Rosen also endured his share of bigotry in those days, it took a few years for he and Doby to warm
up to each other. A lot of that had to do with an incident in 1950
when the two of them came to blows in the visiting clubhouse at
Yankee Stadium. Rosen related,

> *It was a big series against our archrivals, the Yankees—as they all*
> *were—and we were both fierce competitors. I was heading out onto*
> *the field when I saw Doby lying on the trainer's table, and I said*
> *something to the effect "big men play in big series." Well, Larry*
> *shot back, calling me a yellow sonofabitch, and the next thing you*
> *know we're throwing punches. He wound up going home [to New*
> *Jersey] for the weekend because he was pretty banged up, and it*
> *was my fault we lost him for the series. It was not something I was*
> *proud of or ever talked about again. But we gradually reconciled*
> *all of that because we were teammates for a long time. And one*
> *thing is for certain—1954 was his year.*

A primary reason for Doby seeming much more relaxed in '54,
as Lopez maintained, was that for the first time he'd been allowed to
stay with the rest of the team in spring training after Indians traveling secretary, Spud Goldstein, imposed upon the manager of the
Santa Rita Hotel in Tucson to lift its restriction of black patrons.
The manager relented on the condition the Indians' black players
accept rooms on the mezzanine level and not sit in the hotel lobby.
Goldstein agreed to the compromise but neglected to tell Doby or
the Indians' six other black players in camp. "That was okay," Doby
said, "Even if he had told us about them, I would've ignored them."

In taking those two out of three in Yankee Stadium, July 23–
25, and ousting the Yankees from their share of first place, the Indians went home to Cleveland for a three-game series against the
Red Sox feeling pretty good about themselves. Nevertheless, the

Yankee series had taken a toll. In the Friday night 8–2 win George Strickland suffered a double fracture of his chin when, sliding into third base, a ball thrown by Yankee reliever Marlin Stuart struck him. Upon examining him, Yankee team physician Dr. Sidney Gaynor estimated Strickland would be out for at least a month.

"Losing Strickland like that was a big blow," said Rosen. "He was an excellent shortstop and the glue to our infield. He had great range between myself and Avila and wasn't any automatic out at the plate either. We had to go with Sam Dente, who did a good enough job, but he wasn't Strickland."

The thirty-two-year-old Dente was a journeyman utility infielder whom the Indians had purchased from the White Sox the year before and sent to their Triple A Indianapolis farm team for the entire season. He made the Indians' team out of spring training only because Lopez's other backup infielder, Regalado, was more suited for third and second.

Despite the loss of Strickland, the Indians maintained their momentum out of the Yankee Stadium series, taking two of three from the Red Sox and two more from the Senators to close out July, 69–30, two and a half games ahead of the Yankees. The 8–3 victory on July 30 was especially noteworthy because of a spectacular, jaw-dropping catch by Doby that robbed the Senators' Tom Umphlett of a game-tying two-run homer in the third inning. Playing a fairly deep center field, as was customary for him, Doby took off after Umphlett's long fly ball until he reached the five-foot fence in left-center. He then made a leap toward the bullpen canopy behind the fence, grabbed the ball backhanded, and, after seemingly hanging suspended in the air for a moment, tumbled down off the canopy and fell back onto the playing field. As he lay there, semiconscious, left fielder Al Smith rushed to his aid, and the Municipal Stadium crowd of 17,504 went silent. When Smith alertly grabbed the ball out of

Doby's glove to keep Jim Busby, the Senators' base runner from advancing from second to third, second-base umpire John Flaherty signaled Umphlett out. It was another couple of minutes before Doby arose from the ground and the crowd was able to roar its appreciation.

By coincidence, Dizzy Dean and the ABC TV *Game of the Week* crew were again in Cleveland to broadcast the next day's game, and Ol' Diz who, earlier in the season had proclaimed to his audience that Bobby Avila had the best chance of anyone to hit .400, was even more effusive in his praise of Doby's catch. "That was the greatest catch I ever saw in my whole life," Dean gushed. "I've seen Terry Moore, Joe DiMaggio and others make some dandies, but nothing I ever saw was close to this. If I was the pitcher, I'd go up to Larry and say, 'Podner, here's half my salary. You deserve it.'"

Art Houtteman, the beneficiary of the catch, didn't exactly do that, but he did wait until all the other Indian players had left the dugout after the game to thank Doby personally. "I wanted to talk to you alone," the Indian pitcher said. "As long as I live, I'll never forget the greatness of that play."

From his Lakeside Hospital bed, where he was recovering from a heart attack, Tris Speaker, who'd been listening to the game on the radio, said, "Tell Larry he gave this old man a big lift!" And in the next day's *Cleveland Press*, Indians beat writer Frank Gibbons wrote, "If this wasn't the greatest catch of the century, it must be at least a match for any other."

And yet, awe inspiring as all who witnessed it agreed the catch was, it was the story of Larry Doby's life that, two months later, there would be another catch by a much more celebrated center fielder that would render his just another lost and forgotten footnote of the '54 season.

CHAPTER
9

A TREE DIES (SLOWLY) IN BROOKLYN

N EW YORK IN THE 1950S WAS THE CAPITAL OF THE BASEBALL universe, a time and place in which every year, from 1947 until 1957, when the Giants and Dodgers left town for the West Coast, at least one and often two of the city's three teams played host for the World Series. And with television in its small-box, black-and-white infancy, the fans' connection to the games they weren't able to attend in person was mostly through the radio broadcasts and newspapers.

As such, the team voices, Mel Allen of the Yankees, Red Barber of the Dodgers, and Russ Hodges of the Giants, and the newspaper scribes who chronicled the three teams' daily triumphs and travails, most notably Dick Young of the *Daily News*, Jimmy Cannon of the *Post*, and Red Smith of the *Herald-Tribune*, were almost as identifiable to the fans as the players themselves.

Nowhere was this any truer than in Brooklyn, the largest of the five boroughs, with a population of 2.7 million, more than any other city in the United States except Chicago and Los Angeles. Dodger fans were like no others, ingrained as they were with the pathos of having never experienced a world championship banner hoisted up the flag pole at Ebbets Field. Theirs was a love-hate relationship, in which they embraced their heroes like family—a lot of the Dodgers lived right there among them in the neighborhoods—but would lovingly disparage them as "bums" when they lost. The common "bums" reference to the Dodgers was derived from an inspiration from the *World-Telegram* cartoonist Willard Mullin while riding in a taxi cab through Brooklyn after leaving a game at Ebbets Field. As Mullin told it, the cabbie at one point turned to him and asked in his pure Brooklyn-ese, "How did dem bums of ours do today?" How funny, Mullin thought. Brooklynites thought of the Dodgers as bums because of their long history of losing and playing ragged baseball, but they were nonetheless *their* bums, making what seemed to be their disparagement of them actually a term of affection. When Mullin got back to his office he got out a picture of Emmett Kelly, the famous circus performer—who, as a sad-faced hobo character, "Weary Willie," was seen sweeping up the arenas after all the acts—and began to draw a caricature of him in a tattered blue jacket, rumpled gray fedora hat, and pinstriped baseball pants. Mullin's "Brooklyn bum" soon became an everlasting symbol of the Dodgers' and their fans' "wait 'til next year" frustrations. The Dodgers themselves even solicited Mullin to draw the character for the covers of their yearbooks throughout the fifties.

Brooklyn's was largely a blue-collar populace comprised of Italian, Irish, Asian, and Jewish immigrants along with the heaviest concentration of black citizens in the United States, mostly the result of their migration from Harlem when the A-train subway line was connected from upper Manhattan to the Bedford-Stuyvesant section in the 1930s. "The Dodgers were our identity, our civic pride, our family, if you will," said Brooklyn native Bob Rosen, a sports statistician with the Elias Bureau in New York for over forty years who grew up in the Flatbush section of the borough, a fifteen-minute walk from Ebbets Field. "And we followed them through Dick Young."

Of all the New York sports writers at the time, none seemed to have the unique connection to the team they covered the way Young did with the Dodgers. With a daily circulation of just over 2 million and 3.6 million on Sundays, the *Daily News* was the "Big Kahuna" of New York's eight major daily newspapers. (The next largest circulation was the *Mirror*, at just under 900,000 daily and 1.6 million on Sunday.) As a tabloid, the *News* was a "people's paper," appealing directly to the blue-collar masses with its emphasis on local news—cops, crime, scandals, and mayhem up front, celebrity gossip columns by the likes of Ed Sullivan and Bob Sylvester in the middle, and then the heavy emphasis on sports, particularly baseball, which ruled the realm pretty much uncontested in those days before the rise in popularity of the National Football and Basketball leagues.

"What set Dick Young apart from the other baseball writers," Rosen continued, "was the way he wrote. He wrote what I saw. He didn't use a lot of fancy words. He wrote to *us*. Like he was a common fan, just like us. He was anti-owner. He knew Rickey was a cheapskate and got rid of our favorite players to make a buck."

In those days there were the morning papers, with early "night owl" editions that hit the newsstands at seven at night and were comprised mostly of straight news stories with no quotes, and the afternoon papers, which arrived on the stands around noontime and sought to supply fresh angles on the news stories along with more features.

Dave Anderson, the *Brooklyn Eagle*'s neophyte Dodger beat writer in 1954 who later went on to be a Pulitzer Prize–winning general sports columnist for the *New York Times*, said,

> *Dick was like our commissioner. Dick was the first AM writer to go into the clubhouses for quotes from the players after games. The other morning guys didn't give a shit. They just wrote their routine game stories, made sure they had the scores right, and were out of there and on to Toots Shor's or wherever. Dick would supply a PM angle for his AM paper. He beat the afternoon guys at their own game! He was always two days ahead of all the other writers. My graduate school was Dick Young. I learned from him how to cover the team. The other writers just covered the game.*

When Rosen said Young was "like one of us," he wasn't wrong. Young was born in New York in 1917, the son of Jewish parents, and attended George Washington High School in the Washington Heights section of upper Manhattan. But that was about as far as it went with his formal education. He was the product of a broken home—his parents separated when he was in his early teens, and an Italian family, named Barbuto, who were friends with his mother, raised him. When he graduated from high school he went west to Los Angeles to live with his father, who was in the film business and by then had shortened the family name from Youngswick to Young. Young had hoped to attend junior college in LA, but, as he later said, his father, who was then with another woman, was not willing to help him out financially, and "the $75 tuition fee was all the money I had." So, instead, he returned to New York, and in 1936 he joined the Civilian Conservation Corps, which paid $30 a month.

After a year with the CCC, building a state park in upstate New York, Young, at age nineteen, got himself a job with the *Daily News* as a messenger in the publicity department. He later graduated from that to tabulator in the sports department, but he quickly caught the fever of the newspaper business and wanted to write, convincing the sports editor to let him rewrite stories from the Associated Press and United Press wires. In a 1986 radio interview with NBC sportscaster Bob Costas, Young explained, "I guess it was the Walter Winchell thing. I grew up in the Walter Winchell era, wanting to be a news correspondent or a police reporter. Winchell began his radio show, with a Morse code ticker tape in the background, and he'd give you an item, three dots, and another item. Tell the people what's going on and what you think is going on. Meat and potato stuff."

Young would reiterate this whenever he counseled young writers. "Don't try to be a fucking Hemingway," he'd tell them. "Talk to your readers. Don't talk down to them. Whenever possible, give them something different from just the score of the game. They already know that."

In 1943 Young was given the Dodgers as his first beat with the *Daily News*, whereupon he was immediately caught up in an anti–Branch Rickey campaign launched by the *News's* sports editor and columnist, Jimmy Powers. The Powers-Rickey war was ignited when Rickey sold popular outfielder Joe Medwick to the Giants on July 6, 1943, and followed that up three weeks later with the trade of first baseman Dolph Camilli, who'd been the NL Most Valuable Player in 1941, also to the Giants, for cash, a couple of second-line journeymen pitchers, and a utility infielder. It was a known fact that, stemming from his days as general manager for the St. Louis Cardinals in the thirties, Rickey had a clause in his contract that allowed him a percentage, believed to be 10 percent, of all cash payments included in player transactions. Powers, taking up the fans' outrage over the jettisoning of the popular Medwick and Camilli, began referring to Rickey as "El Cheapo" in all his columns about the Dodgers president, and Young likewise made Rickey a frequent target in his writings on the Dodgers. When, in 1947, Leo Durocher was suspended from baseball and Rickey replaced him with his own man, the previously retired, gentlemanly fifty-three-year-old Burt Shotton, who was the polar opposite of Durocher in both temperament and quote-ability for the writers, Young began referring to the new manager disparagingly as "KOBS," for Kindly Old Burt Shotton.

It was in 1950 that Rickey and Dodger attorney Walter O'Malley locked horns over control of the Dodgers in the wake of the passing of John L. Smith, the pharmaceutical mogul and Rickey supporter who, like them, owned 25 percent of the team. For one thing, O'Malley had privately seethed over the clause in Rickey's contract that gave him a percentage of all cash deals he made, and the wily Irishman was thus adamantly opposed to extending Rickey's contract. Upon Smith's death O'Malley was able to win over Smith's voting rights from his widow, now giving him 50 percent control. Realizing that in Smith he'd lost his biggest ally in the Dodger power structure, Rickey wound up selling his share of the Dodgers to O'Malley, but not before extracting maximum value—$1 million—for it. Under the original ownership agreement between Smith, O'Malley, and Rickey in 1945, if any of the three partners received an offer to sell, the other partners would have to match the offer, and Rickey was able to enlist multimillionaire New York real estate developer William Zeckendorf to offer him $1 million for his share of the Dodgers. As news of his bid became public, Zeckendorf indicated he would ask Rickey to stay on as Dodger GM. Skeptical as he was about the legitimacy of Zeckendorf's bid, O'Malley couldn't chance that and reluctantly capitulated to paying Rickey $1 million for his share. (It was definitely a coup for Rickey, who, all the while, had a standing offer from the Pittsburgh Pirates' new principal owner, John Galbreath, to head up the baseball operations of the perennial last-place Pirates.)

Now that he had control of the Dodgers, one of O'Malley's first orders of business was to summon Emil "Buzzie" Bavasi, the general manager of the Dodgers' Montreal Triple A farm team, to Brooklyn. Though Bavasi had originally been a Rickey hire and had worked his way up through the Dodger minor league system, O'Malley was impressed with his business and baseball acumen and named him to replace the new principal owner's now mortal enemy as head of the Dodgers baseball operations. And in one of their first meetings the conversation between O'Malley and Bavasi got around to Dick Young.

"How do you propose we deal with the Dick Young problem?" O'Malley asked.

"I'm not sure what you mean," Bavasi replied.

"Well," O'Malley said, "I'm sure you're aware of the fact that Young and the *Daily News* have been attacking Rickey quite viciously and, by association, Dodger management. We can't have that. We've got to get Young on our side. And so I'm leaving that to you. I'm making you vice president in charge of Dick Young."

According to Roger Kahn, who came on the Dodger beat for the *New York Herald-Tribune* in 1952 and stayed for two seasons until being shifted to the Giants in 1954, Bavasi took his job of neutralizing Young with earnest. "Buzzie was very personable, and he took Young about to the bars and restaurants, bought him clothes, and gave him scoops," Kahn said, adding somewhat bitterly, "Of course, Dick was a good reporter. The leaks just made him better than he was."

But besides his reportorial skill and tireless work ethic—he would most often write six days a week for up to three editions of the *Daily News* when the Dodgers were home and every day on the road, plus his "Young Ideas" columns when warranted— Young had a special gift for turning a phrase. When he was working as a tabulator in the *News*'s sports department he would often send little snippets of news, anecdotes, or different slants on the news—"whatever came to my head," he said—to the *News*'s sports columnist, Jimmy Powers. After a while Powers began using them in his column, without giving any credit to Young. But Young didn't care. He considered that a compliment. And he knew that his talent had been noticed.

When he took over the Dodger beat, Young became just as famous for his clever leads as he did for his scoops. George Vecsey, the award-winning columnist for the *New York Times*, described Young's writing style as having "all the subtlety of a knee in the groin." Indeed, Young's most famous lead, "The tree that grows in Brooklyn is an apple tree," which he wrote when the Dodgers were in the process of blowing the pennant to the St. Louis Cardinals in 1948, playing off the best-selling 1943 Betty Smith novel, *A Tree Grows in Brooklyn*, was the ultimate colloquialism for players "choking." Audacious as it was, Dodger fans did not disagree and once again knew Young had given them their money's worth. Another time, when the Dodgers were on the wrong end of a 17–6 game against the Giants, during which their archrivals clubbed six home runs, Young wrote, "This game belongs on page three with the other axe murders."

When it came to the Dodgers' managerial change from Charlie Dressen to Walter Alston, Young was like all the other writers. He loved Dressen because Charlie could never keep his mouth shut and was always accommodating for a good quote or even an occasional scoop, accidental or otherwise. By contrast, Alston was shy and reticent, and the players viewed his outwardly reserved style, at least initially anyway, as weakness. "I remember on the last stop of our barnstorming trip back home from spring training the writers had a meeting with some of the players at the Shoreham Hotel in Washington in which they implored us to get Alston to talk to them," Carl Erskine related to me in a 2013 interview. "They wanted to know from us what Alston was all about. 'He won't talk to us,' they said." And it became Young's mission to monitor closely—and, when necessary, exploit—this new dynamic between the Dodgers and the rookie skipper, in particular the friction between Alston and Jackie Robinson.

In his 1972 memoir, *I Never Had It Made*, penned just before his death, Robinson detailed his strained relations with O'Malley, and, later by association, the owner's man, Alston, as well as the press after the departure of his benefactor and protector, Rickey, writing,

> *I didn't know whether O'Malley was jealous of [Rickey] because he brought integration into the game. All I know is, after 1950, he seemed furious whenever he heard the name Rickey. O'Malley's attitude toward me was viciously antagonistic. I learned he had a habit of calling me Mr. Rickey's prima donna. My troubles with the Dodger front office, combined with my spirited response on the playing field whenever I felt either my team or I was being shoved around, inflamed the relationship between me and some members of the press. . . . The sportswriter who seemed to be doing his best to make me revert to the old cheek-turning, humble Robinson was Dick Young of the Daily News.*

The differences between Robinson and Young came to a head during the Dodgers' first trip to St. Louis in '54 on April 26–28. The Chase Hotel, where all the teams stayed in St. Louis, was

one of the last bastions of segregation, and when the Dodgers'
bus pulled up to the lobby and the players got out, Lee Scott,
the traveling secretary, hailed taxi cabs to take the black players, Robinson, Don Newcombe, Roy Campanella, Jim Gilliam,
Joe Black, and Sandy Amoros, to the all-black Adams Hotel on
the other side of town. Newcombe, who had just been discharged
after two years in the Army, was outraged that nothing had
changed, at least in St. Louis, in regard to social injustice. Upon
inspecting the conditions at the Adams—tight-quartered rooms
and no air conditioning or dining room—Newcombe declared,
"I've had enough. This is unacceptable. I'm going back to the
Chase," to which Robinson said, "I'm with you."

The two of them had the cabbie take them back to the Chase
and told him to keep the meter running while they went inside
and confronted the manager. When they demanded to know why
they weren't allowed to stay there, the best the manager could
explain was that the hotel didn't want blacks using the pool.

"That's okay, mister," Jackie said. "I don't swim."

"And I don't swim during the season because I don't want to
hurt my arm," Newcombe added.

"Okay," the manager countered. The two could stay, but on
two conditions: they stayed out of the pool and got all their
meals from room service—they were not permitted in the dining room either. Robinson and Newcombe agreed they could live
with that. Erskine said,

*We knew that Lena Horne, when she performed there, wasn't al-
lowed in the Chase lobby and had to go through the kitchen. I was
the player rep, and looking back I wish maybe I'd done more. I think
most of the guys wish they had, but back then we were all on one-year
contracts, just trying to keep our jobs. You have to understand—and*

this is not a cop-out—those were the times and progress was being made, just slowly. When Jackie first broke in, there were a number of hotels—in Chicago, Philadelphia—where he had to stay in private homes or separate all-black hotels. The Chase was the last holdout and, so when Newk and Jackie did what they did, even with the pool and dining room restrictions, we looked at that as a victory. And a big one.

Nevertheless, when Newcombe and Robinson went back to the Adams to tell Campanella and Gilliam, they were somewhat surprised when Campy declined the invitation. "It's a matter of pride," Campanella said. "I don't want to stay anywhere where they didn't want me in the past. I'm no crusader." Gilliam agreed.

Word spread fast of the Dodgers' breakthrough at the Chase, although when the Pittsburgh Pirates followed them into the hotel later that week, Curtis Roberts, the infielder who'd broken their color line to start the season, was subject to the same indignity as Newcombe and Robinson. Roberts's mistake was going down to the dining room in the morning and expecting some breakfast. He waited at his table for close to an hour, ignored by the waiters, until finally getting up in exasperation, checking out, and moving over to the Adams. At least he'd been somewhat prepared: when Branch Rickey informed him in spring training he'd made the team and was going to be the first black player on the Pirates, he counseled him—as he had Robinson in 1947—to maintain an even temper and not to make waves about the many racial slurs and indignities he could expect.

It wasn't until the following year, after Robinson and Newcombe had succeeded in completely integrating the Chase by eating in the dining room as well, that all the Dodgers' black players stayed there. Meanwhile, a few days later Robinson got to talking to Young about his and Newcombe's success in breaking down another racial barrier—and Campanella's decision not to join them.

"That's the trouble with you, Jackie, and the difference between you and Campy," said Young. "I can go to Campy and all he ever wants to talk about is baseball. But with you, it always sooner or later gets back to social issues. I'm telling you as a friend that the newspapermen are saying Campy's the kind of guy they can like, but that your aggressiveness, your wearing your race on your sleeve, makes enemies."

Nearly a quarter-century later Young and Robinson were still sparring with each other over race relations. In February of 1968 Young was in spring training when he wrote a column in the *Daily News* commenting on the withdrawal of several African nations from the 1968 Summer Olympics and a threatened boycott from US black athletes, led by African American sociologist and black power activist Harry Edwards, over the International Olympic Committee's decision to admit South Africa, an apartheid nation, to the Games in Mexico City. The IOC had only accepted South Africa's application after it promised to bring an integrated team that would eat, dress, and travel together as a unit.

"There seems to be a strange new standard for participating in the Olympic Games," Young wrote. "You have to approve of the other guy's form of government. . . . The nations that have been withdrawing from the 1968 Olympics are in a huff about the South Africa situation. South Africa is the last of the apartheid nations, regardless of the preachments of Prof. Harry Edwards, who chooses to place the U.S. in that same category."

The column touched an old nerve with Robinson, who, with his wife, Rachel, was dealing with his own personal problems at the time—the much-publicized drug addiction of his son Jackie Jr. In a letter to Young, Robinson lamented it was particularly frustrating that Young had not changed in his views on race relations. Robinson wrote that Young has no regard for those demanding the same rights that he demands as an American and chastised Young for admonishing him not to push too fast.

Young's response, a week later, was characteristically blunt and uncompromising:

Dear Jackie:

First, I would like to say you're full of shit, and then I will say it was nice hearing from you, and it is always nice hearing from you, and I was saddened to hear of your trouble with your son. Don't blame yourself, the way you seemed to do. Gil Hodges and I were talking today, and we both said it is so much a matter of luck; it could happen to his son, to mine. We all try to do what we think is right for our families, and sometimes it turns out, and sometimes it doesn't.

Now for why you are of full of shit. You guys kill me. Every time somebody disagrees with you, he's a bigot. Christ, I want the perfect world that you want. I want black people eating, sleeping, working with whites, marrying whites. That is our only way, to be one. You should know all the fights I got into in bars in Vero Beach arguing about this. The bartender would say, "if that nigger Robinson, or that nigger Campanella would show up here, he'd have to come around the back door to pick up his bottle." And I'd say, "they're better than you are, you sonofabitch." I'm no hero, but that's how I feel.

I also feel there's a way to do what you're trying to do, and maybe that's not always your way. Maybe you're right, and maybe I'm right, but that doesn't give you the right to call me a bigot, or say "your true colors are showing" because that's a prickish thing to say and you know it.

I never told you that you were pushing too fast for any reason than that I might have fears that bull-in-the-china-shop tactics would do more harm than good. I worry about the white backlash. I know it's wrong, but it's there. (About South Africa, which you seem so upset over, you can't turn a cruddy nation like that around overnight. Take the big step, and accept it. Let some kid in South Africa be the Jackie Robinson of the '68 Olympics.) When you were given the chance by Mr. Rickey, suppose the NAACP had said, no, Jackie Robinson can't play ball for Brooklyn until we have 100 percent integration in the United States. You'd still be standing outside Ebbets Field with your thumb up your ass, and nothing good would have happened yet. Think about that when you get so goddam righteous.

Best to Rae and I do hope all turns out well for you.

Dick

"As great a baseball writer as Dick was, as connected as he was to the Dodger fan base, I don't think he ever understood Jackie as a person," said Tom Villante, the (Dodger sponsor) Schaefer Beer account executive for the giant BBDO advertising agency and the producer of their TV and radio broadcasts, who traveled with the team throughout the fifties. "To Dick, Jackie was just a ballplayer. Dick was only interested in what was going on with the team."

Carl Erskine added,

There was no question, Campy and Jackie had decidedly different views when it came to race relations in baseball. Whereas Campy would say: "Don't rock the boat, we should be happy for everything baseball has given us," Jackie would counter that he was not here just to play baseball but for bigger reasons. To me, they were both right. Baseball did take the lead in a time when the nation still had segregation attitudes, and not just in the South, and Campy recognized that. On the other hand, Jackie wanted everyone to know how he was picked and why he was there.

According to Villante, although the Chase Hotel segregation situation may have been the most notable social injustice that still existed in baseball seven years after Robinson broke the color line, there were plenty of other more subtle indignities the black players were still forced to endure. "I remember every time we'd leave Crosley Field on the last game of a series in Cincinnati the organist there would play 'Bye Bye Blackbird,'" Villante said. "I was always amazed nobody ever said anything about it and the writers never wrote anything about it."

"Sadly, that was still the culture and the climate of the times," said Erskine.

As for Robinson and Alston, theirs was a kind of armed truce at the beginning. Although Alston had a made a point of taking Robinson aside in spring training to assure him he considered him to still be an integral part of the team, Jackie believed the new manager didn't really trust him. Robinson had made no secret of his upset over Dressen's departure, and when Alston said, "I hope you'll play as hard for me as you did for him," Jackie took that as a sign of insecurity.

But after the first two weeks of the season, during which the Dodgers finished April with 9–6 and in first place by a half-game, Alston suddenly had a far more pressing concern than that of his relationship with Robinson. The chip fracture in Campanella's left hand, suffered when he was sliding into a base in a late-March spring training game against the Yankees, had gradually worsened as the reigning NL MVP gamely sought to play through it. On May 1 Campy was hitting .167, with three homers and just eight RBI, when Alston reluctantly benched him. "For the first time in his ball-bashing career, Roy Campanella is benched for weak hitting," wrote Young. "Walt Alston, no longer able to countenance Campy's .167 b.a., announced Rube Walker will be behind the plate for tomorrow's game with Milwaukee."

"There's no doubt the hand bothers him," said Alston. "But to that extent I don't believe it's any worse than it was in spring training and he hit then. I just think it's a slump and a rest might snap him out of it."

Alston was wrong. The Dodgers wound up being rained out all three games in Milwaukee, during which time Campanella had his hand reexamined, and the doctors determined he needed an operation. The surgery was to be performed May 4 at Long Island College Hospital. The recovery prognosis: one month.

"I thought about it all night and I concluded that I've been kidding myself," Campanella told the writers resignedly. "The thing hurts and I can't roll my wrists when I swing, so I'm going to have them cut the chip out right now."

Without Campanella, the Dodgers barely played .500 ball through the month of May. He returned May 31, as they were two games into a string of ten straight victories that enabled them to take a two-game lead in the National League over the Giants. The Dodger streak came within inches of being aborted in the third game of it, on Memorial Day in Philadelphia. After the Dodgers took a 5–4 lead against the Phillies in the top of the twelfth inning their closer, Clem Labine, pitched himself into a jam, with two outs in the bottom of the inning, by walking a pair of pinch hitters, Danny Schell and Mickey Micelotta. That brought to the plate Willie "Puddin' Head" Jones, the Phillies' power-hitting third baseman. On a 1–1 pitch, Jones launched a drive high and deep toward the 405-foot mark in Connie Mack Stadium's expansive left-center field. Dodger center fielder Duke Snider was off in pursuit at the crack of the bat, but when he got to the wall, instead of turning and leaping, he kept right on running. Everyone in the ballpark was astounded as Snider proceeded to scale the wood-faced concrete wall with his spikes and, with a last-second leap, make a spinning, back-handed catch of the ball as it was about to leave the ballpark. As he fell to the ground, his glove hand with the ball triumphantly held high, Snider found himself suddenly mobbed by a bunch of small boys who'd run out onto the field after the catch.

"At first I was a little scared—what were all these kids doing there?" Snider said in an interview shortly before his death in 2011. "One of 'em even stole my cap before the rest of my teammates got out there to get me back to the dugout. Fans—Phillie fans, no less—were mobbing out onto the field, even though I had robbed their team of a victory, they were pummeling me! I guess you could say it was an adrenaline thing on my part. I just kept going until I ran out of room. There's no question it was the best catch I ever made."

In the *Brooklyn Eagle* the next day Dave Anderson described it as "the greatest, absolutely the greatest catch in baseball history," and in the *Post* Dodger pitching coach Jake Pitler, who witnessed it from the bullpen, was quoted as saying, "In my forty years in baseball I never saw a catch like Snider made." And, wrote Young, "To most of the 22,386 fans [Snider running after the ball] seemed like a futile gesture. He took off, dug his spikes into a fence, that didn't seem possible, and went higher—just enough to throw his glove hand high over his head and across his body."

Six days later, in Chicago, Snider made two similar leaping catches up the ivy-covered left-center field wall of Wrigley Field to rob the Cubs' Ernie Banks and Ralph Kiner of extra base hits and help preserve a 6–4 Dodger win in ten innings. The next day he had a double, triple, and a homer in a 7–5 victory over the Cardinals in St. Louis that lifted his batting average to .364. Then, in a three-game stretch from June 10 to 12, Snider went 9-for-14 with two doubles, a homer, and five RBI to take over the NL batting lead at .375. It was now apparent the Duke of Flatbush was having the best season of his career as the all-around driving force keeping the Dodgers in first place.

At the same time Snider was making his spectacular Memorial Day catch in Philadelphia, Dodgers' vice president of player development, Fresco Thompson, was back in Brooklyn completing the paperwork to send Joe Black, the Dodgers' one-time breadwinner right-hander and 1952 Rookie of the Year, to their Triple A Montreal Royals farm team. "He's got to go somewhere to find out whether he can or cannot pitch," Thompson said. "He's lost the confidence he once had. With it, he's lost everything else too." Since that sensational 15–4 season in '52 during which he also attained the distinction of becoming the first black pitcher to win a World Series game, Black had struggled to achieve the same success and was relegated to the back of the bullpen. Alston had used him in only five games in '54, during which he was strafed for eleven hits, including three homers, and nine runs in just seven innings.

The demotion of Black drew the particular interest of Branch Rickey in Pittsburgh. In one of his last acts as Dodger GM before his acrimonious divorce with O'Malley, Rickey had added the final pieces of his "Great Experiment" to integrate baseball by purchasing Black's and Jim Gilliam's contracts from the Baltimore Elite Giants of the Negro leagues at the end of the 1950 season. If there was one person in baseball anxious to know whether Black could still pitch, it was the old "Mahatma," (as longtime New York sportswriter Tom Meany so aptly nicknamed Rickey "because he was a combination of God, your father and a Tammany Hall leader.") A few weeks after Black reported to Montreal, Rickey summoned his trusty aide, Clyde Sukeforth, to his office. It was Sukeforth whom Rickey had dispatched to Chicago in 1946 to look at Jackie Robinson with the Kansas City Monarchs, telling him, "If you like what you see, bring him back to Brooklyn."

"I want you to go down to Richmond where Montreal is playing and take a look at Joe Black," Rickey said to Sukeforth. "I'm thinking of making a deal for him. The Dodgers have clearly given up on him, but I want to know if he's got a sore arm."

Sukeforth, as was his custom, arrived at the ballpark in Richmond midafternoon, three to four hours before the start of the game, and took a seat in the stands to watch the Royals taking batting practice. It wasn't long before his attention focused on a lithe, dark-skinned player shagging flies in right field. After each catch the player unleashed one laser-like throw after another, each of them right on the mark, to home plate. "Who's *this*?" Sukeforth said to himself, looking at his roster sheet.

The player was Roberto Clemente. Sukeforth recounted in a 1996 interview at his home in Waldoboro, Maine:

I didn't know anything about him because there was very little information to be had about him. It turned out the Dodgers were hiding him out in Montreal because he was signed to a minor league contract and not on their forty-man roster, which meant he was subject to the draft that winter, where we were going to have the

number-one pick because of finishing last. I saw him run and throw,
and that was all I needed to see. I went back to my hotel room and
wrote Mr. Rickey a note that said: "I haven't seen Joe Black, but I
have your number-one draft pick. For $4,000 you'll never get this
kind of talent."

Over the years there have been many theories espoused for
why the Dodgers didn't protect a talent like Clemente on their
forty-man roster after having their Triple A Montreal team sign
the nineteen-year-old outfielder from the Santurce team in the
Puerto Rican winter league in 1953 for a $10,000 bonus. After
all, the Giants also heavily pursued Clemente, an acclaimed high
school baseball and track star in Puerto Rico. At the time baseball had a rule that players signed to bonuses of $6,000 or more
had to be kept on the twenty-five-man major league roster for
two years. The Giants, therefore, apparently deciding Clemente
needed more seasoning in the minor leagues, kept their offer under $6,000. Buzzie Bavasi always maintained the Dodgers felt
the same way—that Clemente was a raw talent who would be
overmatched if he went straight to the big leagues, and this is
why they instead signed him to a Triple A Montreal contract.
There was also the theory, which Bavasi never denied, that the
Dodgers only signed Clemente to keep him from going to the
Giants. Years later, after Clemente had established himself as one
of the finest all-around right fielders in baseball history, Bavasi,
in a bit of revisionist thinking, said, "For publicity reasons alone
we couldn't afford to have the Giants have both Mays and Clemente in their outfield."

But the one prevailing theory that no one in baseball would
ever admit was the unwritten, unspoken, unspecified "quota"
of black players that clubs could have on their twenty-five-
man active rosters. With Robinson, Campanella, Newcombe,

Gilliam, Black, and Sandy Amoros (the black Cuban outfielder who won the International League batting title with a .353 average, plus one hundred RBI, at Montreal in '53), the Dodgers figured to have six black players in the majors in '54, two more than the next most-integrated team, the Giants. To add a seventh would make it more than 25 percent of their twenty-five-man roster.

For Sukeforth, the opportunity to heist a potentially great player from the Dodgers was almost as satisfying as it was for Rickey, as his parting from Brooklyn had likewise bitter undertones. In 1951 Sukeforth was the Dodgers' bullpen coach and, therefore, the person who answered the phone when manager Charlie Dressen called down to ask which reliever, Clem Labine or Ralph Branca, was ready to relieve in the ninth inning of the third playoff game against the Giants at the Polo Grounds, with two on, one out, and Bobby Thomson coming to bat. Sukeforth's response was, "Labine just bounced one," to which Dressen said, "Okay, send me Branca." But after the game, after Thomson had connected for the "shot heard 'round the world" a couple of feet over the Polo Grounds' short left field porch, Dressen told reporters he'd relied on Sukeforth's opinion. "Only at the Polo Grounds [where the home run landed barely 296 feet away] was that a bad pitch," Sukeforth, still bitter forty-five years later, said. "Of course Charlie didn't hesitate to point the finger. That was it for me. I couldn't work there anymore. Mr. O'Malley later came to me and told me he wanted me to stay, but I told him the same thing. I also already had an offer to rejoin Mr. Rickey in Pittsburgh."

On his way out of the ballpark after scouting Clemente shagging those flies, as the classic fox in the hen house, Sukeforth related he couldn't resist chiding Montreal manager Max Macon. "I told Max to take good care of our boy."

A week after Snider saved the Memorial Day victory over the Phillies, the Dodgers had another close call in their winning streak when they escaped with a rain-abbreviated five-inning 7–6 win over the Braves in Milwaukee. It was a fiasco of a game, played amid 40-degree temperatures, driving rain, two stoppages of play, and a vehemently protested missed count by home plate umpire Lee Ballanfant. When it was finally called, at 12:18 a.m., with the Dodgers declared victors, Dick Young unleashed a torrent of outrage in his story for the Brooklyn faithful:

> *Milwaukee—This is directed to Warren Giles, president of the NL, or Ford Frick, Commissioner of Baseball, or to Sen. Joseph McCarthy (R-Wis.) if necessary. Somebody should investigate the fraud that was committed here tonight under what is left of the good name of baseball. By playing in almost constant rain they managed to get in five innings by the time the travesty was called at 12:18 in the morning. Because the Dodgers were ahead at the time, 7–6, they took first place away from the Braves. But what is evidently more important to the powers-that-be, the cash wound up in the till and 34,044 rain checks were avoided.*

The Dodgers' May-into-June winning streak finally came to an end on June 12, with a 5–1 loss to the Reds in Cincinnati. After taking the second two games of that series, they returned home to Brooklyn, where they lost two out of three to the Braves to fall out of a first-place tie with the surging Giants, who had won nine of eleven.

It was absurd to think this was the turning point of the Dodgers' season, that they would never again enjoy the fruits of first place, especially after they swept the next four games against the lowly Cubs, whose only ray of hope for better times ahead had been the play of Gene Baker and Ernie Banks, their new double-play combination and graduates of the Negro Leagues. Banks was batting .282 with seven homers, and Baker was at .271 before being sidelined May 30 when he was hit on the wrist with a pitch. The Dodgers completed their thirteen-game Ebbets Field homestand by winning five of the final six against the Reds and Cardinals. But the Giants were even hotter on their homestand, winning eleven of thirteen leading up to their three-game showdown with the Dodgers at the Polo Grounds.

Despite the Dodgers' continued hot play after falling out of first place, there was unsettling news for Alston regarding his pitching. On June 23 Johnny Podres, the brilliant young lefty whose 7–4 record led the staff, underwent an emergency appendectomy after complaining of stomach cramps for several days. The twenty-one-year-old Podres, from upstate Glens Falls, New York, was already showing himself to be one of the top young pitchers in the National League after a meteoric one-and-a-half-year apprenticeship in the Dodgers farm system, during which he completely dominated the Class D Mountain States League in '51 with a 21–3 record and league-leading 228 strikeouts and 1.67 ERA. He was jumped all the way to Triple A Montreal the next year and earned a spot on the big club's pitching staff out of spring training in '53. It was Podres who'd beaten the Giants, 5–3, on May 30 in the last meeting between the two rivals, but now he would be sidelined for a month—a critical loss for Alston. In addition, Newcombe, after struggling to a 5.16 ERA in his first nine starts, was shut down with a sore arm for two weeks from June 7 to 18.

Big Newk was back for the Giants' series and pitched creditably—seven innings, five hits, two runs—in the first game on June 29, but he was not a factor in what was another classic encounter between the two borough rivals. Sal Maglie took a five-hit, 2–0 shutout into the ninth inning, only to be undone by

Campanella's two-out, game-tying homer. Into extras it went as
the bullpens—Marvin Grissom for the Giants and Jim Hughes
and Billy Loes for the Dodgers—kept it deadlocked into the thirteenth. In the top of the thirteenth Dodgers' rookie Don Hoak
broke the tie with a solo home run. That also broke a string of
seventeen consecutive scoreless innings of relief for the thirty-
six-year-old Grissom, who'd been mostly unhittable all season
for the Giants and came into the game with a 1.48 ERA. But
in the bottom of the inning Loes encountered a lapse of control and walked the bases full before yielding a two-out, two-run
game-winning pinch-hit single to Dusty Rhodes, Leo Durocher's
ultimate man in the clutch.

The Giants won the next game, 5–2, when they again vic-
timized the Dodger bullpen with three eighth-inning runs on
Hughes's two-out, bases-loaded walk to Alvin Dark as well as
a two-run single by Whitey Lockman. On Thursday, July 1,
they completed the sweep, 5–2, to expand their first-place lead
to four games over the Dodgers. And once again it was Durocher's magnificent "ice man," Rhodes, who delivered the winning blow with yet another two-run, pinch single, this one in
the eighth after the Dodgers had tied the score, 2–2, an inning
earlier with a pair of solo homers by Campanella and Carl Furillo. The Giants' winning rally had been set up by a rare error
of judgment and then commission by Campanella, who fielded
Hank Thompson's bunt and ill-advisedly tried to get Lockman,
who'd gotten a good jump and was almost at the bag, at second. Campy's throw then sailed into center field for a two-base
error. From his perch in the press box Young watched, aghast,
the Dodgers' collapse and all but conceded the season to the
Giants in his story the next day, in which he wrote, "What else
but a team touched with star dust could have benefited from the
worst play Roy Campanella has made in his entire, magnificent

career? The boys will resume this relationship in Brooklyn next Tuesday, Wednesday and Thursday, where The Faithful have revised their motto to 'Wait 'til Next year.'"

He wasn't far wrong. The three-game series at Ebbets Field resulted in another Giants' sweep, this one by a combined score of 26–6, in which Durocher's men clubbed eleven homers, three off Erskine and two off Newcombe. With their second-place deficit now swelled to six and a half games, Alston called a team meeting after the embarrassing 11–2 finale and aired his troops out. "You can be sure I didn't hand out any praise," the manager said with a trace of irritation. "What would you tell players who had just lost three straight—that they were just dandy?" Then he ordered them back out to the field for extracurricular practice. Later Bavasi took further punitive action by shaking up the roster with the second recall of Amoros, hitting .361 at Montreal, as well as the demotion of outfielder Dick Williams and reserve first baseman Charlie Kress.

The addition of Amoros to the major league roster set the stage for another racial "quota" being broken in baseball, even if it, surprisingly, got very little attention. Following the Giants' sweep, the Dodgers bounced back to close out the homestand by beating the Phillies three out of four. But then they went into Milwaukee for a five-game set with the third-place Braves and lost three out of the first four. On the July 17 getaway day, when the Dodgers escaped with a 2–1 win in eleven innings, Alston had Newcombe on the mound and, for the first time in history, four other black players in the lineup: Robinson at third, Gilliam at second, Campanella behind the plate, and Amoros in left field. Never before had a manager fielded a lineup with more black players than whites, but in the newspaper coverage the next day only Dick Young seemed to realize this was one social issue far more significant than the baseball game.

Mike Gavin in the *Journal-American* made no mention of it at all; Roscoe McGowen in the *Times* buried it as his third "game note" at the bottom of his story; Gus Steiger in the *Post* didn't get to it until the seventh paragraph of his story, in which he wrote, "With Amoros in left field, there were five colored players in the Dodger lineup, thereby disproving the theory that the club was reluctant to have more Negroes on the field at one time than white players." Roger Kahn, in the *Herald-Tribune*, said he'd wanted to lead with it, but out of concern his editors would frown on leading with the social aspects of the game, waited until his third paragraph before writing, "Five of the Dodger starters were Negro players, and there are those who have hinted in print and said directly that a clandestine baseball law prohibited one team's use of more than four Negro players at any one time. If such a law existed, Walter Alston appeared to be unaware of it."

Young, however, addressed the issue head-on in his lead: "The Brooks made baseball history today by playing five Negroes in the starting nine. They also made a bit of history by winning for a change. Both developments took considerable time." But for the rest of his story Young wrote about the game and made no mention of the unspoken, implied quota that had existed in baseball once teams like the Dodgers began employing more than four black players.

A run of seven wins in eight games at the end of July enabled the Dodgers to get back to within two games of the first-place Giants. Suddenly, however, there was an interloper in the race in Charlie Grimm's Braves, who were in fourth place, fifteen and a half games behind two weeks earlier, when they began a 25–5 tear that closed them, on August 15, at a scant three and a half games from the lead. In the process they swept a three-game series from the Giants at the Polo Grounds and took three out of four from the Dodgers at Ebbets Field, July 30–August 2. In the third game of the Dodger series, Braves first baseman Joe Adcock tied one major league record and broke another by becoming only the fifth player in history to hit four home runs in a game while also accumulating eighteen total bases. Adcock connected off four different Dodgers pitchers, Newcombe, Erv Palica, Pete Wojey, and Podres, who had just returned from his appendectomy surgery.

Afterward Adcock revealed he'd achieved his feat using a borrowed bat. "I broke my regular bat last night," Adcock said, "so I used one belonging to [reserve catcher] Charlie White. I could hardly lift the bat! It's the heaviest on the team. If I played for the Dodgers I'd hit 35 homers a year in this park, easy."

Adcock was a one-man wrecking crew against the Dodgers. In the Friday night 9–3 Braves win he'd had a homer, a double, and three RBI against Erskine, and the five homers and seven extra base hits in two games had also tied a major league mark. After all that Adcock had to know there would be retribution, and it came in his third at-bat on Sunday, after he'd stroked another double. The Braves were in the process of completing a third-straight rout, this one 14–6, when Adcock came to bat in the fourth and was struck by a pitch behind his ear by Dodger reliever Clem Labine. Though conscious, Adcock was carried off the field on a stretcher. Fortunately, he suffered only a headache, and for that he credited the plastic helmet he was wearing that, ironically, was the creation of Branch Rickey, who'd made it a prerequisite for all his Pittsburgh Pirate hitters.

"When a fellow throws me high and tight, I don't mind. I can duck those," Adcock said. "But when he throws behind your head, he means business."

Labine, however, insisted the "hit" wasn't deliberate. "I was only trying to brush him back," he said, "but instead of twisting back, he actually ducked into the pitch."

Another key factor in the Braves' second-half surge was the emergence of the rookie Hank Aaron in the cleanup spot. In a fifteen-game stretch from July 24 to August 10 Aaron had fifteen RBI while raising his batting average from .264 to .283. On August 7 William Brower of the *Chicago Black Defender* wrote proudly about how three black players, Aaron and the Cubs' Ernie Banks and Gene Baker, were all leading contenders for the NL Rookie of the Year award: "Tan performers are thick in the competition for the honor this year. Aaron, the 20-year old cleanup hitter for the Braves, and Baker, who has shown surprising power for the Cubs, right now are among the leaders for the coveted designation."

Brower then went on to write, with clear distress, "The American League is bereft of outstanding Negro rookies. After a fast start on the mound, Bob Trice deteriorated so rapidly that he requested the Philadelphia Athletics to option him to Ottawa where he was 20–10 last season. His former teammate, Vic Power, has been a disappointment as well. Tried in both the outfield and first base, Vic has not hit up to expectations."

It did look as though Aaron had an excellent shot at winning the National League's top rookie honors, filling the Braves' offensive void, as he had, after the loss of Bobby Thomson to a broken ankle in the spring. But then, in going 4-for-4 in the second game of a doubleheader against the Reds on September 5, Aaron suffered the exact same fate as Thomson: he broke his ankle sliding into third base on a triple. He was hitting a solid .280 at the time, with thirteen homers and sixty-nine RBI in 122 games. A week later the Braves were dealt another blow when a pitch from the Dodgers' Newcombe struck Adcock on the right wrist, end-ing his season as well. The Braves were 80–54, in second place, four games behind, when Aaron went down. They went 9–11 the rest of the way without him and finished third, eight games out. Their one consolation: on September 6 the Braves became the first NL team in history to draw 2 million fans at home—in little ol' Milwaukee, no less—an achievement that set off further alarm bells for Walter O'Malley in his frustrating haggle with the New York City parks commissioner, Robert Moses, over a new stadium in Brooklyn to replace Ebbets Field.

Regarding that season, Aaron later said,

> *I wound up finishing behind Wally Moon of the Cardinals. Who knows what would've happened if I hadn't broke my ankle. I did struggle adjusting to major league pitching the first half of the year, and I wasn't flashy. I didn't steal a lot of bases. Moon hit .304 that year, and I'd probably have had a hard time catching him. But it was still a very satisfying season for me because I knew I belonged in the big leagues.*
>
> *I especially enjoyed playing all those games against the Dodgers because I got to see Jackie up close. I watched his mannerisms and copied everything he was doing—the way he took infield and batting practice. That was who I wanted to be.*

However, throughout most of his twenty-three-year career, Aaron demonstrated it was not in his nature to be as outspoken and in-your-face confrontational as Robinson.

In their surge into the pennant race the Braves were equal-opportunity intruders, with a second three-game sweep, August 6–8, of the Giants in two weeks. Suddenly the Giants, who had maintained a comfortable lead over the Dodgers in the standings most of July and August, were appearing to slip. On Friday the 13th they invaded Ebbets Field for a three-game series, only to suffer yet another sweep, enabling the Dodgers to close to a scant half-game of them, the closest the Dodgers had been to first place since June 13.

"Even though we'd lost those two series to the Braves and Dodgers almost back to back, there was no panic among us," said Monte Irvin later. "Maybe if it had been the previous year, when the Dodgers were overwhelmingly the best team in the league, but we knew this year was different. We had the pitching and we had Willie. I remember Leo telling us, 'Just keep plugging, fellas. We're all right.'"

Dick Young, however, wasn't so sure. "The Giants isn't dead, but they're growing sicker by the moment," was his lead after the Dodgers' 9–4 win on Sunday completed the sweep.

Except it was a moment that passed. After staggering out of Ebbets, the Giants proceeded to win nine of their next ten games. At the same time the Dodgers went 3–4 in their next seven games against the Phillies and Pirates, and once again it was an opportunity lost as their deficit was back to four games.

And even when a six-game winning streak at the end of August—capped by a couple of 12–4, 11–4 retribution drubbings of the Braves in Milwaukee—moved the Dodgers back to a game and a half of first place, they promptly lost eight of their next ten to fall six games behind. As the maddening losses mounted, so too did the tensions between Robinson and Alston. It was Robinson's contention that Alston simply wasn't an adequate leader—too laid back, not nearly the game tactician that Dressen was, and incapable of instilling confidence in his team. Finally, on September 1, the simmering Robinson-Alston tinder box exploded at Wrigley Field in Chicago.

"Jackie's problem was that he tried to be too aggressive, and too often that was to his detriment," recalled the Giants' Monte

Irvin. "Pee Wee [Reese] was the captain of the team, but sometime you'd never know it. Jackie'd be yelling all this stuff from the dugout, daring us to come get him or whatever, and we'd yell over to Pee Wee, 'Hey Pee Wee, aren't you the captain?'"

The Dodgers had lost the last two games of the Milwaukee series to close out the month of August, and now in the third inning at Wrigley they were in the process of wiping out a 4–0 deficit to the Cubs when Snider sliced a liner into the left-center field bleachers that should have been a game-tying two-run homer. But between the sun and all the white-shirted fans in the bleachers, third-base umpire Bill Stewart apparently lost sight of the ball, and when it wound up bouncing back onto the field, he ruled it a double. As soon as Stewart made his call, the enraged Robinson charged out of the Dodger dugout, right past Alston, who was in the third-base coach's box, and confronted the umpire. For a couple of minutes Robinson raged at Stewart until suddenly realizing no one had followed him out there. Embarrassed, he turned and trotted back to the dugout. He was not through venting, however. Citing the fact that Alston, who had a far better view of the ball from third base, made no effort to argue the call with Stewart, Robinson fumed after the 9–5 loss, "If that guy [Alston] hadn't stood standing out there like a wooden Indian, this club might go somewhere. That was a play that meant a run in a tight ballgame, so whether I was right or wrong, it was close enough for him to protest. But not him. Not Alston. What kind of manager is that?"

Indeed, it had been a rocky and unsettling maiden season for the Dodger skipper; the old guard Dodgers—Robinson, Snider, Reese, and others—were not at all convinced he had the stuff for managing a veteran major league team. The pitching Alston had so worried about in the spring had also proved worthy of that concern, as Erskine regressed mightily from his twenty-win season the year before; Newcombe was nowhere near his preservice, twenty-win form; Podres was never the same after his appendectomy; and Labine's ERA ballooned more than a run per game. Somewhere out in Oakland Charlie Dressen was smiling, while Dick Young's blue-collar Brooklyn constituency was already beginning its seemingly eternal lament of "wait 'til next year."

CHAPTER
10

TWILIGHT OF THE GODS

A S JULY TURNED TO AUGUST IN THE SUMMER OF 1954 AMERICANS braced for the schools' integration fallout from the May 17 *Brown vs. Board of Education* Supreme Court decision. At the time of the decision seventeen southern and border states along with the District of Columbia were required by law to have segregated elementary schools. In the years to come, there would be lawsuits and widespread violence in the South in response to federal orders that school systems and the state universities become integrated.

For the time being, however, 1954 remained a quieter time in America, where the only changes in the offing from what the country had grown accustomed to for much of the postwar era appeared to be on both the pop music cultural front, where singers like Perry Como, Patti Page, and Nat King Cole had regularly topped the Billboard charts, and in baseball, where the

Yankees regularly finished atop the AL standings. Though they didn't realize it at the time, the pop crooners, Como & Co., who at the conclusion of World War II had gradually replaced the Big Bands of Tommy Dorsey, Glenn Miller, and Benny Goodman as the most popular music in America, were now themselves about to give way to the Rock 'n' Roll invasion. At the same time the Yankees, after a dominance of six world championships in the last seven years, were also showing signs of vulnerability.

The record that was considered to be the forerunner to the 1950s Rock 'n' Roll/Doo Wop wave, *Sh-Boom* by the Crew Cuts, arrived on the Billboard pop charts in midsummer '54. It had been recorded earlier in the year by the Chords, a black rhythm-and-blues group, and was one of the first crossover hits from the R&B charts. With its goofy lyrics of mostly gibberish, "Hey nonny ding dong, alang, and alang alang. Boom ba-doh, baddoo ba doodle day" and "Every time I look at you, something is on my mind—dat-dat-dat-dat-dhu," the record was a sharp departure from the pop standards. It rose quickly to the number-one spot by August 20 and remained there for the next seven weeks, all the while evoking hand wringing and the distressed cries from parents, as though there was some sort of innate sexual connotation in it all: "What kind of a song is that? What is it saying? It has no lyrics!" In May 1954 Bill Haley and the Comets recorded what would later be acclaimed as the definitive Rock 'n' Roll anthem, "Rock Around the Clock," although it would not become so until the following spring, when it was used as the background song for the hit movie *Blackboard Jungle*, about juvenile delinquency in America. And in July Elvis Presley launched his career as the "King of Rock 'n' Roll" when, at a recording session for Sam Phillips, the legendary music impresario for Sun Records in Memphis, Tennessee, he cut his first commercial single, "That's All Right."

Meanwhile, after spending most of the first three months of the season in the unaccustomed position of third place, the Yankees climbed into second at the beginning of July and briefly tied the Indians for first on July 20, only to fall back into second the next day when they absorbed a 15–3 drubbing from the White Sox. On August 1 they were still in second, two and a half games behind the Indians, and for the season had spent a total of only three days in first place. This was in stark contrast to the previous five straight world championship years, during which the Yankees spent a total of 465 days in first place.

Casey Stengel was in an uncharacteristically wistful and reflective mood the night of July 30 as he celebrated his sixty-fourth birthday at a dinner with the Yankee beat writers in downtown Baltimore. Earlier that day the pitiful Orioles, who would go on to lose one hundred games their first year in Baltimore as the transplanted St. Louis Browns, had climbed out of last place in the American League by pummeling the Yankees, 10–0, as Allie Reynolds took only his second loss of the season against ten wins. Considering how so many of his spring training concerns had been realized—he'd already used eight different starting pitchers, with nobody stepping up to replace Vic Raschi adequately as a durable top-of-the-rotation big winner; Phil Rizzuto, nearing thirty-six, had gone even further back at shortstop and was hitting a paltry .202; second baseman Jerry Coleman, at .235, had failed to regain his preservice hitting form of three years earlier; Eddie Robinson, with just two home runs and eleven RBI, had been a complete bust as the supposed power-bat replacement for Johnny Mize at first base; and Enos Slaughter had missed nearly two months with a broken wrist—Casey had every reason to feel grateful the Yankees were only two and a half games behind the Indians at the end of July. What had especially heartened Stengel was the emergence of surprise stars of 1954—his guy, outfielder Irv Noren, and rookie right-handed starting pitcher, Bob Grim—and this had helped offset a lot of the other adversity. Given the chance to play regularly in the outfield when Slaughter went down, Noren had made the most of it, batting .350 and playing all three outfield positions, while first-year man Grim, 8–3 as a spot starter and middle reliever the first three months of the season, pitched himself into the starting rotation by hurling a five-hit shutout over Washington on July 4, then reeled off four more wins in July.

On this night, however, Stengel seemed more consumed with the Yankees' inability to overtake the Indians for four months. "I am paid by the Yankees to win, just as the players are paid to win," he said, "and if we can't do it, they should get rid of me and get someone else who can."

"Did we hear you right, Casey? You're saying the Yankees should fire you if they don't win, after you've won five straight world championships?" one of the writers asked agitatedly.

"Yep, that's what I said," Stengel replied. "If I can't win for them, they ought to fire me and get someone else. The whole history of this ballclub is that of getting fellers who can win and getting rid of those who can't. The same thing should go for the manager. They got rid of someone else to get me, didn't they? Well, if I don't come through, they should go out and get someone to win."

Stengel's distress was quickly eased when the Yankees won the next three games in Baltimore in preparation for another huge three-game series in Cleveland with the Indians, who continued to maintain their two-and-a-half-game lead. Following a Monday off day, Whitey Ford beat the Indians in the opener, tossing a complete game, 2–1, a four-hitter, with the only Cleveland run being a solo homer by Larry Doby in the first inning. After the Indians won the next day, 5–2, knocking out Reynolds after just four innings, Grim, aided by a pair of homers from Mickey Mantle, outdueled Early Wynn by hurling six and two-thirds innings of shutout ball in a 5–2 Yankee win that again reduced their deficit to one and a half games. Once again it had been Doby who provided the only Indians' runs in the loss, with a two-run homer off reliever Johnny Sain in the eighth.

For the Yankees it was by far their biggest win of the year. A loss would've dropped them five games behind in that column to the Indians. Otherwise, four months into the season the two teams couldn't be more evenly matched. In their seventeen games against each other to that point, the Yankees had a 9–8 advantage and had outscored the Indians by a scant one run, 84–83. Since June 8 the Yankees had had to play .750 ball (42–14) at the same time the Indians were 40–16, just to stay close. They had done so despite constant scrambling and patching on Stengel's part with his starting rotation, as compared to his counterpart, Al Lopez, whose mainstay starters, Bob Lemon, Early Wynn, and Mike Garcia, and rotation back-enders, the veteran Bob Feller and Art Houtteman, had pitched consistently well and were all headed for double-digit victory totals.

With the thirty-seven-year-old Reynolds and fellow rotation senior, thirty-six-year-old Eddie Lopat, both showing signs of wearing down, Yankees general manager George Weiss signed veteran Ralph Branca, the former Dodger who'd been bothered by arm troubles the previous two seasons, off waivers from the Tigers for rotation insurance. (For Weiss, it was becoming an especially trying season. On July 27 Arthur "Red" Patterson, the popular Yankees public relations director who the year before had gained nationwide fame by taking a tape measure to determine the distance of Mickey Mantle's tremendous home run hit out of Griffith Stadium in Washington, announced his resignation from the team, citing a clash of personalities with the Yankees general manager. Patterson had become disgruntled when Weiss passed him over for the assistant general manager's job in April, and the final straw for him was when Weiss castigated him for giving a couple of free passes to a game to the elevator operator at the Yankees' Fifth Avenue offices.)

After the August 5 victory over the Indians Stengel was effusive in his praise of Grim, who, out of nowhere, had now emerged as his top winner at 14–4. The son of a Brooklyn bartender, Grim was signed by the Yankees in 1948 off the same Queens-Nassau, Long Island, sandlots where they found Whitey Ford. The Giants, Cubs, and Braves had also pursued him, but the Yankees were the most persistent and signed him for $3,000. He was moving gradually up through the Yankees' minor league system, all the way to Class A Binghamton of the Eastern League, where he was 16–5 in 1951, when he was drafted into the Marines for a two-year hitch. It was after noticing he'd gone 23–4 in his second year with the Camp Lejeune, North Carolina, Marine Corps team, that the Yankees decided to invite him to their '54 pre-spring training instructional league camp in St. Petersburg. Stengel said,

> The kid was outranked by quite a few pitchers in our instructional league last February. But where are they now? He showed me plenty in the school and even more all spring, even though he wasn't even on our [forty-man] roster. I kept hoping he would lose so I could send him back, but he was our best pitcher in camp. He don't have any one above-average pitch, unless it's his slider, which they tell me he taught himself. But he knows how to pitch, keeps the ball down, pitches to his spots. But for Grim and Whitey Ford [11–6 with a team-leading 2.79 ERA to that point], we'd be out of the race by now. Now I just gotta make sure when he's in his daddy's tavern he doesn't get behind the bar anymore and start pourin' drinks. When he goes there from now on, he's gotta understand he's a Yankee.

"My baseball experience with the Marines was very important to me," Grim said. "I was always physically fit. I always studied pitching. I studied the batters. As we rarely ran into the same opposition more than twice, you had to reach conclusions on batters fast. I throw a slider, fastball, and curve ball—I'm not fooling around with any other pitches—and I have always had control."

Following Grim's August 5 win the Yankees lost two out of three to the Tigers in Detroit, suffering a significant casualty in the Sunday finale when Gil McDougald, Stengel's second-base/third-base "swingman," suffered a wrist injury that would sideline him for a month. But then the Yankees embarked on a ten-game winning streak to maintain their stubborn two-and-a-half-game deficit to the Indians as they went into Boston for a three-game series with the Red Sox. Before their August 18 game against the Athletics in Philadelphia they were taken aback when Rizzuto, their aging, slumping former AL MVP, appeared on the field wearing eyeglasses. According to Rizzuto, his left eye had been bothering him, so a few days earlier Weiss had ordered him to see an optometrist, who recommended he try using specs. "Guess I'm getting old," Rizzuto said with a weak laugh. "The left lens is an optical glass. The right one is just plain glass because that eye is all right."

Around the batting cage before the first game in Boston two days later Yogi Berra greeted Rizzuto, teasing him, "How ya doin', 'Specs'?"

"You know what, 'Yog'?" Rizzuto said. "I was thinking before of the time Lefty Gómez started wearing glasses. I never believed him, but the story he told me was that he got out on the mound and put on his glasses and suddenly noticed Jimmie Foxx was at the plate. It was such a terrifying sight, Lefty said, that he tore off his glasses and never wore them again!"

At that point Enos Slaughter joined the conversation with a story about Paul Waner, the great Pittsburgh Pirates hitter who won three batting titles in the twenties and thirties. "Paul Waner once tried wearing glasses," Slaughter said, "even though everyone knows what eagle eyes he had. The story I heard was that when he was wearin' his glasses he said the baseball looked as big as a baseball, but when he didn't wear 'em, it looked as big as a grapefruit."

"Let that be a lesson to you, Phil," laughed Berra.

"I'll tell you what I'm discovering," Rizzuto said. "They help me in the field, but when I'm at bat, they're not quite wide enough. I'm looking part out of the glasses and part not looking out of them. I'm gonna have to get a pair of wider lenses."

The Boston series was a disaster, beginning Friday when Grim suffered his first loss, 4–3, in over a month. At least Stengel's curious decision to start the rookie Bill Skowron at third base and in the leadoff spot, both unnatural places for him, proved inspired when the hulking righty slugger went 2-for-4 with a homer. But Red Sox righty Willard Nixon gave up only two other hits over eight innings, and Boston overcame a 3–1 deficit with a two-run double by rookie Harry Agganis off Grim in the seventh and another RBI double by Nixon in the eighth. To that point in the season Nixon had pretty much been the difference in the pennant race, with a 4–0 record against the Yankees, as opposed to 0–4 against the Indians.

The next day one of those classic Fenway Park slugfests was a killer loss for the Yankees, as they'd managed to come back from 5–1 with a five-run rally in the eighth inning on an RBI single by Skowron, an RBI double by Gene Woodling, and a three-run homer by Hank Bauer, only to blow the one-run lead in the ninth when Agganis tied it with an RBI triple off Yankee reliever Johnny Sain. Both teams then scored a pair of runs in the tenth before the Yankees went ahead again, 9–8, in the twelfth on a sacrifice fly by Ford, whom Stengel had summoned for a rare relief appearance after a tiring Sain had given up a single and a two-run homer to Red Sox catcher Sammy White to start the tenth. But in the bottom of the twelfth, after striking out Ted Lepcio to start the inning, Ford proceeded to load the bases on a single and a pair of walks, and this was where Red Sox left fielder Don Lenhardt ended it with a two-run walk-off single. Compounding the loss, Berra, the Yankees' leading RBI man, was thrown out of the game by home plate umpire Bill Grieve for arguing a 3–1 pitch leading off the tenth inning. "This was a game the Yankees never should have lost," wrote Joe Trimble in the *Daily News.* "With great effort they came from far back to go ahead in the eighth inning. But Johnny Sain, whose brilliance seems to be dimming with overwork, couldn't hold it. He went within one strike of victory in the ninth and gave up the tying run . . . and in the 12th with victory in his big left paw, Whitey Ford went wild."

The lost weekend in Boston was completed with an 8–2 Yankee loss on Sunday when the Red Sox tagged Harry Byrd for eight hits and five runs in six innings, including a two-run homer and a two-run double by Ted Williams, and then added three more off Reynolds in relief. Making the sweep even more painful, however, was the news that Woodling would be lost for the season after X-rays revealed a broken right thumb, suffered while making a futile effort to catch Agganis's triple off the left field wall the day before. Though he was having a bit of an off year, with just three homers and his average some thirty points below his lifetime .280, the thirty-two-year-old left-handed-hitting Woodling had been a Yankee mainstay throughout the 1949–1953 world championship years with a .318 average for those five World Series. He was also a particular favorite of Stengel, who first became impressed with his hitting prowess in the Pacific Coast League in 1948 when Casey was managing in Oakland and Woodling won the batting title with a .385 average for San Francisco. Now Woodling was reduced to a spectator as the Yankees prepared to mount their last run on an unwavering Indians team, which won three straight against the Orioles to increase their lead to five and a half games while Stengel's men were being swept in Boston. And unforeseen in all of this was the fact that Woodling, a five-ring Yankee warrior, had played his last game for them.

With the season seemingly slipping away, Weiss was running out of responses. After the Sunday game in Boston he announced he had purchased the contract of veteran right-hander Jim Konstanty, the 1950 NL Most Valuable Player, from the Phillies in hopes that, if nothing else, the fading thirty-seven-year-old reliever might be able to take some of the burden off Sain in the bullpen. (Weiss would have one more move left in his desperate effort to overtake the Indians: his September 3 purchase of veteran left-hander and notorious "wild man" Tommy Byrne from Seattle of the Pacific Coast League. Byrne, who'd begun his career as a Yankee in the forties, was jettisoned to the last-place Browns in '51 after co-owner Dan Topping became exasperated with his chronic control issues, and from there he'd drifted to the White Sox, Senators, and, finally, the minors.)

"I never saw a team try so hard as this one did in Boston," Stengel told the writers the following Tuesday when the team was back at Yankee Stadium for the start of a nine-game homestand. "The effort's been there all season. When you lose two men, first Slaughter and now Woodling, because they run into walls chasing fly balls you know the effort is there. Now it's up to me to get 'em out of this streak. That's where the manager comes in. And don't forget, there are five more games with Cleveland. We ain't helpless yet."

From mid-July it had been essentially a two-team race. For the first three months, however, the Chicago White Sox, who had not won an AL pennant since 1919 or finished fewer than ten games out of first place since 1940, had been an unlikely intruder. They led the league as late as June 12, largely on the efforts of one Orestes "Minnie" Miñoso, a (believed to be) thirty-two-year-old native of Cuba, who, in a brief nine-game cameo with the Indians in 1949, had earned the distinction of being the first black Hispanic player in the major leagues. Though by August the White Sox had faded to third, seven games behind, after being beset with critical knee injuries to first baseman Ferris Fain, the defending AL batting champion, as well as five-time All-Star third baseman George Kell, Miñoso was having himself a Most Valuable Player–caliber season. With four runs batted in, on a homer and a double in the second game of a doubleheader against the Athletics on August 1, Miñoso found himself atop the AL batting leaders at .332 and tied with the Indians' Al Rosen for the RBI lead with seventy-eight. The "Cuban Comet," who'd hit over .300 the previous two seasons and led the American League with eighteen triples in '53, had officially come into his own, now universally recognized by the press and the baseball establishment as one of the best all-around players in the game.

"When I was playing in Cuba [in 1945–46], I knew there was discrimination in the US because there was discrimination in Cuba, just not nearly as bad," Miñoso said in a 2013 interview. "As far as I knew, I couldn't play in the US because it was the law. But I just made my mind up that I was either going to keep playing, always with the thought I would one day go to the major leagues, or not. I was either gonna live or die. I chose to live."

When Jackie Robinson broke baseball's color line by signing with the Dodgers in 1946, Miñoso said, "Now I have a chance to be there. If I don't make it, it won't be because I'm black."

Miñoso was playing for Alex Pompez's New York Cubans of the Negro Leagues when the Indians acquired him in 1948 for $12,000. After spending the 1949 and '50 seasons with the Indians' Triple A San Diego farm club in the Pacific Coast League, he made the big club out of spring training '51 as an outfielder/third baseman, only to be abruptly traded to the White Sox in a three-team deal on April 30.

"I remember being upset about having to leave Cleveland," Miñoso said, "until the general manager, Hank Greenberg, he told me, 'We didn't want to trade you, but they [the White Sox] really wanted you.' I was okay then, and I couldn't wait to get to Chicago."

"I had seen Minnie in the Pacific Coast League for two years when I managed Seattle," said White Sox manager Paul Richards years later. "He had played every position for San Diego. I knew he could run, throw, and hit. I think Cleveland was willing to trade him because they didn't think he could play a position. When [White Sox general manager] Frank Lane asked me where I would play Miñoso, I told him, 'Just get him. I'll find a place for him.' I just knew he was a ballplayer."

According to Miñoso, Richards, a native of Waxahachie, Texas, held a team meeting before Minnie showed up from Cleveland and essentially laid it all out to the White Sox players about what their new teammate could bring to the club—much the same as Leo Durocher did with the Giants players in spring training '54 regarding Willie Mays. "[White Sox shortstop] Chico Carrasquel told me years later that Richards held this meeting in which he said, 'we're getting ourselves a black ballplayer here, and I want everyone here to do the right thing with him. He's here to help us, and he will.'"

As the first black Hispanic player in the majors, Miñoso was faced with two barriers to overcome: the racial one and the lan-

guage one. He did both by sheer force of his effervescent personality and all-out, hustling style of play.

"When I first reached the majors to stay, in '51, there was no
manager harder on me than Jimmie Dykes [of the Athletics],"
Miñoso said. "On the field he called me all kinds of names, a lot
of them racial slurs, then I would see him in the hotel lobby and
he'd call me 'Mr. Miñoso.' He was a lot louder in Philadelphia
than he was in Cleveland and Chicago."

In addition, Miñoso believed it was no accident that, from
1951–1960 he led the American League ten times in hit-by-
pitches. "I have no doubt," he said, "a lot of them were on purpose
because I was black, but I just took it. It really didn't bother me.
I always tried to play with a smile on my face. The way I looked
at it, my job was to play the best that I could, to entertain the
fans. I understood that I had to run everything all out—or else."

For the final six weeks of the '54 season, his team out of the
race, Miñoso had to be content to be part of the subplot involving the Yankees and Indians—the AL batting race that was en-
joined in early August by the Yankees' Noren once he'd reached
the necessary qualifying plate appearances. Miñoso had been
leading most of the summer, with an average hovering around
.330, with the Indians' Rosen and Bobby Avila not far behind.
By late August it had become a three-man race among Noren,
Miñoso, and Avila. On August 29 the Yankees beat the White
Sox, 4–1, for their sixth-straight victory. Noren was 2-for-4,
with an RBI double in the game to raise his league-leading average to .341, while Miñoso went hitless in three at-bats to fall
into a tie with Avila for second at .329. More importantly for
the Yankees, however, was that the six-game winning streak
had gotten them back to within four games of the front-running
Indians on the eve of their final three-game series at Yankee
Stadium.

When Early Wynn shut them down on two hits, 6–1, before a near-capacity crowd of 58,859 in the series opener, it appeared as though the Yankees' season might be about to end right there, at home, without so much as a September stretch. Wynn had indeed made them look flat, tossing no-hit ball into the seventh until Noren broke it up with a homer. But then the next day, September 1, the crafty old lefty Eddie Lopat, backed by Berra's two-run homer, infused new life in the defending champs by stymieing the Indians time and again with his array of off-speed flotsam, scattering nine hits in a complete-game 4–1 win. And when Ford came back and outdueled Bob Lemon in the series finale—a 3–2 Yankee win in which Noren made a saving catch on a long fly ball to the barrier in front of the left-center wall by Cleveland's Hank Majeski with a runner on base in the eighth, and Doby hit a solo homer off Reynolds in relief in the ninth—Stengel could hardly contain himself with the reporters afterward. "We're back in business," he crowed before taking the opportunity to apologize for lifting Ford after eight innings. "Whitey didn't want to come out, but he was working on only three days' rest. I just didn't want to risk anything, which is why I brought in Reynolds."

Any thoughts the Indians may have been shaken by losing two out of three in New York or that this might be a foreboding to a September collapse reminiscent of 1951, when the Indians were in first place as late as September 15 and lost seven of their last ten games to finish five games behind the Yankees, were quickly put to rest when they won seven of their next nine. At the same time Stengel's Yankees faltered again, first losing two out of three to the lowly Senators and then splitting each of their ensuing two-game series with the Red Sox, Orioles, and White Sox. As they headed to Cleveland for the crucial September 12 Sunday doubleheader, they found themselves six and a half

games behind the Indians, their largest deficit of the season. After the gut-wrenching 6–5 loss to the White Sox in Chicago on
Saturday, during which Konstanty gave up the winning run on
a two-out RBI single to Carrasquel in the tenth inning, Stengel,
looking weary and deflated, had little to say other than the obvi-
ous: the Yankees had to win both games of the doubleheader in
Cleveland the next day. The beat writers were equally downcast,
fidgeting nervously while engaging in small talk with Stengel
in an attempt to shift the attention from the deteriorated state
of his team. As they stood there, they couldn't help but notice,
laying on his desk, was a copy of the just-released September
Book-of-the-Month baseball novel, *The Year the Yankees Lost the
Pennant*, by acknowledged Yankees hater Douglass Wallop. It
was about a middle-aged Washington baseball fan who sells his
soul to the devil and is then transformed into a superstar slugger
who comes out of nowhere to lead the perennially losing Senators to an improbable pennant.

"What's this, Casey?" one of the scribes finally said, pointing
to the book. "I hope this isn't some premonition or something."

"It don't mean nothin'. I ain't read it. Some guy sent it to me,"
Stengel snapped. "It's fiction."

AS HE SIPPED MARTINIS IN THE ENGLISH GRILL OVERLOOKING THE
Rockefeller Center skating rink on a warm afternoon in early
September, Roger Kahn was becoming more and more perplexed by the questions his new editor was asking him. A couple of weeks earlier the twenty-six-year-old Kahn had made the
decision to leave the newspaper business and his job as a baseball beat writer for the *New York Herald-Tribune* to sign up with
Time-Life publishing titan Henry R. Luce's new weekly sports
magazine, *Sports Illustrated*, which launched its maiden issue on

August 16, 1954. This was to be the final link in Luce's publishing empire, the perfect companion to his other three weekly
magazines, *Time*, *Life*, and *Fortune*. Whereas his flagship, *Time*,
was established as the dominant newsweekly, found on the desks
of just about every office in the halls of Congress, not to mention the White House itself, *Life* was the most commercially
successful, appealing to the masses with its spectacular array of
photographs of world events, sports, the arts, and Hollywood
personalities. And, with *Fortune*, the signature journal of postwar American business, sports represented the one venue of
American life into which Luce had not yet made a journalistic
foray. Since 1946 McFadden Publications' monthly, *Sport*, with
its lengthy features and profiles (many of them authored by the
nation's foremost writers), quizzes, season previews, and brilliant color photos had been the only mainstream sports publication, with a circulation of around three hundred thousand. But
as a monthly, it was hindered from being topical. Luce's weekly
SI would now fill that in-depth sports news void.

The first issue of *Sports Illustrated*, which featured a cover
photo of Braves slugger Eddie Mathews taking a full cut at the
plate before a packed house crowd in Milwaukee, was 144 pages,
74 of them devoted to advertising, and featured an on-the-spot
by-lined story from Vancouver of the nationally televised race
between the only two four-minute milers, Roger Bannister and
John Landy, two days before deadline; a full-color photo spread
of the Rocky Marciano–Ezzard Charles heavyweight title fight;
a three-page color foldout of reproduction 1954 Topps baseball
cards, along with an accompanying feature on the bubblegum
card war between the Topps and Bowman companies; along with
columns by Red Smith on baseball, Budd Schulberg on boxing,
Billy Talbert on tennis, and Herbert Warren Wind on golf—
all acknowledged authorities on their respective sports. At the

outset *SI* was a huge success, both at the newsstands and, with 350,000 charter subscriptions, the largest circulation launch in magazine history.

But as Roger Kahn was fast discovering in his first week at *SI*, the editors whom Time-Life president Roy Larsen put in charge of the fledgling sports magazine came primarily from the news divisions of *Time* and *Life* and knew precious little about sports or what the hard-core sports fan wanted. This became more and more evident in the subsequent issues, which featured covers of a golf bag, a woman swimmer, yachting, the rodeo, a sports car driver, and a woman horseback rider. In particular, Jack Tibby, the editor with whom Kahn was consuming martinis that September afternoon at the English Grill, appeared to be totally clueless as he discussed the upcoming Yankees-Indians Sunday doubleheader showdown that he had assigned Kahn to cover.

So just who was going to win those important games in Cleveland? Tibby asked at one point.

Kahn, momentarily dumbfounded by the question, replied that he had no idea, that there was no set script like in the theater—this was why he went to the ballpark to find out. Tibby pressed on, suggesting that the writers and reporters, as professionals, knew more than the spectators and, as such, absolutely had a good idea as to who was going to win—so who was it that was going to win on Sunday?

As Kahn related it, into his second martini, Tibby finally wore him down, and Kahn blurted out, flippantly, "Time's up for the Yankees. It's the Twilight of the Gods"—a reference to the Wagnerian opera *Gotterdammerung*, and the Norse mythology about a series of major events being foretold as the result of the death of a number of gods. To Kahn's amazement, Tibby immediately ran with it, and when they got back to the office the editor got out a piece of paper from his desk and began to sketch the outline of the four-page spread he planned for Kahn's story on the doubleheader. And across the top of the first page he scribbled in what he declared to be Kahn's "marvelous headline": The Twilight of the Gods.

So there it was. Kahn was off to Cleveland, armed already with the knowledge of who was to going to win. Now all he needed was for the Yankees to provide the details to be written around his own marvelous headline. On Sunday morning he was having breakfast in the Hotel Cleveland, where the Yankees were staying, when Stengel approached him and congratulated him on his new job, though not without also offering him a word of caution: "You gotta watch them magazine people. They'll make your stuff look funny."

By midmorning, streams of fans, by car and by foot, were making their way down East Ninth and West Third Streets to Cleveland's mammoth Municipal Stadium on the shores of Lake Erie where, by day's end, they were to have formed the largest crowd in history, 86,563, to witness a baseball game, in this case two baseball games that would decide the AL pennant. (Part of the reason for the record crowd was the television blackout of the games. Indians general manager Hank Greenberg had been offered $60,000 for a national telecast of the two games, but he refused to change club policy, in which the Indians had not televised any home games all season, for, in his view, a few extra dollars.)

In the opener Stengel opted for Ford to start over his veteran ace, Reynolds, and Whitey proved up to the task by limiting the Indians to one run and five hits over the first six innings before being forced to leave the game with a muscle pull in his shoulder. Bobby Avila, who had pulled ahead of the Yankees' Noren and the White Sox's Miñoso in the batting race on September 6, broke a scoreless tie between Ford and the Indians' Bob Lemon with a two-out RBI single in the fifth. The next inning the Yankees tied it when Mantle led off by bouncing a double over Dave Philley's head in right field. He was only able to make it to third when Philley nearly made a shoestring catch of Yogi Berra's single. However, Mantle subsequently scored on Noren's sacrifice fly. Any hope of further scoring in the inning on the Yankees' part was snuffed out when Indians' catcher Jim Hegan threw out Berra as he attempted to steal second.

From there Lemon was practically untouchable, limiting the Yankees to only one more hit over the last three innings. In the seventh the Indians provided him with the lead he would not surrender when Reynolds—of whom Harold Rosenthal of the *New York Herald-Tribune* wrote, "the mere mention of his name used to strike terror into the Indians' hearts"—came on to relieve Ford and gave up a one-out bunt single to Al Smith, a walk to Avila, and a back-breaking, two-run double to right-center to Al Rosen. The two RBI gave Rosen his fifth straight hundred-RBI season. He was out of the lineup in the second game, however, resting a sore leg muscle, and after the first inning of the nightcap Larry Doby, also suffering from a leg injury, joined him on the bench.

It didn't matter. Despite the absence of their two best hitters, the Indians shrugged off Berra's two-run homer off Early Wynn in the first inning to scratch together a three-run winning rally off the newly purchased Tommy Byrne in the fifth. To that point Byrne had limited the Indians to just two singles, but with two out in the fifth, he seemed to let up on Wynn, who smacked a down-the-middle breaking pitch into center field for a single. Another single, by Al Smith, moved Wynn to second. Byrne was becoming a bit unraveled now, as Avila scored Wynn with the third-straight single of the inning and took second on the throw home. That brought to the plate the veteran Wally Westlake, Doby's center field replacement, who doubled into left-center for two more runs that proved to be the difference in the ballgame.

As dusk began settling over Municipal Stadium, the Indians had dealt the Yankees their first doubleheader loss of the season, 4–1 and 3–2, to boost their first-place lead back up to eight and a half games, with eleven remaining. Avila had gone 5-for-8 in the doubleheader to lift his league-leading average to .340, whereas Noren, 0-for-5 for the two games, was now down to .325.

"The Yankees were buried with simple honors today and had the best attended funeral ever," wrote Joe Trimble in the *Daily News.*

"This is the way we wanted it," said Al Lopez. "We wanted to beat the Yankees ourselves."

Some fifty-five years later Noren said in an interview with me,

That was maybe the worst day of my life. I roomed with Ford on the road, and I remember him saying to me at breakfast that morning, "I got to get Avila out for you." The overflow fans were all lined up behind the fence in leftfield, and all through the two games they were throwing paper and stuff at me. It had been my best season, and I really wanted to win the batting crown. I read the papers every day, and I could see how Avila was coming and coming. He caught up to me in early September and just kept hitting.

The next morning, as the Yankees gathered in the Hotel Cleveland lobby to leave for the train station and the trip back to New York, Stengel admitted to the writers that for the first time he felt "frightened" over the eight-and-a-half-game deficit, but he still refused to concede the pennant to the Indians. Only after he learned most of the writers were not going to accompany the Yankees back to New York because their editors had instructed them to stay with the Indians for the rest of the season did Casey suddenly turn pale. "You mean they ain't coming?" he exclaimed to traveling secretary Bill McCorry. "Jesus! I've lost my writers!"

A few days later *Sports Illustrated* hit the newsstands with its sixth issue—the one with the rodeo on the cover—with its lead story Roger Kahn's by-lined account of the Indians' triumphant doubleheader sweep of the Yankees under the bold headline, "The Twilight of the Gods." In the first paragraph, after declaring the Indians had demonstrated they were a better team than the five-time world champion New York Yankees, the story summed up, "As drama, it might well have been entitled The Twilight of the Gods. While a band played brassily in left field, the Yankees followed Thor and Wotan into eclipse."

It was a metaphor easily lost on the common fan and one, according to Kahn, that was solely the handiwork of *SI* news editor John Knox "Jack" Tibby.

DEM WUZ SOME GINTS

Talkin' Baseball, the Man and Bobby Feller
The Scooter, the Barber and the Newk
They knew 'em all from Boston to Dubuque
Especially Willie . . . Mickey and the Duke

—TERRY CASHMAN

THE GREAT DEBATE, WHICH RAGED ON FOR YEARS IN NEW YORK saloons and on street corners and sandlots throughout the metropolitan area—Who's the best center fielder in New York: Willie Mays, Duke Snider, or Mickey Mantle?—was at its fever peak in the summer of 1954, if only because all three were also central figures in the pennant races involving their respective Giants, Dodgers, and Yankees, and each had stellar performances in the All-Star Game, in which Snider went 3-for-4 with two runs scored, Mays 1-for-2 and one run scored for the Nationals, and Mantle 2-for-5 with a run scored for the Americans.

At the midway point of the season Mantle was hitting .316, with sixty-four RBI and leading the American League with eighteen homers; Snider was leading the National League in batting at .367, with twenty homers and seventy RBI; and Mays, after his slow start, was hitting .328 and leading the National League with thirty-one homers and seventy-three RBI. And everyone, it seemed, had an opinion and a personal favorite. The *Sporting News* devoted a full-page spread to the Mays-Snider NL portion of the debate, with its Dodgers correspondent, Roscoe McGowen of the *Times*, and Giants correspondent, Joe King of the *World-Telegram*, presenting their cases:

"Twenty-five years ago, Earl Clark, Boston center fielder, caught 12 fly balls against the Dodgers for a record that still stands," wrote McGowen, "but the entire dozen wasn't worth the single catch Snider made high against the wall in Philadelphia on May 31. The Duke had made a lot of other fine catches before and since but that one was the greatest of his career. A box score may show that the Duke made a half-dozen putouts in center field but does not reveal the kind of catches he made. A carload of statistics can not reveal the true measure of Snider's excellence."

King countered, "Duke Snider is one of the outstanding players in the National League, but Willie Mays is one of a kind. It seems drama just waits around until Willie is ready. It is doubtful if any other player in the league can match the electrifying quality of Willie's presence. And when you consider value to the team, Mays is the difference in lifting the otherwise leaderless Giants into the raging fire-eaters they have become this year."

In a late-June column Shirley Povich of the *Washington Post* posed the Willie, Mickey, or Duke question to Garry Schumacher, the longtime Giants publicist, and got an emphatic but predictable response: "They run out there with tape measures on Mantle's long homers and try to make him a big shot personality," grumped Schumacher. "They're trying to build him up as the greatest center fielder since Speaker, and what happens?

Mantle isn't even the best center fielder in town! He runs a bad third to Mays and Snider."

Long after the three retired from baseball, the debate lingered on in the minds of New Yorkers, fueled by the trio's subsequent election to the Hall of Fame and the undying wave of fifties nostalgia, along with the now-classic baseball ditty, "Talkin' Baseball—Willie, Mickey and the Duke," written by baseball balladeer Terry Cashman and performed by him over the years in every major league park. It wasn't until the New York Baseball Writers dinner on January 22, 1995, the last time Mays, Snider, and Mantle ever appeared together, that Mantle deemed to settle the issue once and for all. Citing Mays's .302 career average, 660 homers, and 1,903 RBI to Snider's .295–407–1,333 and his own .298–536–1,509, Mantle told the audience, "I've been asked the question for years, all of us have, but I have to say right here and now: Willie Mays was probably the best of the three of us . . . just look at the statistics."

Monte Irvin added in response,

> *There's no question Willie had the statistics, but he was so much more than just about the stats, especially in 1954. In '54 Duke had the statistics too, but he had so many other guys on the Dodgers who were just as important to their success—Campy, Pee Wee, Jackie. Willie made us a different team, and he had so many different ways to win a ballgame for us. It was like Leo always said about him: there was nothing on a ballfield—hit, hit with power, run, throw, field—he couldn't do. The only thing Willie didn't do was lead us, at least in a spiritual sense. Willie led by example, by his deeds on the field.*

> *Our spiritual leader was Alvin Dark, just like Pee Wee was the Dodgers' leader and Rizzuto for the Yankees. I've often said that if Pee Wee and Rizzuto are in the Hall of Fame, Dark should be too. He was every bit the shortstop they were and the guy on the field we took our lead from.*

As close knit as the 1954 Giants were, with their uniquely blended core of Negro League graduates, Mays, Irvin, and Hank Thompson, and the southern whites, Dark, Whitey Lockman, Dusty Rhodes, Davey Williams, and others—their summer-long stay in first place was not without its moments of in-house friction, most of it generating from the manager.

In the early season Durocher seemed bent on replacing Wes Westrum as his first-string catcher because of his poor hitting. In four seasons as the Giants' number-one catcher, Westrum had barely hit .225. But he was an excellent defensive catcher and handler of pitchers. After first trying Ebba St. Claire, the catcher acquired in the Bobby Thomson trade from Milwaukee, Durocher tried to force-feed rookie Ray Katt, calling him "my number-one catcher." When Katt proved not up to the task defensively, the Giant pitchers implored Durocher to restore the regular catching duties to Westrum because of the confidence they had in him. Durocher finally agreed, and after June 16 the Giants went on a 29–5 streak with Westrum behind the plate.

Then there was Irvin, a .309 lifetime hitter, who was forced to suck up his pride and bite his tongue on the numerous occasions Durocher pinch hit for him or benched him altogether against a right-handed pitcher in favor of the lefty-swinging Rhodes. And there was the game on September 12 against the Cardinals, which the Giants lost 4–3. Durocher curiously sent Rhodes up to pinch hit for the likewise left-handed Don Mueller in the eighth inning against left-handed St. Louis starter Harvey Haddix. Rhodes struck out looking, and Mueller, hitting .331 at the time, was deprived a final at-bat to continue his twenty-one-game hitting streak. Conversely, Rhodes was periodically subject to the manager's wrath—and similarly confined to the bench—because of his fielding lapses. And Dark was only half-kidding in the spring, after watching Durocher fawning over Mays and bestowing daily gifts of clothes and jewelry on the returning prodigy, when he asked Irvin, "Does Leo know there are other guys on this team?"

In fact, other than Mays, Durocher played no favorites with his troops, and when displeased by their performance, he did not hesitate to be openly confrontational. The most public example of that occurred on July 29 in the fifth inning of an 8–0 Giants loss to the Cardinals. Following a six-game losing streak that included a three-game sweep by the resurgent Braves in Milwaukee, the Giants' lead over the Dodgers had shrunk to two games. They snapped the slump with a 10–0 win over the Cardinals, with Johnny Antonelli running his record to 15–2 backed by Rhodes's three home runs. But now, the next day, they were losing again when, with two out in the fifth, Lockman hit a ground ball to first base and, in Durocher's eyes, didn't run it out. When Lockman came back to the dugout Durocher was seen raging at him. "Tell him off, Whitey!" Cardinals' manager Eddie Stanky needled loudly from across the field. The incident became further magnified when the Giants went back on the field and Bobby Hofman had replaced Lockman at first base. Upon realizing he'd been benched, the respected Lockman, who was also the Giants' player rep for what was then a loose-knit players association, threw a glove, a ball, and a towel at Durocher before confronting him in front of the water cooler.

The Durocher-Lockman flap quickly passed, as did most of Leo's confrontations with his players, especially after the Giants manager learned the field had been freshly watered and Lockman had, first, tripped running to first and then thought the ball had gone foul. That was Durocher's way. He'd have it out with a player, and the next day it was a clean slate. He didn't hold grudges, and, besides, the twenty-eight-year-old Lockman, an elite defensive first baseman and .293 lifetime hitter to that point, was actually one of his favorites. (Years later, after his retirement, Lockman served on Durocher's coaching staff with the Cubs and, in 1972, was hand-picked by Durocher to succeed him as manager.)

Lockman grew up in tiny Paw Creek, North Carolina, a suburb of Charlotte, and signed with the Giants as an outfielder straight out of high school in 1943. It took him less than a half-season to work his way up to their Triple A Jersey City farm club in the International League. In 1945, his third season at Jersey City, Lockman, just nineteen, was hitting .317 when the Giants called him up to the Polo Grounds. In thirty-two games for them he was hitting a robust .341 when he was drafted into the Army and later sent to the Pacific for the final months of World War II. His career was further stalled when he suffered a backward dislocation of his right ankle and a broken fibula trying to break up a double play against the Indians in spring training '47, and was sidelined for nearly the entire season. Said Giants manager, Mel Ott: "There is not a player on this team we could spare less."

Midway through 1948, Lockman's first full season with the Giants, Durocher replaced Ott as manager and immediately took a liking to the agile, intense, six-foot-one line-drive hitter with the fluid left-handed swing. "Lockman shows me something new every day," said Durocher. "I didn't realize he was so fine a player. They used to kid me when I first came over to the Giants from Brooklyn and I talked about my kind of ballplayer. Well, I'll tell you about my kind of ballplayer. He's alert, he's quick on the trigger and he wants to win so bad it hurts. No, not wants to win—*has* to win. That's what I'm seeing in Lockman: The perfect ballplayer."

But not so perfect Durocher didn't still want him to change positions. In the spring of 1951, having become convinced that incumbent first baseman Tookie Gilbert, a one-time $50,000 bonus baby who'd hit just .220 in 1950, wasn't going to cut it,

Durocher asked Lockman to make the switch to first from the outfield. Like everything else about Lockman, the transition was smooth, as though he'd played there all his life. A year later he was the NL All-Star first baseman. It didn't matter to Durocher that Lockman was not a power hitter, in a position where you ordinarily would want that. He liked the fact that Lockman's approach was to meet the ball wherever it was pitched and use all the fields. He was one of the few left-handed hitters in the league opposing teams had to play straightaway because of his ability to get extra base hits, even homers, to the opposite field. "He's just magnificent," Durocher gushed. "Becoming a first baseman made him great. He's a guy who'll kill the other side any way you can think of. He goes into the hole, he hits-and-runs, he steals and he never misses a sign."

It may well be that Durocher calculated jumping on Lockman the way he did in that game against the Cardinals as a means of firing up his floundering team. If he did, it certainly worked: the Giants won their next six to up their lead to five games over the Dodgers.

One of the factors in the Braves' belated charge into the pennant race was the return of Bobby Thomson, who had been sidelined the first three and a half months by the triple-fractured ankle he'd suffered in spring training. When Thomson was first activated on July 14 the Braves were in fourth place, one game below .500 at the midpoint of the season and fifteen and a half games behind the Giants. The no-hitter that right-hander Jim Wilson pitched against the Phillies on June 12 was about the Braves' lone highlight to that point in the season, and it was to be the only no-hitter of the entire '54 season. However, for the first month back Thomson was limited to pinch-hitting duties. On July 23, the first game of the Braves' three-game sweep of the Giants at Milwaukee's County Stadium, the two teams were locked in a tense 2–2 game in the ninth when singles by Andy Pafko and Del Crandall put runners at first and second with two out against Giants reliever Hoyt Wilhelm. Braves manager Charlie Grimm summoned Thomson to pinch hit for starting pitcher Bob Buhl, and the old Giant hero drove a single to left to bring home the winning run.

"That was one of the big moments in what had otherwise been a lost season for me," Thomson recalled in an interview shortly before his death in 2010. "Even though the ankle had healed, I wasn't able to really run on it yet, and all I could do was sit on the bench and wait for Charlie to get me an at-bat. It was frustrating, but at least I was back and helping the team whenever I got the opportunity."

From July 22 to August 15 the Braves went on a 20–2 tear, including that July three-game sweep of the Giants in Milwaukee and another at the Polo Grounds on August 6–8, to close to within three and a half games of first place. The second sweep gave the Braves a 9–8 season advantage head-to-head with the Giants, the only team in the National League to have gotten the better of them. During that stretch Thomson hit .444 as a pinch hitter, albeit with no homers, but his mere presence on the bench had seemed to invigorate the Braves.

Durocher had every reason to be concerned about the Braves, who were younger than the Giants, had three formidable starting pitchers in perennial All-Star Warren Spahn; Lew Burdette, a fifteen-game winner in '53; and the six-foot-eight rookie Gene Conley, who led the American Association with twenty-three wins in '53 and was 11–5 with a 3.01 ERA after beating the Giants on August 6. (Conley, it should be noted, had a dual career as a pro basketball player with the NBA Boston Celtics in '52 and '53 and later from 1958 to 1964.) The Braves were also regarded as the best defensive team in the National League. But the three and a half games on August 15 were the closest the Braves would ever get to the Giants. They lost four of their next five games, while Durocher's men, after subsequently losing three straight to the Dodgers, got back on track and finished out the month of August winning twelve of their last fifteen games. The surge enabled them to enter September with a restored lead of three and a half games over the Dodgers and six and a half over Milwaukee.

The day after that mid-August three-game sweep by the Dodgers in Ebbets Field the Giants defeated the Phillies, 8–3, with Antonelli raising his record to 18–3. Once again Durocher sought to ignite his team by getting into a furious argument with third-base umpire Augie Donatelli over a ball Hofman hit into the left field stands that bounced back onto the field with two outs and Mays on first. Donatelli, thinking a fan had interfered with the ball, initially ruled it a ground rule double, with Mays being placed at third. But Durocher could see from the dugout that the ball, in fact, reached the stands on the fly and should, therefore, have been a home run. Charging out onto the field, Durocher first confronted Donatelli, then persuaded the other umpires to consult on it, whereupon the home plate umpire, Jocko Conlan, agreed it was a clean home run. For Hofman, who had been given a rare start by Durocher after being used mostly as a pinch hitter and late-inning defensive replacement, it was his second homer of the game, prompting Leo to keep him in the starting lineup for the next seven games.

The easy-going twenty-nine-year-old Hofman grew up near the Italian-populated Hill section of St. Louis—where he was boyhood friends with Yogi Berra and Joe Garagiola—and was a manager's delight in that he could play almost every position, had a knack for pinch hitting, and did not complain about his limited playing time. (It was during one of their teenage St. Louis sandlot baseball games in the early forties that Hofman happened to notice Berra sitting along the basepath with his legs crossed. "Lookie there at Lawdie," he yelled. "He looks like one of them yogis!" And from there on Larry Berra became the one and only Yogi.)

Prior to his August 17 two-homer game Hofman had homered three other times in '54, all of them as a pinch hitter. Along with Rhodes, who tied for second in the majors with fifteen pinch hits, he was a principal in Durocher's "magic wand" pinch-hitting corps in '54 that set the record with ten pinch homers and hit .282 (46-for-163) as a unit. On June 20 Hofman and Rhodes set a major league record with pinch-hit homers in the same inning in a 7–6 Giants' win over the Cardinals. For the season Hofman was 11-for-36 (.306), with two doubles and three homers as a pinch hitter while also playing twenty-one games at first, ten at second, and eight at third.

Because of his versatility, Hofman was much too useful to Durocher as a bench man. Rhodes, however, was so proficient with the bat that he forced Durocher into finally playing him mostly every day. Beginning on August 18, when Rhodes hit two homers and drove in five runs out of the number-five hole in the lineup against the Phillies, Durocher started him in the outfield in thirteen of the next fifteen games, and in that span he maintained a .370 average. In an August 29 doubleheader against the Cardinals in St. Louis Rhodes hit two triples in the opener and two homers and two doubles in the nightcap to tie a major league record of six extra base hits in a doubleheader, while raising his average to .389. The game was played in sweltering 100-degree heat, but as Rhodes, the native Alabaman, said afterward, "I never mind the heat. Heat only bothers pitchers. Why, one time I played a doubleheader in Mobile when the heat was 124 degrees!"

"How did you do?" a reporter asked him.

"Seven-for-eight," Rhodes replied with a grin.

When it came to hitting, Rhodes had supreme confidence in himself. He was hitting .347 with eighteen homers and sixty-nine RBI in ninety games at Double A Nashville in the Southern Association in 1952 when the Giants acquired him for two players and $30,000. But after a disappointing '53 season with the Giants, during which he hit just .233, with eleven homers in seventy-six games, he knew he had to make some adjustments if he was to stay in the major leagues. In particular, opposing clubs put a shift on him to the right side, figuring—correctly—he could not get out of the habit of trying to pull everything to right field for homers.

During the Giants' goodwill tour of Japan after the '53 season Rhodes approached Don Mueller, who, despite a lack of power, had batted .333 in '53 and, with his ability to hit the ball to all fields, had impressed Durocher enough to bat him frequently in the middle of the order. "Last year, I went for homers, but that meant strikeouts too, and nobody likes a pinch hitter who fans," Rhodes said. "Man, that shift they tried on me had me sitting up in bed at night, trying to figure out a way to make them honest again. Meeting the ball was the only answer. I figure my job is to get on base with any kind of a hit, and to do that was to forget about trying to pull the ball for homers and just meet the ball for average."

In a 2008 interview at his home in Henderson, Nevada, a year before his death at age eighty-two, Rhodes recalled that heat-scorching doubleheader in St. Louis that convinced Durocher he had to be in the lineup in left field over the popular veteran and quiet team leader, Irvin:

The Cardinals could hardly get me out. I went 6-for-7 in the two games. At one point I said to Monte, "All the times I've hit for you,

I know you're pissed," and he said to me, "Dusty, don't apologize. You're the greatest left-handed hitter I ever saw."

That was the way we were, as a team. We didn't have any race issues . . . blacks and whites—we all got along as one. We never thought a thing about it. I grew up with blacks in Alabama, and I didn't know or care a thing about race. Willie, Hank Thompson, and Monte were probably my best friends on the team. Monte was like a brother to me, and Henry? God rest his soul. He died young [of a heart attack at age forty-three in 1969 after spending four years in a Texas penitentiary for holding up a liquor store]. *After our careers were over we wound up working together at the Casa Grande hotel in Arizona where the Giants trained. Henry worked the pool, and I was the bartender. What a pair we were! As for Willie, he's always been one of my best friends in life. I visited with him and stayed at his house many times after I retired.*

On September 3 the Giants began a three-game weekend series with the Dodgers that was the last meeting of the season between the two rivals at the Polo Grounds. Behind eighth-inning RBI singles by Mueller and Davey Williams and three innings of shutout relief by Hoyt Wilhelm, the Giants won the first game, 7–4, and followed up with a 13–4 pummeling of the Dodgers on Saturday, during which Hank Thompson had a grand slam homer, and the backup catcher, Katt, had a two-run shot. Now the lead was five games, their largest since August 5, and the Dodgers prospects for a third-straight NL pennant were looking more and more gloomy.

"There wasn't much we could do about it," said Dodgers manager Walt Alston after the 13–4 rout. "They just whaled the tar out of us—with the bats and their pitching."

Durocher, however, was not about to start making World Series preparations. "Things are getting better all the time," he said. "But don't get me wrong. I'm not claiming anything. And we're gonna keep playing 'em one at a time and the big one is tomorrow's game. By that I mean every tomorrow's game until we run out of tomorrows."

By the time the two teams met again, for a three-game series at Ebbets Field, September 20–21–22, the Giant lead was still five and a half games, except now there were only seven remaining in the season. As far as the pennant race was concerned, the Dodgers were about out of tomorrows. Not close to being decided, however, was what had become a furious three-man race for the NL batting crown among the Dodgers' Snider and the Giants' Mays and Mueller. Here it was again, the NL part of the "who's the best center fielder in New York" debate, with Mueller an unsung interloper.

With the exception of two days, Snider had led the league in batting since June 12 and, as late as August 20, by as much as twenty points (.353–.333) over Mays and Mueller. By September 9 the race had tightened, with Snider at .350 and Mays at .342. Over the next nine days Snider showed signs of late-season strain, going 9-for-38 with just one homer, his average dipping to .342, just one point better than Mays. In the middle of that span Snider had a disastrous 1-for-10 doubleheader against the Cubs.

Then came Monday, September 20, the first game of the last-stand three-game series against the Giants at Ebbets Field and the darkest day of the 1954 season for Snider and the Dodgers. Behind a fourteen-hit support, three each by Mays and Hank Thompson, the wily Dodger-killer Sal Maglie put them out of their misery with a five-hit, 7–1, complete-game victory that clinched the pennant for the Giants. Upon fielding Roy Campanella's bouncer and throwing over to first for the final out, Maglie was mobbed at the mound by his jubilant Giants teammates. "This was much tougher than in '51, when we beat them in the

Polo Grounds," Maglie said later. "Back in '51 we were really not expected to win. We were playing each game with only hope. This time we had the thing in the bag, but if we lost, we would have been kicking ourselves the rest of our lives."

In the solemn Dodger clubhouse afterward Walter O'Malley made a rare appearance to deliver a farewell speech. "This one is over," the owner said. "It was a rugged season. I feel sorry for you. I feel sorry for the fans, particularly because we lost to the Giants. I don't feel our record was as good as it should have been, but let's just forget about this season now. I hope everybody has a good winter."

The headlines in the tabloids the next day—"Dem Gints!" and "Gints Oust Bums"—said it all in pure Brooklyn-ese.

Meanwhile, Maglie had held Snider hitless in three at-bats to relinquish the batting lead to Mays, .344 to .340. The day began for Snider by hitting into a double play after Maglie had walked the first two batters in the first inning, and it ended with a strikeout looking in the eighth.

"Looking back, I probably lost the batting title in that doubleheader against the Cubs," Snider said years later. "I was really worn down by September. It was a really tough season, although maybe the best of my career, and we managed to stay close to them, but in the end it was Willie's year."

After the game Durocher vowed to continue playing his regulars the final six games, at least until second place was decided between the Dodgers and Braves. The next day the Giants won again, 5–2, with Mays and Mueller each going 2-for-3 to raise their respective averages to .346 and .339, and Snider went 1-for-4 to remain at .340. Snider elected to sit out the series finale with a bruised shoulder against the Giants' new ace, the twenty-one-game-winning Antonelli, and in doing so, he at least afforded himself a front-row seat for one of the most spectacular pitching debuts in baseball history.

With both Don Newcombe and Billy Loes nursing sore arms, Alston decided to give himself a sneak preview of the Dodgers' top young pitching prospect, a chunky, five-foot-ten, 185-pound twenty-three-year-old left-hander named Karl Spooner, who'd been a late September call-up after his attention-grabbing season at Class AA Fort Worth, where he was 21–9 and led the Texas League in both strikeouts (262) and walks (162) in 238 innings. The hard-throwing Spooner proved every bit as good as advertised, and without the wildness, setting a major league record by striking out fifteen batters in his first game in the big leagues, walking only three, and outpitching Antonelli for a 3–0 Dodger win. Spooner struck out the side three times in the game and gave up only three singles, one of them to Mays, whom Durocher lifted for a pinch runner in the third inning. Watching the performance from the box seats behind the Dodger dugout was Greg Mulleavy, the scout who'd signed Spooner out of high school for $600 in 1950 after getting a letter from a newspaperman in Oriskany Falls in upstate New York urging him to just take a look at the kid.

Roy Campanella, who caught the game, could not contain himself. "He's the greatest young pitcher I've ever seen," Campy gushed. "I couldn't believe it! And, buddy, I put him to the test. I didn't let him rely on his fastball. I called for the curve and the changeup, and damn, if he didn't get strikeouts on them too! But his fastball is his pitch. It's the damndest thing I ever saw. It takes off sometimes a foot. His stuff even amazed the umpire."

Home plate umpire Frank Dascoli confirmed as much, allowing how he'd called a ball on a curveball in the ninth that broke over the plate on Rhodes. "It broke so much it fooled me," Dascoli said. "I hope they don't try to teach him anything, like a knuckle-ball or something, next spring."

"The thing I liked most about him was the confidence he showed," said Alston. "I intended to pitch him against Pittsburgh [the next day] but when Loes got a sore arm, I didn't have anyone else to pitch against the Giants. I asked him if he'd pitch against the Giants instead of Pittsburgh, and he said it didn't make any difference to him—and it didn't. That's what I like."

Four days later, the final game of the season for the Dodgers, Spooner made one more start and pitched almost as brilliantly, shutting out the Pirates, 1–0, on three singles and striking out twelve more batters. Only one other pitcher in NL history, Allan Worthington with the Giants the year before, had broken into the majors with two consecutive shutouts. "This kid is a cinch to win 20 next year," wrote Dick Young in the *Daily News*. "No, make that 25."

Amid all the buzz over Spooner and the Giants' pennant clinching, it went largely unnoticed that Mueller, in his characteristically quiet, unassuming way, had made it a three-man race for the batting title. The most noise about Mueller was being generated by the writers suddenly taking notice of the quiet Missourian's emerging challenge to the two New York center field icons, especially after Durocher's baffling decision to pinch hit Rhodes for him back on September 12 against the Cardinals' lefty, Haddix, with runners on first and second and the Giants trailing 4–2. At the time Mueller had a twenty-one-game hitting streak going and a .331 average against both lefties and righties. Joe King of the *World-Telegram* was one of the few writers who'd dared to question Durocher's genius, did it often during the season, and this move in particular served to make his case.

"At the time Mueller was lifted, a sound baseball man at the game was quoted as saying, 'What is this? What is a free-swinging lefty like Rhodes doing up there against a clever southpaw like Haddix? Everybody knows Rhodes cannot hit good lefties and Mueller does," King wrote, and then quoted a Dodger player who'd been watching the game on TV as saying, "Durocher is in a spot where he needs a single to set him up and he takes out the guy who has the most hits in the league! He's working for us today."

On September 18 Mueller had a 3-for-4 game in the Giants' 9–1 rout of the Phillies, lifting his average to .338 and becoming the first Giant since Jo Jo Moore in 1936 to amass two hundred hits in a season. In the next-to-last game of the season Mueller went 2-for-5 against the Phillies to barely surpass Mays, who went 0-for-4, for the batting lead. With one game to go, the batting race stood a virtual three-way tie, with Mueller at .3426, Snider at .3425, and Mays at .3422.

For the two Giants the final game posed a most formidable task: the Phillies' durable, hard-throwing right-hander, Robin Roberts, who already had a league-leading twenty-three wins and twenty-eight complete games. By contrast, Snider's opponent was Pirates rookie right-hander, Jake Thies, who'd been 3–8 as a back-end-of-the-rotation starter for them. In their first times up against Roberts, Mueller and Mays both singled. Then, after each made out in their second at-bats, Mays took charge of the race with a triple leading off the seventh and a double in the eighth to finish 3-for-4—with one intentional walk from Roberts—at .345. Mueller went 2-for-6 in the eleven-inning, 3–2 Giants win to wind up at .342. Back at Ebbets Field Snider was held hitless in three at-bats by Thies to finish at .341. With his clutch effort against the best right-hander in the league, Mays became the first Giant since Bill Terry, with a .401 average in 1930, to win the batting crown. But that wasn't all. His .667 slugging percentage was twenty points higher than the next National Leaguer, Snider, and he also led the league with thirteen triples.

"Usually when you win, you get a chance to rest, but Leo made me play that last game against Roberts," said Mays in a 2008 interview at the Baseball Hall of Fame. "I know people always said that Mueller and I pushed each other and Duke and I pushed each other for the batting title. But I didn't care about those things. I didn't play for that. I played to win."

(Nevertheless, a month later the Baseball Writers Association overwhelmingly voted Mays the NL Most Valuable Player, 283–217, over Ted Kluszewski, the Cincinnati Reds' muscled slugging first baseman, who had hit .326 and led the league in homers (41) and RBI (149). Mays got sixteen first-place votes to Kluszewski's seven. Antonelli, who would have surely won the Cy Young Award for pitchers had there been one, was third, with 154 votes, and Snider was fourth, with 135.)

Not surprisingly, Roberts pitched the entire eleven innings for the Phillies while Durocher used the last game to give Antonelli a two-inning tune-up for the upcoming World Series before turning it over to his bullpen. This was a different time, when starting pitchers strived to finish what they started, and nobody embodied that work ethic more than Roberts, who led the National League in complete games five straight seasons, from 1952 to 1956, and had five straight league-leading seasons of three hundred or more innings from 1951 to 1955. It didn't matter to Roberts that it was the last game of the season. "Why would I come out of a game I had a chance to win?" he said. "There's no World Series for us this year. I've got all winter to rest now." In besting Roberts, the Giants finished the season 97–57, five games ahead of the Dodgers. For Antonelli especially, it had been quite a momentous maiden season as a Giant. His twenty-one wins were tied with Warren Spahn for second in the NL behind Roberts, and he led the league in both ERA (2.30) and shutouts (6). "In the last couple of years, Johnny's become a real big leaguer," said Spahn. "If nothing happens to his arm, he should be a 20-game winner for many years to come."

The winter trade that had brought Antonelli over from the Braves for Bobby Thomson had indeed turned out to be a bonanza. From afar in Milwaukee there was grumbling and second-guessing aplenty over the trade that also gave the Giants lefty Don Liddle, who was 9–4 as a number-five starter and long reliever for them, at the same time that poor Thomson missed most of the season with his broken ankle. Much of the criticism was directed at Braves owner Lou Perini, who will also be remembered for having provided the Giants with the cornerstones of their 1951 NL pennant-winning team with his trade of Alvin Dark and second baseman Eddie Stanky to them in 1949. "[Perini] keeps giving the Giants the one thing they didn't have," one of the veteran Braves players was quoted as saying in the *Milwaukee Sentinel*. "This year it was a left-handed pitcher. In fact, he gave them two left-handed pitchers. If that's smart business, then I'm a Chinaman!"

In the visiting clubhouse at Connie Mack Stadium, after the last game, Eddie Brannick, the venerable, seventy-two-year-old traveling secretary who'd been in the Giants' employ since 1905 and had been front and center for all of their previous fourteen pennants since 1900 except their first one in 1904, was talking to a group of writers about this latest team, with all its diversity and togetherness. One of the writers noted that three times the Giants had had their mettle tested: when their lead was trimmed from seven games to two in late July; when it got down to a scant half-game on August 15, and when it was slashed to one and a half games on August 29. And all three times they rebounded with winning streaks. Brannick replied,

This is a sound club, and it has as much spirit as I've ever seen on any Giant club in my time. Everybody pulls for each other and we didn't have any disputes or anything like that all season. Collectively, it has as many good players as any I've ever known. I thought in the spring, back in Phoenix, we had a good chance to win, but that it depended on what kind of a job Antonelli could do for us. Pitching was the big question mark then, and I figured Johnny would have to come through if we were going to win. Looking back, he and Willie Mays made all the difference.

CHAPTER
12

DUSTY AND "THE CATCH"

Didn't it seem . . . like he ran forever?
They all said, he'd never catch that ball
Then he tapped his glove
And Monte knew Willie had a play
But he still wonders to this day
How . . . did he ever catch that ball?

—TERRY CASHMAN, "THE CATCH"

I N THE TINY VISITING CLUBHOUSE MANAGER'S OFFICE OF DETROIT'S
Briggs Stadium, barely larger than a closet, a horde of news-
men who had pushed their way through the door, pens and notebooks in hand, practically pinned Al Lopez to his desk to get
his postgame synopsis on the AL pennant-clinching that had
occurred on the field about fifteen minutes earlier. It had been a
long, hard journey for the Indians who, in dethroning the five-
straight world champion Yankees, had been pushed to play over
.700 baseball (107–40), a feat only seven other teams since 1900
had achieved, and, as Lopez was saying now, that push could be

expected to continue through the last week of the season. Lopez said, as he wiped the sweat off his brow,

> *I guess I borrowed Stengel's crystal ball. Seriously, though, I believe we won because of the vast improvement in two departments—our pitching and our bench. We had a lot of important injuries, but they never kept us from winning because substitutes, like Sam Dente at shortstop, Hal Naragon behind the plate, Wally Westlake and Dale Mitchell in the outfield, stepped in and played just as well. Of course, a great deal of credit has to go to the pitching staff— Bob Lemon, Early Wynn and Mike Garcia, our big three. But as great as they are, we couldn't have won the pennant without Bob Feller, Hal Newhouser, Art Houtteman and the two youngsters in the bullpen, Don Mossi and Ray Narleski. The great work of those five enabled me to give my big three more rest between starts and saved me from tiring them out in relief.*

"So, Al, are you gonna go' for the '27 Yankees' record?" a reporter asked in reference to the 1927 Yankees' AL record of 110 wins.

"I think the fellas want to," replied Lopez. "Put it this way, just because we've clinched, we're not letting up."

Besides, there were individual achievements to consider.

Even though he had sufficiently distanced himself from the White Sox's Minnie Miñoso and the Yankees' Irv Noren in the batting race, Bobby Avila played all seven of the Indians' remaining games and went 9-for-27 to finish up at .341, twenty-one points higher than the runner-up Miñoso. Actually, Ted Williams of the Red Sox hit .345, but because he missed the first month and half of the season with the broken collarbone suffered in spring training, he did not have the necessary plate appearances to qualify for the title. Nevertheless, Williams's twenty-nine homers were good enough for second behind Larry Doby's thirty-two for that crown. Both Doby, who was battling Yogi Berra for the RBI lead, and Al Rosen were hurting with leg injuries yet determined not to rest. Whereas his average had been as high as .338 at the start of July, despite playing with that broken finger, Rosen started four of the Indians' last seven games, went 2-for-16, and finished at an even .300. Doby, meanwhile, started every game the last week and was able to wrest the RBI title from Berra, 126–125, by driving in eleven runs over the final seven games to Yogi's one. Six of those RBI for Doby came in one game, on September 21 against the White Sox, by virtue of his thirty-second homer, a double, and a sacrifice fly. The Indians lost that game, 9–7, but won the four others they needed to finish with 111 victories and surpass the great "Murderers' Row" '27 Yankee team of Babe Ruth, Lou Gehrig, and Co. for the AL record. (The second-place Yankees' 103 wins were also the most from any of Casey Stengel's teams in his twelve-year tenure as their manager.)

One would have thought leading the league in both homers and RBI for a team that won a record 111 games was sufficient to warrant Doby winning Most Valuable Player honors. After all, since the award's inception in 1934 there had never been a player on a winning team who led the league in homers and RBI who had not won the award. But when the Baseball Writers Association announced the vote in October, Berra had outpointed Doby, 230–210. Berra also received the most first-place votes (seven) of any player in the balloting, to Doby's five.

"I always wondered about that vote," Doby said. "Not taking anything away from Yogi, but we won. Was it prejudice on the writers' part? I guess we'll never know."

Upon further examination of the voting, however, it would appear Doby was probably not the victim of any racial prejudice but rather the overall greatness of his own team. Avila, whose league-leading batting average was nearly 70 points higher than Doby's .272, finished third in the balloting, with 203 points, and likewise got five first-place votes. (Unlike the new-age sabermaticians who have pretty much dismissed batting average as a worthwhile factor in determining a player's value, in the fifties winning the batting title was considered far more prestigious than even leading the league in RBI and, thus, carried considerable weight with the voters.) In addition, Bob Lemon, whose twenty-three victories tied with Indians' teammate Early Wynn for the most in the American League, also received five first-place votes and finished fifth in the balloting with 179 points, and Wynn was sixth. Clearly, the voters were torn as to who was the Indians' own MVP, the AL batting leader, the American League's top winning percentage pitcher at 23–7, or the home run and RBI leader. It's unlikely the voters took defense into account either, and too bad for Doby that his fantastic catch off Washington's Tom Umphlett back in July was made in relative obscurity, as there was no TV on that day and neither the local Cleveland newspapers nor the wire services got photos of it.

ON SEPTEMBER 29, 1954, A PERFECT WARM, SUNNY FALL DAY, THE Polo Grounds was packed to capacity with over fifty-two thousand fans and hundreds of the nation's sportswriters, who had gathered to witness the first World Series game in history with players of color on both teams. In large part, of course, this had to do with the absence of the Yankees, winners of six of the previous seven World Series and who remained the most prominent of the four teams (the Red Sox, Tigers, and Phillies were the others) who had still not integrated, even after a full seven years since Jackie Robinson broke the baseball color line. "The Yankees," said Al Rosen, "were the white supremacists of the baseball world and, until 1954, had dominated that world."

Oddly, there was no mention of this historical fact in any of the advance or day-of coverage in all the newspapers. It was as though nobody noticed, or if they did, deemed it to be somehow inconsequential. Even the black papers danced around it without getting into its historical significance.

The *Chicago Defender*:

This World Series being played this year between the New York Giants and the Cleveland Indians must be an awful ordeal for Negro sports fans accustomed to supporting teams because they have Negro players. This year, the record number of eight Negroes—four on each team—are eligible to see action before the Series end. The fact that the number of Negroes on each team is exactly the same adds to the frustration of the race conscious Negro fan. To add to this perplexity, he has to pick between Willie Mays, the National League batting champ and Larry Doby, the home run king of the American League, on the Indians.

Similarly, in the *Atlanta Daily World*, under the headline, "Eight Sepia Stars on Indians, Giants Series Roster," the record number of black players in the World Series was duly noted, but curiously skirted was the fact that this was the first-ever Series in which they were on both teams: "The New York Giants, seeking world championship No. 5, and the Cleveland Indians, vying for No. 3, will have a million dollar collection of bronze talent aiding their collective efforts. The Giants have four whiz bang players in Willie Mays, Monte Irvin, Hank Thompson and Reuben Gomez. The Indians can counter with Larry Doby, Al Smith, Dave Pope and Dave Hoskins."

Instead, much of the pregame banter between the press corps
and the two rival managers, Leo Durocher and Al Lopez, cen-
tered on the odds, the pitching matchups, and the Giants' starting left fielder.

The oddsmakers installed the Indians as 8–5 favorites, citing
their deeper pitching and those overwhelming 111 victories. "I
don't have anything to do with the odds," said Lopez. "I just
think we have a good chance to win. I think we have a helluva
club. You'd have to be to win 111 games." When a newsman
countered, "Yeah, but it was in a lousy league," Lopez took um-
brage. "You said that. We had to beat a team that's won the last
five World Series," he said, a trace of anger in his voice.

On the other side of the field Durocher scoffed at being the
underdog. "Odds don't mean a thing to me," he said. "You win
them on the field, not with bets. Naturally, my guys feel they're
gonna win it."

Of much more interest to the writers was Durocher's choice
of Sal Maglie to start Game One against the Indians' Bob Lemon
instead of his twenty-one-game winning ace, Johnny Antonelli,
whom he'd slated to start Game Two, and Durocher's refusal to
divulge his left fielder until game time. "I'm going with Maglie
because I want to be sure of having him again in the Series with
reasonable rest and even relieve with him in the seventh game if
I have to. Antonelli's only 24 and, if need be, can come back on
two days rest. I'm not saving anyone, that's for sure."

"Who's your leftfielder, Leo?" a writer asked.

"I don't know yet," said Durocher. "I'm still thinking about it.
Could be Rhodes. If it is, he'll bat fourth. If not, Mays will bat
fourth."

Only after the writers had retreated to the press box was the
Giants lineup posted: no Rhodes. Rather, Durocher had opted for
the righty-hitting Monte Irvin in left, batting sixth against the

right-handed Lemon. The crowd had barely gotten to their seats and Perry Como had just finished singing the National Anthem when Maglie hit Al Smith, the first batter of the game, with a pitch, and Avila followed with a base hit to right. With runners at first and third and the heart of the Indians' order coming up, Maglie bore down and retired Doby on a foul pop behind third base and Rosen on another pop up to Whitey Lockman at first. That brought to the plate the lefty-swinging Vic Wertz, who had settled in at first base for the Indians after coming over from the Orioles on June 1 and had been a major force in the middle of the lineup, with fourteen homers and forty-eight RBI in ninety-four games while hitting .275 for them after just .202 for the Orioles. Before the Series Lopez had cited Wertz as potentially his most dangerous hitter at this juncture, given the leg injuries that had rendered Doby and Rosen something less than 100 percent, and in his first World Series at-bat, Wertz reaffirmed that by launching a long drive of some four hundred feet into the gap in right-center that was good for a two-run triple even for him, with his limited speed.

The 2–0 Indians' lead was short lived, however. In the third the Giants nicked away at Lemon for two runs of their own on singles by Whitey Lockman and Al Dark, an RBI infield force-out by Don Mueller, and an RBI single by Hank Thompson. Prior to Thompson's hit, Lemon pitched carefully to Mays, eventually walking him with Mueller at first base, thus putting the tying run in scoring position.

From there the game evolved into a tense pitching duel between Maglie and Lemon, with no scoring and only one base runner apiece advancing as far as third base through the seventh inning. For a moment in the sixth it looked as though the Indians were going to break through with a run when Wertz led off with a single to right, took second on a throwing error by Mueller, and

advanced to third on an infield groundout. After George Strickland popped to short for the second out, Indians catcher Jim Hegan hit a hard bouncer to third that Thompson initially fumbled
as Wertz raced to the plate. The ball then dribbled away into foul
territory as Thompson chased after it. Reaching down, he made
a desperate last-instant grab of it, and fired over to first to get
Hegan by a half-step for the final out.

"When that ball squirted away, all I could think was, 'I gotta
get that son of a buck over to first base!'" Thompson said.

"If Thompson hadn't stayed with that ball the way he did, we
would've won the game right there," said Lopez.

Maglie had been experiencing trouble with his curveball all
day, especially against left-handers. He began the eighth by issuing a walk to Doby, followed by an infield base hit by Rosen.
With runners at first and second, nobody out, and Wertz, who
was already 3-for-3, due up, Durocher went to the mound to relieve Maglie, summoning the little lefty Don Liddle, whom he'd
used as both a fifth starter and long reliever during the season.

On Liddle's first pitch Wertz hit a high drive just to the right
of straightaway center field, which at the Polo Grounds and its
"bathtub-like" contour was 483 feet, as opposed to 279 feet along
the lines. At the crack of the bat Mays began racing toward the
high, green center field wall, his back to the plate . . . racing and
racing, never looking back, until, finally, about 25 feet from the
warning track and some 460 feet away from home plate, he began tapping his glove as the ball came down over his left shoulder and fell safely into it. He then whirled and, as his cap flew
off, threw the ball back into second base, keeping Rosen from
advancing from first after Doby, who'd been almost to third, had
to hustle back to second, tag up, and race back to third.

"What made the catch so remarkable was not the catch itself
but rather how fast Willie wheeled and got the ball back to the

infield," said Rosen. "That was the play. Everybody had to hold up. I thought I could score from first base on a ball hit that far, and Doby should've been able to easily score from second. The throw was unbelievable. Most center fielders with all that room would've been happy just catching up to the ball and making the catch."

From his perch in the camera box behind home plate *New York Daily News* photographer Frank Hurley was shooting the game with his new Hulcher 70 camera, with a twenty-inch lens and its new technology capable of taking anywhere from five to ten pictures or frames per second. The camera was originally built to enable the armed services to photograph rockets and flying missiles.

"The Hulcher performed as if it had been built just for this job," Hurley wrote in a by-lined story in the *Daily News* a couple of months later, after his five-sequence shots of the catch received nationwide acclaim. "It had both the ball and the speeding Willie in focus. The ball passed the zenith of its arc and began to fall. At precisely the right instant, Willie raised his hands and the ball smacked into his glove. Another fraction of a second, Willie whirled, threw a strike to second base and two amazed base runners were chained to the bags. And every detail of the action was recorded on high speed panchromatic film."

Once everyone in the ballpark had recovered from the shock of the play they had just witnessed, Durocher marched to the mound again, this time to bring in right-hander Marv Grissom. As Grissom approached the mound, Liddle handed the ball to Durocher and quipped to his successor, "I got my man."

Liddle later revealed that, in spring training the following year Mays gave the Rawlings HH glove he'd used to make the catch off Wertz to Liddle's son, Craig. "You take care of it and it'll take care of you," Mays said, and Craig Liddle used it all through Little League before putting it away for safekeeping and eventually loaning it to the Hall of Fame in Cooperstown, where it was still on display as of 2014, sixty years after its seminal catch.

"People have always said that was the greatest catch ever and all that," said Mays, "but the truth is I made plenty of catches that were better. I knew I had that ball all the way. It was high enough that I could catch up to it. The throw was the issue. As soon as I caught it I said, 'Where you gonna go now?' And in one motion I was able to get the ball back to the infield and only one guy advanced. That was the key."

And even though it may have seemed like it, the inning was far from over. The first batter Grissom faced, pinch hitter Dale Mitchell, walked, loading the bases and prompting Lopez to send up another left-handed pinch hitter in Dave Pope. But Grissom was able to escape the jam by striking out Pope and retiring Hegan on a fly to left.

With a tense hush having enveloped the Polo Grounds, the 2–2 tie continued on through the ninth and into the tenth, when the relentless Wertz struck again with a leadoff double off Grissom to complete a 4-for-5 afternoon of a triple, two singles, a double, and the only two Cleveland RBI—along with the longest out in World Series history. Rudy Regalado, pinch running for Wertz, was then sacrificed over to third, and Pope was issued an intentional walk. Once again Lopez called down his bench for yet another left-handed batter, this one Bill Glynn, to pinch hit for Hegan. But Glynn struck out, and Lemon, hitting for himself, lined out to first to end the inning.

If Lemon, who had allowed eleven base runners over the first nine innings, was tired, he wasn't about to tell Lopez, and the manager, who had supreme faith in his ace, wasn't about to ask. "There was no tougher competitor than Lem," said Rosen. "No way was he coming out of that game."

With a new battery-mate in third-string catcher Mickey Grasso, Lemon struck out Don Mueller leading off the bottom of the tenth before carefully pitching around and walking Mays again. All of a sudden Mays lit out and stole second, surprising the Indians, as the shortstop, Dente, was barely able to contain Grasso's errant throw in the dirt. Lopez then ordered an intentional walk to Thompson in hopes of setting up a double play with Irvin coming to bat. Now, however, it was Durocher's turn to go to his bench for the first time in the game, and here came Rhodes, the weapon he'd been holding back all game after deciding not to start him in left field. Mays recounted,

> *My stolen base was a key because it set everything up. They'd pinch hit for Hegan, and now they'd brought in this catcher [Grasso], who'd hardly had time to warm up in the bullpen. I saw all of that and I said, "How he gonna throw me out when he just came in from the bullpen?" There was no way! Leo always gave me the green light, so I was goin'. So with first base open, they had to walk Thompson, and that played right into Leo's hand because this was the perfect moment to bring in Rhodes to hit for Monte.*

James Lamar Rhodes, a rugged six-footer with broad shoulders, a jut jaw, and a monosyllabic manner with the sportswriters, was born in the tiny town of Mathews, Alabama, a suburb of Montgomery. His formal schooling ended in the eighth grade, and as a teenager he picked cotton, "side by side with the black folks," and worked in a grocery store. When he was seventeen he joined the Navy and, upon being discharged two years later, joined up with a semipro baseball team in Montgomery called the Gaels. The way he told it, he was having an accidentally spectacular game for the Gaels one day, hitting a home run through the window of a house across the street from the ballfield, along with two triples, all the while playing barefoot because he had just come out to watch the game that day only to be pressed into service when one of the regular Gaels players failed to show up. That was how a local scout named Bruce Hayes, who worked for the Nashville club in the Double A Southern Association, discovered him. "Hayes was at that game, and afterward he gave me a contract to play for Hopkinsville in the Kitty League," Rhodes related. "First thing I said to him was, 'Where the hell is Hopkinsville?' I'd never heard of the place. I took the contract to a friend of mine, Elmer Wood, and he signed it instead of my parents. I didn't know what was in it. I didn't care. I just wanted to play."

Rhodes spent five years in the minor leagues before finally making it up to Nashville in 1952. He was hitting .347 there when the Giants purchased his contract after getting a recommendation letter on him from a former Giant catcher, Jack Aragon, who was managing the nearby Knoxville team in the Tri-State League. "I never saw a player with more confidence in his own ability," Aragon wrote Giants farm director Jack Schwartz. "His timing has improved and he is the best left-handed hitter in this league. If he has any weakness it's he still has some trouble with the changeup."

It was on the Giants' goodwill tour to Japan the previous fall when Rhodes went to Don Mueller about changing his approach at the plate, from trying to pull everything to just meeting the ball. It happened after one of the Japanese pitchers struck him out on a changeup. "Dammit!" Rhodes screamed when he came back to the dugout. "I could be playing at the damn North Pole and some stinkin' Eskimo could pop out of an igloo and say, 'Ha ha. Can't hit the change!'"

Now here he was, a year later, being called upon to pinch hit in his first World Series for his friend Irvin, with one out and runners at first and second, against one of the premier right-handed pitchers in baseball. "I was going up there looking to swing at the first pitch, just as I always did, if it was anywhere near the plate," Rhodes recalled.

From the mound Lemon studied Rhodes for a moment, then unleashed his pitch. But instead of the fastball Rhodes had anticipated, it was a changeup—*a damn changeup*. Rhodes swung, a tad late, and lofted what initially appeared to be a fairly routine pop fly to shallow right field. Avila drifted back from second base in anticipation of making the catch, only to stop in his tracks as the ball kept drifting into the wind toward the right field foul pole. Then it was Indians' right-fielder, Pope, who thought he had a bead on it, as long as the ball didn't hit the overhanging ledge of the Polo Grounds' upper deck. It didn't—but it didn't come down in Pope's glove either. Rather, it landed in the first row of the right field stands, barely 10 feet fair of the pole and 260 feet from home plate, where it bounced off the chest of a fan in the $7 standing-room-only row and skittered back onto the field. For a moment the 52,751 fans stood quiet, unsure whether the ball had been fair or foul. Only when right field umpire Larry Napp, running into the corner, raised his right arm to signal *home run* did the Polo Grounds erupt in delirium.

"Maybe it wasn't much of a hit," said Durocher afterward, "but you had to have a ticket to catch it."

As Rhodes circled the bases behind Mays and Thompson, Lemon stood motionless on the mound, staring out to right field in utter disbelief over being beaten by a 260-foot home run. Finally he heaved his glove in the air in anger and frustration. "Lemon's glove went farther than my home run," Rhodes joked years later.

When it came to cheap-shot home runs, this one had no doubt been the dandy of them all. It was the accepted slang of the day to call such shots "Chinese home runs," and Dick Young of the *Daily News* was quick to seize all over that theme in his lead the next day:

> *The story of the Giants' 5–2 victory over Cleveland in yesterday's World Series opener should be written vertically, from top to bottom . . . in Chinese hieroglyphics. It was won on a 10th inning homer that was not only sudden death but pure murder . . . right out of a Charley Chan yarn. Ming Toy Rhodes, sometimes called Dusty by his Occidental friends, was honorable person who, as a pinch hitter, delivered miserable bundle of wet wash to first row in rightfield of Polo Grounds, some 259½ feet down the block from the laundry.*

Young's characterization of the home run, in addition to all the subsequent "Chinese homer" references on the radio and other newspapers, created a furor in the Chinese community in New York. In what may have been the first public outcry for "political correctness," Shavey Lee, the unofficial "mayor" of New York's Chinatown, presented a petition to Giants' secretary Eddie Brannick, objecting to the term and demanding the cessation of its use. "It isn't the fault of the Chinese if you have 258-foot fences," Lee wrote. "Why should we be blamed all the time? What makes a cheesy home run a 'Chinese' home run?"

Lee's petition, which was made public when Brannick posted it in the Polo Grounds press box the next day, prompted hundreds of congratulatory letters and phone calls to his house from Chinese citizens across the country. The story was put on the television show *What's the Story?*, and after that a writer for the *Sporting News*, Jack Orr, tracked Lee down at his restaurant in Chinatown and said to him, "You have a point. Writers shouldn't be using that term. But what took you so long to get around to protesting?"

"To tell you the truth," Lee said, laughing, "all of us Americans of Chinese descent have been thinking for years that this was an unpleasant reference. I guess it goes back to Matty's [Christy Mathewson] time in the early part of the century when they were referring to a 'Chinaman's chance'—which meant no chance at all at beating the Giants. We didn't like it in those days either, but we're patient people and we just bided our time."

He paused for a moment and then added with a wink, "But the real reason I haven't led any protest is because I'm a Giant fan!"

His "cheapo" home run heroics notwithstanding, Rhodes found himself back on the bench for Game Two the next day as Durocher sent his same lineup, with Irvin in left field, out against the Indians' other twenty-three-game winner, Wynn. And like Game One, this one evolved in a tight pitcher's duel between Wynn and Antonelli, although by his own admission, the Giants' young lefty did not have his best stuff. Part of that may have had to do with Durocher's decision to keep Wes Westrum behind the plate. During the season backup Ray Katt had been Antonelli's catcher of choice, mostly, he said, because Katt was able to squat lower than the muscled Westrum and was thus able to get closer to the ground for Antonelli's sinkers. Antonelli, the first Giants lefty to win twenty games since Cliff Melton in 1937, had been 12–0 when Katt caught him during the season, as opposed to 9–7 with Westrum.

And for a stunning initial moment it looked as though this might indeed be a brief outing for the National League's ERA leader when Indians' leadoff hitter, Al Smith, hit Antonelli's first pitch of the game deep into the left field seats, bringing an immediate hush to the Polo Grounds crowd of 49,099. After getting the next two Indian batters Antonelli walked both Rosen and Wertz and then was touched for a single to center by Wally Westlake that loaded the bases. He was able to get out of that by retiring Indians shortstop George Strickland on a pop to first base, but was right back in trouble again in the second when Jim Hegan led off with a double and Wynn sacrificed him to third. Again Antonelli escaped by striking out Smith and getting Avila to hit a foul pop-out behind third base. He would strand two more runners in the third after a two-out single by Wertz and another walk, to Westlake, while in the fourth Thompson saved him with a sensational diving stab of Avila's scorching liner to the left of third base following a two-out walk of Smith. Through the first five innings Antonelli had already stranded seven base runners and issued four walks.

"To be honest I'm surprised Leo didn't yank me," Antonelli said in his 2012 memoir. "I was in trouble just about every single inning that day. He could have pulled me several times and I wouldn't have complained. I didn't have command of my stuff. All I can say is, thank God they didn't rely on pitch counts in those days or I would've been gone in the fourth inning."

By contrast, Wynn retired the first twelve Giants in order before issuing a leadoff walk to Mays in the fifth. When Thompson followed with a single to center, advancing Mays to third, Durocher seized the opportunity to make his Rhodes-for-Irvin move a little earlier this time. The Polo Grounds crowd was on their feet as Dusty strode to the plate. Out in center field, Doby had moved twenty to thirty feet further toward the far-reaching wall, respecting Rhodes's power. It was a fatal mistake. On Wynn's first pitch Rhodes dunked a "Texas League" pop-up into short-center, scoring Mays and sending Thompson to third. On the throw in, Dusty wound up at second. Later in the inning, after Wynn walked Westrum, a .187 hitter for the season, Antonelli's grounder to second scored Thompson. Just like that, Wynn, who had been perfect through the first four innings, found himself trailing 2–1.

Rhodes, however, wasn't finished. Durocher allowed him to stay in the game in left field, and in his next time up, leading off the seventh against Wynn, he hit another home run, this one entirely legit, to deep right field, making it a 3–1 game.

The Indians' day-long futility was manifested in the ninth when their first two batters, Smith and Avila, reached with singles, only to be left standing at second and first respectively when Antonelli retired the next three batters, the last being Wertz on a fly out—fittingly—to Rhodes in deep left. In all, the Indians stranded thirteen base runners, same as in Game One.

Afterward Rhodes found a telegram in his locker from Bill Chan's Gold Coin restaurant on Second Avenue, inviting him "to restore your energy with our homer producing Chinese food." There was no such levity in the visitors' clubhouse, however, where Al Lopez was growing more irritated with the postgame inquisition from the writers, particularly one writer who kept asking him for the turning point in the game.

"I don't understand what you mean," Lopez responded.

"Well, uh," the scribe pressed on, "did you not believe Doby was playing too deep on Rhodes' single in the fifth?"

"Now goddam, what are you doing?" Lopez snapped. "Asking the goddam questions and answering them at the same time? Nobody could've caught that ball, not even Willie Mays. It was just a bloop hit."

Needless to say, the Indians couldn't wait to get out of the chamber of horrors the Polo Grounds had been and back home to their own Municipal Stadium that, gigantic as it was, with its three-tiered, nearly eighty thousand–seat capacity, at least had normal field dimensions. There was no off day, however, to clear their minds of Rhodes, who was once again on the Giants' bench, lying in wait for yet another ambush of one their vaunted pitchers.

The Indians' third-game starter was the California Mexican, Mike "Big Bear" Garcia, who was 19–8 during the regular season with a league-leading 2.64 ERA, in a distinctly Latin matchup against the Giants' Puerto Rican righty, Rubén Gómez. This time it was the Giants getting the jump on scoring, staking Gómez to a quick 1–0 lead in the first on an RBI single by Mays. Two innings later was when it all came unraveled for Garcia.

After singles by Alvin Dark and Mueller to start the third, Mays hit a grounder to third that resulted in Dark being thrown out in a rundown at the plate, with the runners winding up at second and third. Lopez then elected to walk Thompson intentionally to pitch to Irvin. After all, no way Durocher would pinch hit Rhodes this early, would he? As a matter of fact, that was precisely what Durocher intended to do. Dusty was in the on-deck circle before Garcia even completed the walk to Thompson. And once at the plate, he again swung at the first pitch and lashed a single into right, scoring Mueller and Mays for a 3–0 Giants' lead. Next up, Davey Williams attempted to sacrifice Rhodes over to second, but after fielding the bunt, Garcia threw wide to first, allowing Thompson to score from third. For all intents and purposes Garcia's day was over. Lopez brought on Art Houtteman to start the fourth, and the Giants added another run off him in the fifth inning on a double by Thompson and an RBI single by, of all people, the light-hitting Westrum.

Buoyed by all this run support that had pretty much taken the Cleveland crowd of 71,555 out of the game, Gómez went on to limit the Indians to just three hits into the eighth, one of them a leadoff homer by the still-rampaging Wertz in the seventh, before asking to be removed because his sinus condition was acting up. With the help of one and two-thirds hitless innings of relief from Hoyt Wilhelm, he earned the distinction of the first native-born Puerto Rican to win a World Series game, and this was so noted by the governor of Puerto Rico, Luis Muñoz Marín, who cabled a message to him saying, "I am certain all Puerto Ricans share my rejoicing over your brilliant work on this occasion Puerto Rico has been represented by a pitcher in a World Series game."

When they arrived back in the visitors' clubhouse, the Giants were greeted by a blunt message on the bulletin board: *Have your bags packed and in the hotel lobby at 10 a.m. tomorrow. We're leaving by bus to the airport immediately after the game. Invite your wives to the victory dinner at the Biltmore Hotel tomorrow night.* It was unsigned, but there was no doubt as to who had authored it. Durocher had the broom out, and there were no plans for an extended stay in Cleveland and a Game Five two days hence.

In the manager's office the writers were all querying Durocher about having now beaten the Indians' "Big Three"—Lemon, Wynn, and Garcia. "Sure they got good pitching," he said, "but my pitchers don't exactly throw bean bags. We won 69 games in which the other team scored two or less runs. Look it up." He then announced his Game Four starter would be Don Liddle.

So much had been made of the Indians' deep pitching and how it seemingly gave them a big edge in this Series. Suddenly it looked like a mirage, especially when Lopez announced he was starting Lemon on two days rest to pitch Game Four. Bob Feller, for one, felt Lopez panicked after losing the first two games in New York. Originally Lopez had Feller penciled in to pitch Game Three, but after Lemon and Wynn were defeated he switched off to Garcia and left Game Four open. Granted, the thirty-five-year-old Feller was past his prime and no longer possessed the 97–98 mph heater that enabled him to amass six twenty-win seasons from 1939 to 1951, interrupted by four years in the Navy in World War II. But as the Indians' number-five starter in '54, he'd fashioned a 13–3 record and his lowest ERA (3.09) since

1947. At the very least he seemed like a better Game Four bet than Lemon on two days rest.

"It was the biggest disappointment of my career," Feller told me in an interview at the Hall of Fame in 2008. "The one thing I hadn't accomplished was winning a World Series game, and I really thought I was going to get my chance in '54. Al never told me why he didn't pitch me. I can only surmise he didn't think I could win for him because I didn't have the blazing fastball anymore."

He was right in that assumption. In a March 2004 interview at his home in Tampa the then-ninety-five-year-old Senor told me bluntly, "I just thought Feller was through. In that situation, with no tomorrow, I felt like I had to go with my best, and that was Lemon."

It proved to be a fatal decision. Lemon was anything but ace-like. He was already behind 3–0 going into the fifth inning when the Giants scored four more runs to turn the game into a run-away. When singles by Alvin Dark and Mueller and a walk to Mays loaded the bases with nobody out, Lemon was relieved by the veteran Hal Newhouser, who walked Thompson to force one run home and was rocked by a two-run single by Irvin. Suddenly it was 6–0 Giants—all on a day when Dusty rested!

At the same time, the soft-throwing Liddle was the beneficiary of a clearly deflated Indians team, resigned to its fate. Through the first four innings they managed just one hit, a double by—who else?—Wertz. Even their supporters in the press box had resorted to gallows humor. When Mays caught Dente's fly for the third out of the second inning and then fired a throw to the plate, thinking there were only two away, Frank Gibbons of the *Cleveland Press* rose to his feet and shouted, "We finally found his weakness! He can't count!"

But in the fifth the Giants had an uncharacteristic defensive breakdown when Liddle and Davey Williams at second both made errors on ground balls, opening the door for Hank Majeski's pinch-hit, three-run homer to deep left field. Having done his job and provided the Giants their last dividend from the Bobby Thomson trade, Liddle turned the ball over to Hoyt Wilhelm with two out in the seventh. In the eighth Avila reached on an errant strike-three Wilhelm knuckleball, and Rosen singled to left-center to put runners at first and third with one out. In the Giants' dugout prior to that inning Dark, the team captain, told Durocher that, because of the shadows creeping in over the top of the stadium, it was becoming more and more difficult to see pitches from a left-hander. "It was right then I made up my mind to bring in Antonelli if we got into any further trouble," Durocher said.

And so, with Wertz and Westlake due up, Durocher went for the kill. Antonelli came on and struck out both of them to snuff out that threat and, after issuing a leadoff walk to Dente in the ninth, retired the last three Indians for the save.

The Giants had done it in stunning fashion—swept the winningest team in AL history, outscoring them 21–9, while holding Doby, Rosen, and Avila to a combined 7-for-43 with no RBI or extra base hits. In the four games the Indians stranded thirty-seven base runners. Rosen later said,

The truth is, we should've never kept playing the way we did at the end of the season just to get the record. Doby and I should've both sat out and rested that last week. We were all banged up. We never talked about it for publication, but the writers saw it. The first game was probably the turning point. We got beat by a catch on a ball that would've been a home run in any other ballpark in baseball, and a home run that would've been an out in any other park. If the Series had opened in Cleveland, the Giants would've been down 0–2.

"We laughed at those odds," said Irvin. "Before the Series Leo said to us, 'Just do what I say and I'll outmanage Lopez nine days out of ten.' What people didn't understand was we *knew* them from all those twenty-one games we played against each other in spring training. We knew their weaknesses. We knew we could hit their pitchers. The only one Leo said he was a little worried about was Feller, and Lopez never used him."

HALF A CENTURY LATER DENNIS MINOGUE, WHO HAD WORSHIPPED THE Giants as a kid growing up in Washington Heights, a short subway ride from the Polo Grounds, and later rhapsodized them in song under his "nom de tune," Terry Cashman, now found himself, quite unexpectedly, in their midst for the first time. They were all three thousand miles away from the shadows of Coogan's Bluff and the long-ago demolished Polo Grounds— at SBC Park in San Francisco, where the Giants, in their new stadium, were preparing a fiftieth anniversary celebration of their New York roots and that season of Willie. A few months earlier the Giants had contracted Minogue and asked whether he would like to be part of the festivities, performing one of his classic baseball songs or, even better, could he write a new one, just for this occasion? For Minogue, this was the gig of a lifetime. Just to be in the presence of his boyhood idol, Willie Mays, he'd have done it for nothing. It took him less than a day to compose "The Catch," his ode to Mays and 460-foot catch off Vic Wertz.

They were gathered in one of the ballpark's restaurants for a late lunch reception before Friday night's on-field celebration—seventeen surviving '54 Giants, including most of the principals of the championship team: Mays, Monte Irvin, Don Mueller, Johnny Antonelli, Marvin Grissom, and the sons of the South, Alvin Dark, Whitey Lockman, Dusty Rhodes, Davey Williams, and Hoyt Wilhelm. Minogue stood quietly off to the side, not wanting to be an intruder in their camaraderie.

"You know," shouted Rhodes, who, after his retirement from baseball worked as a ticket taker at the 1964 World's Fair in Queens and later as a deck hand and cook on the Staten Island Ferry, "I never could buy a drink in New York for the rest of my life! I'm surprised I'm still living!"

"I can't believe the Giants haven't won a world championship since," said Mueller. "I would've thought they'd won a bunch of 'em."

"Especially with Willie," said Dark, "the greatest baseball player I've ever seen. The best all-around player. The greatest."

With that, they all began applauding, and Mays stood up, and the room went silent.

"You guys here," he said, "are responsible for me learning how to play baseball. I could do everything, but I learned the art of the game from you fellows."

Then, looking down at Dark, the team captain, who lived his whole life in the South and, years earlier, as manager of the Giants, had been accused of having inherent racist views when a New York sportswriter for *Newsday* quoted him as questioning the "mental alertness" of black and Hispanic players, Mays said, "I just want everyone here in this room to know I learned more about baseball from Alvin Dark than anyone else. More than from Monte here, more than from my father, more than from Leo. I love you, Alvin."

For a moment Dark sat there and wept. Then he rose to embrace Mays, as the rest of his teammates got up from their tables to do the same.

"It was just an extraordinary scene," said Minogue. "All these guys, a lot of them southerners, in some areas from the Deep South, and there was this certain respect for Willie. I don't know if I've ever been anywhere in my life where you could feel so much love in one room."

EPILOGUE

A WEEK BEFORE THE END OF THE '54 SEASON THE YANKEES ANNOUNCED the re-signing of Casey Stengel as their manager to a two-year contract at $70,000 per season. In making the announcement Yankees co-owner Dan Topping said, "We didn't agree with Casey's idea of quitting because we lost." Stengel, for his part, admitted he had told the writers back in July that if he didn't win, the Yankees should fire him, just as they got rid of players who didn't perform up to their expectations. "But they wanted me back, so here I am."

Stengel said there were two conditions in particular he wanted from the Yankees: he would not have any reduction in salary and the front office would promise to rebuild. He got both. In mid-November general manager George Weiss addressed the team's biggest need—young, quality starting pitching—by executing a seventeen-player trade, the largest in baseball history, with the

Baltimore Orioles in which the Yankees obtained twenty-four-year-old right-hander Bob Turley, who'd led the American League in strikeouts in '54, along with another promising righty, Don Larsen, in exchange for a bunch of minor league prospects, right-hander Harry Byrd, who had come over the previous winter from the Philadelphia Athletics in the Vic Power trade, and the popular veteran outfielder Gene Woodling.

The remaking of the Yankee starting rotation was underway. When Weiss sold three-time twenty-game winner Vic Raschi to the St. Louis Cardinals the previous spring he was right about Raschi being nearly washed up (he was 8–9 with a 4.73 ERA for St. Louis and had the distinction, which he wouldn't realize until years later, of giving up the first of Hank Aaron's 755 career homers). But Weiss was wrong about the Yankees being able to win without Raschi. Byrd did not live up to the Yankees' expectations in his one year as one of their principal starters, and Stengel had to constantly juggle his rotation, which was no match for Cleveland's trio of aces, Bob Lemon, Early Wynn, and Mike Garcia, along with fifteen-game winner Art Houtteman and the veteran five-time former All-Star Bob Feller. After the surprising Bob Grim, whose 20–6 record earned him AL Rookie of the Year honors, and sixteen-game winner Whitey Ford, the next highest win total by a Yankee was thirteen from Allie Reynolds, their ace from 1947 to 1953, who in January announced his retirement because of a chronic back condition.

Two of the prospects the Yankees surrendered in the Oriole deal were catchers Gus Triandos and Hal Smith, both of whom had been slated to compete with Elston Howard for the backup job behind Yogi Berra in '55. A couple of weeks later the Yankees announced that Howard, who'd hit .330 with twenty-two homers, 109 RBI, and a league-leading sixteen triples while on loan to the International League Toronto Maple Leafs in '54, had been signed to a major league contract and was being sent to San Juan of the Puerto Rican Winter League to both catch and play the outfield. Very subtly, the Yankees had made a statement: after losing the pennant for the first time in five years, they were finally ready to integrate.

In the borough of Brooklyn, where the Dodgers were likewise experiencing the second-place blues, they announced that Walter Alston, despite his unsettling maiden season as manager, was being rewarded with a new one-year contract. In giving Alston a vote of confidence, Dodgers president Walter O'Malley said the low-key Ohioan, a career minor leaguer before being tapped to succeed Charlie Dressen after the '53 season, should be much more comfortable in '55 now that he'd had a year to familiarize himself with all the Dodgers veterans. "Alston did all right," O'Malley said. "He was in no way to blame for Roy Campanella's hand injury or Johnny Podres's appendectomy." O'Malley then took the occasion to pass out attendance figures to the assembled press corps that showed the Dodgers had led the National League with home attendance of 12,378,242 and road attendance of 14,508,779 for the nine-year, postwar period. In reference to the recurring rumors that the Dodgers were considering a move to Los Angeles, O'Malley said, "It is inconceivable that the Dodgers should play any place except Brooklyn in light of these figures."

O'Malley went on to say he wasn't sure what, if any, changes in personnel the Dodgers would be making, although there was one particular player transaction out of their control, which the Dodgers had nonetheless been anticipating with a sense of dread.

On the morning of November 22, in a gathering of baseball executives from the sixteen major league teams at the Biltmore Hotel in New York for the Rule Five Major League Draft of players not protected on the forty-man rosters, Branch Rickey

Jr., son of the former Dodgers general manager who had moved on to head up the Pittsburgh Pirates baseball operations, rose from his chair and announced, "The Pittsburgh Pirates, with the first pick, select Roberto Clemente, outfielder with the Montreal club of the International League." The drafting fee was $4,000.

"Clemente was No. 1 on the lists of four or five other clubs," Rickey Jr. told the assembled writers. "We had several men scouting him. Clyde Sukeforth did a very thorough job on him."

Later, back in Pittsburgh, Rickey Sr. acknowledged that the twenty-year-old, five-foot-eleven, 170-pound Clemente, who'd hit .257 with two homers and twelve RBI in a limited eighty-seven games for the Dodgers' Triple A farm in '54, was still a "raw product" in many ways, especially with the bat. "But I had a good line on this boy. On the reports, I would've paid more than the $4,000 it cost the club. I would've paid $10,000 or even $30,000 for him. We are confident he will be able to hold his own in the majors with us next year. All of our reports on him are that he has all the qualities to become a substantial major league player."

At the time Clemente was hitting .361 in the Puerto Rican Winter League, prompting White Sox general manager Frank Lane to say, "I think the Brooklyn club outsmarted itself on the kid. It should have never let him play winter ball. That's where he got all the attention. I doubt if a club would have taken him based on his .257 average at Montreal."

Meanwhile, in Milwaukee, Braves' executives, still hearing the criticism from the February trade of pitchers Johnny Antonelli and Don Liddle—both of whom played key roles in the Giants' winning of the world championship—for Bobby Thomson, continued to do their best to rationalize the deal with their fans. After all, they said, Antonelli had never won twenty games before, and who knew Thomson was going to break his ankle in spring training? It was Braves manager Charlie Grimm, however, who put the deal in the best perspective for them. "Had it not been for Thomson's injury," he said, "we'd have never gotten to see how good Hank Aaron was. Bobby going down opened up the outfield spot for Aaron and he just took it from there. Otherwise, we'd have sent him back to the minors. If Aaron himself hadn't broken his ankle in September, with three weeks still to go, he might have won the Rookie of the Year Award. He hit .280 which was the same as Thomson's lifetime average, and showed real power."

The Giants' winning of the 1954 World Series broke a streak of seven seasons in which the American League—mostly the Yankees—had ruled the baseball world. The National League had not won back-to-back World Series since 1933–1934. But that was about to change—as was the overall balance of power in baseball.

Upon the dawning of the 1955 season, *Sports Illustrated*'s April 11 baseball preview issue featured on its cover a photo of Willie Mays, Leo Durocher, and Durocher's wife, actress Laraine Day. In the photo Day is in between the Giants manager and the reigning 1954 NL Most Valuable Player, with her arms around both. In its first cover to feature a player of color, *Sports Illustrated* sought to combine baseball and show biz, and if the idea was to bring attention to the fact that America was changing in terms of racial attitudes, it surely did that too. Reaction from the South in *SI*'s "19th Hole" Letters to the Editor two weeks later was, to say the least, fierce and emphatic:

> *Up until now, I have not found anything in particularly bad taste in SI, but by golly, you print a picture on the cover in full color, of a white woman embracing a negro (with a small letter) man, you make it evident that even in a magazine*

*supposedly devoted to healthful and innocent sports, you
have to engage in South-bating. . . . I care nothing about
these three people, but I care a heck of a lot about the proof
this picture gives that SI is part of a giant plan to flaunt all
decency, so long as the conquered of 1865 can be reminded
of their eternal defeat.* —Shreveport, La.

*To tell you that I was shocked at SI's cover would be putting
it mildly. . . . The informative note inside that this Mrs. Leo
Durocher, a white woman, with her arm affectionately around
the neck of Willie Mays, a Negro ballplayer. . . . Let me say to
you, Sir, the most appalling blow ever struck at this country, the
most disastrous thing that ever happened to the people of America, was the recent decision of the Supreme Court, declaring
segregation unconstitutional.* —Nashville, Tenn.

*Please cancel my subscription to SI immediately. . . . This is an insult
to every decent white woman everywhere.* —Fort Worth, Tex.

*Such disgusting racial propaganda is not fit for people
who are trying to build a stronger nation based on racial
integrity.* —New Orleans

As far as social change, integration, and adherence to *Brown
vs. Board of Education* in 1954, most of the South was still saying,
"count us out." Of the two high-ranked Double A minor leagues,
the Texas League did not get its first black player until 1952,
when pitcher Dave Hoskins, who would win nine games for the
Cleveland Indians the following year, was added to the Dallas

Eagles' roster, and the Southern Association, throughout its entire existence up until when it folded in 1961, had but one black player, catcher Nat Peeples, who appeared in two games for the Atlanta Crackers in 1954. Actually, Crackers owner Earl Mann, who had a working agreement with the Milwaukee Braves, had anticipated getting Hank Aaron for the '54 season. Aaron had spent '53 at Class A Jacksonville, and the natural progression was for him was to start '54 at Class AA, until the Braves decided to promote him all the way to the big club.

Nevertheless, when compared to the other two professional sports leagues, the National Football League and the National Basketball Association, baseball, despite its unspoken, unofficial seventy-one-year segregation policy, was clearly in the forefront in 1954 in terms of not just integrating but also doing so with star-quality black players. The NBA did not integrate until 1950, when guard Earl Lloyd joined the Washington Capitols, but by 1954 still had only seven black players, out of 110, on the rosters of its nine teams. The NFL went from 1927 until 1946 as an all-white league and likewise had less than 7 percent black players in 1954.

A big reason, of course, for the dearth of black talent in both professional football and basketball was the fact that three of the leagues' primary "feeder" collegiate athletic conferences, the Southeastern, Southwest, and Atlantic Coast, did not get around to integrating until 1963, nine years after *Brown vs. Board of Education.* And it wasn't until 1971, for instance, that the Southeastern Conference athletic programs were fully integrated. With so many gifted young black athletes in the South denied the opportunity to play football and basketball at all the major southern universities, baseball became their natural sport of choice. "I'm sure I could've been a real good football player—that's what my mother wanted me to be," Aaron told me in 2012. "But I didn't see any future there. Not in Alabama anyway. I wasn't going to college. All I wanted when I got out of high school was to get on with my baseball career and follow Jackie to the big leagues."

In 1954 Major League Baseball had 38 black players, out of 536, on its rosters during the season, or 7 percent. That percentage gradually increased every year to a high of 28 percent by 1986, when it began declining again. By 2013 the number of African American players on the major league rosters was down to about 8.5 percent. Not coincidentally, the decline began in the mideighties, when the major southern collegiate conferences' football and basketball teams were now predominantly black. It's anyone's guess how many potential Hank Aarons and Willie Mayses, who grew up in the South, baseball lost to football and basketball.

ELSTON HOWARD BECAME THE FIRST BLACK YANKEE IN 1955, APPEARING in ninety-seven games as a backup catcher and outfielder, hitting .290 with ten homers and forty-three RBI. After a one-year hiatus the Yankees made it back to the World Series where, for the first time, the Dodgers defeated them. "Next year" finally came for the Brooklyn faithful, who had known nothing but despair in seven previous World Series, five of them against the Yankees. In providing the National League its second-straight World Series championship, the Dodgers needed the full seven games to deal Casey Stengel his first Fall Classic loss with left-hander Johnny Podres hurling a nifty 2–0 shutout in the finale. The game was ultimately decided, however, on a sensational defensive play by Dodgers black Cuban reserve outfielder Sandy Amoros. In the bottom of the sixth inning Dodgers manager Walter Alston inserted Amoros in left field as a defensive replacement, a move that would go down as one of the most inspired in baseball history when, with no outs and Yankees at first and second, Yogi Berra hit a long fly ball into the left field corner that looked for certain to be a game-tying extra base hit. And had Amoros not been left-handed, it might have been. Racing full tilt into the left field corner, Amoros reached out at the last instant with his right glove hand and made the catch. He was then able to whirl and get the ball back to the infield to the relay man, Pee Wee Reese, who fired over to first to double off Gil McDougald and stifle the last Yankee threat against Podres. For Alston, the Series triumph was redemption for a rocky first season as Dodgers manager, during which the Dodgers veterans had frequently questioned his leadership, toughness, and game strategy. He would go on to sign twenty-one more one-year contracts and win three more world championships en route to his election to the Hall of Fame in 1983.

Elston Howard went on to play in eight more World Series for the Yankees and, in 1963, became the first black player to win the AL Most Valuable Player award. By then, however, it had become readily apparent how the Yankees-led resistance to integrate in the American League had swayed the balance of power in baseball. Beginning in 1954, with the triumph of Willie Mays and the Giants and the impressive debuts of Hank Aaron and Ernie Banks, the first generation of black superstars began making their mark in baseball—and most of them were in the National League. Roberto Clemente would debut with the Pittsburgh Pirates in 1955, followed by Frank Robinson for the Cincinnati Reds the following year, Orlando Cepeda with the Giants in 1958, and, all in 1959, Bob Gibson with the St. Louis Cardinals, Willie McCovey with the Giants, and Maury Wills with the Dodgers.

From 1949 to 1962 Jackie Robinson, Mays, Roy Campanella, Don Newcombe, Aaron, Banks, Frank Robinson, and Wills combined to win eleven of the fourteen NL Most Valuable Player Awards, while at the same time the AL MVP remained an all-white affair. Both Robinsons, Jackie and Frank, as well as Mays, Aaron, Clemente, Campanella, Gibson, McCovey, and Cepeda all also went on to earn plaques in the Hall of Fame. And whereas, in the years prior to 1954, the Yankees-led American League had dominated Baseball, winning seven straight World Series after the color line was broken in 1947, the National League was 13–10 in the Series from 1954 to 1976 and, even more tellingly, won twenty-four of the twenty-six All-Star Games from 1960 to 1982 during the heydays of Mays, Aaron, Clemente, Banks, Cepeda, McCovey, and others.

"I guess we showed them pretty good," said Aaron, "what most of America was missing for the first seventy years of baseball."

ACKNOWLEDGMENTS

A S MUCH AS THIS BOOK PROJECT WAS A LABOR OF LOVE BECAUSE of my admiration for all of the baseball players of my youth from whom I developed my appreciation of the game, it was also a labor of labor, which could not have been completed without the assistance of many people. To all of the following, my heartfelt thanks:

Moss Klein, my close compadre and relentless, nonpareil fact checker, who gave of his time to make the editors' jobs at Da Capo Press so much more seamless.

Bill Francis of the National Baseball Hall of Fame and his boss, Jim Gates, who gave me the run of the Hall of Fame library and hours of their time to provide me with much of the research material used for this book.

My coworkers at the *New York Daily News* library, especially Vinny Panzarino, Scott Widener, Scotty (Sheriff) Browne, and head librarian Victoria Luther, who poured through the *Daily News* archives to uncover many of the historical accounts of the '54 season that were part of the basis of the book. In addition, they came through as always whenever it came to locating "missing persons" I needed to interview for the book.

Colin Myler, editor-in-chief, Teri Thompson, sports editor, both of the *New York Daily News,* and Tony Puterio, editorial/ finance director of the *Daily News,* who gave me the time and support along with all the newspaper's resources to do this book, and Eddie Fay, former *Daily News* VP of operations, who provided support early on.

Angie Troisi and Claus Guglberger of the *Daily News* photo department, who helped in selecting and procuring most of the photos in this book.

Vern Morrison of the digital production unit of Cleveland State University who assisted in procuring photos from the university's Michael Schwartz Library.

The Dick Young family, who graciously provided me access to their father's personal letters and permitted the use of them in this book.

The guys at the Elias Sports Bureau in New York—Steve and Tom Hirdt, Bob Rosen, John Labombarda, Bob Waterman—who provided much of the statistical research in the book.

Sean Forman of Baseball-Reference.com website. Although we will never agree on WAR, everyone agrees his is the most invaluable, comprehensive baseball research vehicle on the planet, without which this book would've taken years more to complete.

Matt Boylan, of the New York Public Library, who helped in all the research of New York City in the 1950s and the New York newspapers.

Dave Kaplan of the Yogi Berra Museum and Learning Center, who provided research material on Larry Doby and Dick Young.

Lou Hernandez of the Chicago White Sox, for his assistance in the Minnie Miñoso interview.

Bob DiBiasio, senior VP of public affairs of the Cleveland Indians, who provided assistance in obtaining photos as well as other research material from the Indians' archives.

Lee Lowenfish, friend and baseball historian, who helped in Roberto Clemente and Branch Rickey research.

Jerry Izenberg, respected fellow scribe who provided correspondence and other research materials from his friend Larry Doby.

Ira Berkow, David Fisher, Art Berke, and Christopher Longinetti, all of whom provided support, editorial assistance, and continued bond-ship.

And lastly . . .

Dan Ambrosio, my editor at Da Capo Press (no finer in my opinion), who "got" this book from the very beginning and let me run with it.

Rob Wilson, my agent who persevered in finding the right place for this book and has never wavered in his support, advice, and encouragement.

and

Lillian Madden, my first read and sounding board, whose love, support, encouragement, and, yes, even critical comment were invaluable.

BIBLIOGRAPHY

Antonelli, Johnny with Scott Pitoniak. *Johnny Antonelli: A Baseball Memoir*. Rochester, NY: RIT Press, 2012.

Bryant, Howard. *Shut Out: A Story of Race and Baseball in Boston*. New York: Routledge, 2002.

Creamer, Robert W. *Stengel: His Life and Times*. New York: Simon and Schuster, 1984.

Dark, Alvin, with John Underwood. *When in Doubt, Fire the Manager: My Life and Times in Baseball*. New York: E. P. Dutton, 1980.

Durocher, Leo, with Ed Linn. *Nice Guys Finish Last*. New York: Simon and Schuster, 1975.

Feller, Bob, with Bill Gilbert. *Now Pitching, Bob Feller*. New York: Birch Lane, 1990.

Greenberg, Hank, with Ira Berkow. *Hank Greenberg: The Story of My Life*. New York: Times Books, 1989.

Grimm, Charlie, with Ed Prell. *Jolly Cholly's Story: Baseball, I Love You!* Chicago: Henry Regnery Co., 1968.

Kahn, Roger. *Memories of Summer: When Baseball Was an Art and Writing About It a Game.* New York: Hyperion, 1997.

Lowenfish, Lee. *Branch Rickey: Baseball's Ferocious Gentleman.* Lincoln and London: University of Nebraska Press, 2007.

MacCambridge, Michael. *The Franchise: A History of Sports Illustrated Magazine.* New York: Hyperion, 1997.

Maraniss, David. *Clemente: The Passion and Grace of Baseball's Last Hero.* New York: Simon and Schuster, 2006.

Martin, Charles H. *Benching Jim Crow: The Rise and Fall of the Color Line in Southern College Sports, 1890–1980.* Urbana, Chicago, and Springfield: University of Illinois Press, 2010.

Moore, Joseph Thomas. *Larry Doby: The Struggle of the American League's First Black Player.* Mineola, NY: Dover Publications, 1988 and 2011.

Robinson, Jackie, with Alfred Duckett. *I Never Had It Made.* New York: G. P. Putnam's Sons, 1972.

Rosengren, John. *Hank Greenberg: The Hero of Heroes.* New York: New American Library, 2013.

Swaine, Rick. *The Integration of Major League Baseball: A Team by Team History.* Jefferson, NC: McFarland & Co, 2009.

Veeck, Bill, with Ed Linn. *Veeck as in Wreck: The Autobiography of Bill Veeck.* New York: G. P. Putnam's Sons, 1962.

CREDITS

INDEX